WINDOWS & SKYLIGHTS

By the Editors of Sunset Books

Sunset Books
President and Publisher: Susan J. Maruyama
Director, Sales & Marketing: Richard A. Smeby
Marketing & Creative Services Manager: Guy C. Joy
Production Director: Lory Day
Editorial Director: Bob Doyle

Sunset Publishing Corporation
Chairman: Jim Nelson
President/Chief Executive Officer: Stephen J. Seabolt
Chief Financial Officer: James E. Mitchell
Publisher: Anthony P. Glaves
Circulation Director: Robert I. Gursha
Director of Finance: Larry Diamond
Vice President, Manufacturing: Lorinda B. Reichert
Editor, Sunset Magazine: William R. Marken

Windows & Skylights was produced in conjunction with
St. Remy Press
President/Chief Executive Officer: Fernand Lecoq
President/Chief Operating Officer: Pierre Léveillé
Vice President, Finance: Natalie Watanabe
Managing Editor: Carolyn Jackson
Managing Art Director: Diane Denoncourt
Production Manager: Michelle Turbide

Editorial staff for *Windows & Skylights*
Senior Editor: Heather Mills
Editor: Alfred Lemaitre
Assistant Editor: Jennifer Ormston
Senior Art Director: Francine Lemieux
Art Director: Normand Boudreault

Book Consultants
Richard Day
Giles Miller-Mead
Don Vandervort

Special Contributors
Eric Beaulieu, Michel Blais, Marc Cassini, Robert Chartier,
François Daxhelet, Hélène Dion, Jean-Guy Doiron, Lorraine
Doré, Dominique Gagné, Michel Giguère, Christine M.
Jacobs, Solange Laberge, François Longpré, Geneviève
Monette, Jacques Perrault, Judy Yelon

COVER: Design by Susan Bryant.
Photography by John Sutton.

ISBN 0-376-01769-4
Library of Congress Catalog Card Number: 95-070327
Printed in the United States

For more information on *Windows & Skylights* or any other
Sunset Book, call 1-800-634-3095. For special sales, bulk
orders, and premium sales information, call Sunset Custom
Publishing Services at (415) 324-5577.

Acknowledgments
Thanks to the following:
American German Roll Shutters, Inc., Scottsdale, AZ
American Homeowners Foundation, Arlington, VA
American Institute of Building Design, Westport, CT
Andersen Windows, Inc., Bayport, MN
Bristolite Skylights, Santa Ana, CA
Can Wind Roll Shutters, St. Catharines, Ont.
City of Stockton Permit Center, Stockton, CA
Decorative Window Coverings Association, St. Louis, MO
Edward Gertler, Ottawa, Ont.
Keller Building Products, Miami, FL
Kenergy Skylights, Orlando, FL
Kolbe & Kolbe Millwork Co., Inc., Wausau, WI
Marvin Windows & Doors, Warroad, MN and
  Mississauga, Ont.
Michael J. Shingle Project Management, Pittsburgh, PA
National Association of Home Builders Remodelors™
  Council, Washington, DC
National Association of the Remodeling Industry, Arlington, VA
ODL Incorporated, Zeeland, MI
Pittsburgh Corning Corporation, Pittsburgh, PA
Roto Frank of America, Chester, CT
Stry-Buc Industries, Sharon Hill, PA
Tom Miller Handyman Service, Huntington Beach, CA
Velux-Canada Inc., Baie-d'Urfé, Que.
Vinyl Tech, Venice, FL
Wasco Products, Inc., Stanford, MA
Watertown Bureau of Code Enforcement, Watertown, NY
Window Covering Distributors, Inc., Norcross, GA

Picture Credits
p. 4   Tom Wyatt
p. 5   *(both)* courtesy Marvin Windows & Doors
p. 6   *(upper)* Steve W. Marley
p. 6   *(lower)* courtesy Kolbe & Kolbe Millwork Co., Inc.
p. 7   *(upper)* courtesy Andersen Windows, Inc.
p. 7   *(lower)* courtesy Marvin Windows & Doors
p. 8   *(both)* Steve W. Marley
p. 9   *(upper)* courtesy Marvin Windows & Doors
p. 9   *(lower)* courtesy Andersen Windows, Inc.
p. 10 *(upper)* courtesy Andersen Windows, Inc.
p. 10 *(lower)* courtesy Kolbe & Kolbe Millwork Co., Inc.
p. 11 *(both)* Steve W. Marley
p. 12 *(upper)* Tom Wyatt
p. 12 *(lower left)* courtesy Kolbe & Kolbe Millwork Co., Inc.
p. 12 *(lower right)* courtesy Andersen Windows, Inc.
p. 13 *(upper)* courtesy Pittsburgh Corning Corporation
p. 13 *(lower)* Steve W. Marley
p. 14 *(upper)* courtesy Velux-Canada Inc.
p. 14 *(lower)* Rob Super
p. 15 *(upper)* courtesy Velux-Canada Inc.
p. 15 *(lower)* courtesy Velux-Canada Inc.

CONTENTS

WINDOW AND SKYLIGHT POSSIBILITIES

Windows and skylights are more than just holes in the fabric of a house. They bring in natural light, connect a home with outdoor views, provide architectural accents both inside and out, add a sense of openness, and can even contribute warmth to a home's interior spaces.

Windows often add character to a room: If they're dramatically sized or unusually shaped, they can highlight a view; colorful stained glass or glass blocks can add a more subtle design accent. Skylights bring their own special drama to a room. They can direct light deep into a room, maximizing their potential for adding and balancing light.

In this chapter, we feature windows and skylights used in both functional and aesthetic ways. The designs range in style from traditional to contemporary, from budget-conscious to downright extravagant. If you have been thinking about building your dream home or are just anxious to do something about that sunless bathroom, or enlarge a tiny window that faces the best view, read on: This chapter may just nudge you into action.

This curved-eave greenhouse section encloses a deck off the living room to add indoor space. The dark tile floor soaks up warmth by day, releasing it at night. Motorized windows at the top open to admit cool air on warm days. Tinted film applied to the upper panels prevents excessive heat buildup. (Architect: Donald K. Olsen)

Ensuring that new windows fit in well with the existing ones is an important part of a remodeling project. The four new double-hung windows in the remodeled breakfast nook at left harmonize with the style of the rest of the house. Different muntin arrangements are available, to accommodate a range of existing styles.

Many window manufacturers provide replacement sash for double-hung windows, such as those shown at right. By replacing only the sash and jamb liners, you can have new, energy-efficient windows while keeping your original interior and exterior trim. In addition, many types of double-hung windows can be tilted into the room for easy cleaning.

WINDOW AND SKYLIGHT POSSIBILITIES **5**

The windows in this attractive seating area allow anyone sitting here to feel surrounded by the view, yet also sheltered. The opening casement windows help direct fresh air into the room. (Design: MLA/Architects)

Like a regular casement window, these French casements can direct cooling breezes into the room. In addition, the lack of center mullion allows an uninterrupted view.

Combine fixed and opening windows to fill your rooms with light. The fixed glass in the specially shaped frames at the top allows in plenty of light, while the opening awning windows at the bottom provide fresh air.

Fixed glass needn't be flat. The special corner window in this kitchen allows the interior space to be used efficiently, without sacrificing light and view.

A multistory light shaft brings sunshine into all levels of this tall house; the dining room shown is on the lowest level. The double-glazed windows facing south are designed for energy efficiency; mini-blinds allow for control of direct sunlight. The light shaft also allows air circulation between levels. (Architect: The Hastings Group)

Neatly encapsulated mini-blinds fit between panes of double-glazed casements. They offer sun control but never need dusting. (Design: William Young)

Adding a bay or other projecting window can open up a room, creating a sense of space and enlarging the view. Projecting windows, like the angled bay above this kitchen sink, provide a perfect place for growing plants or displaying favorite treasures.

Many bay windows have fixed glass in the middle section and opening windows on the sides. But all three windows in the angled bay shown at right are operable double-hung windows, allowing for maximum fresh air.

Projecting windows also add architectural interest to the outside of your home. The roof of a bay window can be finished with the same roofing materials as the rest of the house, or with copper for greater impact.

Greenhouse windows, or garden windows as they're sometimes called, often fit right into existing window openings. Glazed on all sides, they're ideal year-round environments for plants; a ventilating top or side helps prevent condensation.

These south-facing clerestory windows admit the warmth of low winter sun. An exterior overhang above them blocks sun in summer. The relationship between the size of the windows and the depth of the overhang was carefully thought out for a region with cool winters and hot summers. (Architects: Jacobson/Silverstein/Winslow)

This country home is heated almost entirely by a south-facing glazed wall. Double-glazed windows and clerestories admit winter sun that's absorbed by the insulated concrete floor, and reradiated at night. The overhanging roof above the clerestories and the roller shades on the lower windows provide summertime shade. (Architect: J. Alexander Riley)

The open ceiling in this remodeled kitchen creates a light, airy feeling. The arched window enhances the desired effect at minimum expense; just try to imagine the room without it. (Architect: William B. Remick)

The divided lights in the octagonal window above create patterns of light and shade inside as the sun moves across them.

Specially shaped windows can enhance interior design elements; the oval window at right harmonizes with the curved top of the adjacent bookcase, brightening the area at the bottom of the staircase.

Glass blocks provide ample natural light at countertop level without sacrificing overhead cupboard space.

A beguiling stained glass window fits into a modern casement frame. The window contributes light and privacy to a bathroom, while the casement action allows easy cleaning of both surfaces from inside.
(Design: Michael Felix)

Combined with many glass doors and a half-circle fixed glass window, these skylights help create a feeling of spaciousness in this dining area. The opening skylights allow air to circulate, and provide a vent for rising warm air.

A glazed roof is an ideal source of light for this ceramics studio. Tempered glass assures safety; the floor—tile over concrete—stores solar heat to help warm the room.
(Architect: Ron Senna)

Splaying the light shaft of a skylight allows maximum light penetration per square foot of glazing; the blinds provide sun control. An opening skylight is ideal for a bathroom, where fresh air is in high demand.

Roof windows in a sloping ceiling can be a key part of a renovation, providing light and air circulation in a perhaps otherwise unused area; semicircular fixed glass sections add extra interest to the design. These roof windows tilt in for easy cleaning of both surfaces from inside.

PLANNING FOR WINDOWS AND SKYLIGHTS

The choices for windows and skylights are almost limitless—large or small, clear or tinted, modest or spectacular. Your first step in choosing a window or skylight is to define your goals so you can decide where you want your openings and what will work best for you.

To realize their full potential, windows and skylights must be carefully planned. Otherwise, they can be a source of unwanted heat gain and glare, or of excessive heat loss. Between 15% and 35% of a house's total heat loss comes from windows and skylights, so poorly insulated or incorrectly oriented windows and skylights can be a costly liability, allowing an unwanted exchange of heat between the inside and outside of your home.

In this chapter, you'll learn the facts about lighting and light distribution, as well as other considerations to be aware of as you plan windows and skylights. Beginning on page 24, we'll show you three basic window types—sliding, swinging, and fixed—as well as windows for special situations *(page 26)*. You'll find out how you can reduce energy loss *(page 29)*. Turn to page 32 for information on the different types of skylights, and how to choose the right one for your roof. You'll learn how to make informed choices about the openings you already have, and any additions you may be planning.

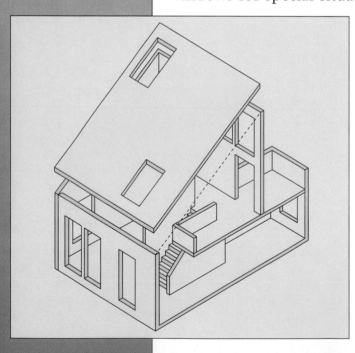

Before you cut holes in your walls or roof for windows or skylights, you can make a model to test your ideas.

WINDOW OR SKYLIGHT?

Whatever else windows and skylights may be used for, one of their key purposes is to admit light into a home. If you're building a new house or planning a major addition to an existing one, you can orient rooms, and design windows and skylights so they bring in light exactly where you want it. And you can choose between windows and skylights, or use a combination of the two. If you're not involved in major construction, your alternatives will be more restricted. Walk around your property; study the site and look for any obstructions that might prevent the light from falling where you want it, and observe where the sun falls, both in the morning and afternoon.

Whether you choose windows or skylights will depend on what you want the openings to do for your home. If you want to highlight views, increase ventilation, and add design accents, windows are probably the answer. If you want to let in light without sacrificing privacy, or avoid direct sun and glare, skylights may be a better choice.

The best way to anticipate what effect the windows or skylights you're considering will have on the lighting inside your home is to build a model. Follow the instructions on page 23 to construct and use a model of your home to help test your ideas.

The type of window you choose should be influenced by the function of the space outside the room. For example, in rooms that open onto porches or walkways, sliding windows are a better choice than swinging windows because they won't interfere with people passing by outside. A window, especially a bay or a bow *(page 28)*, can also add character and space to a room. By adding a window or greenhouse section to a south-facing wall, you'll ensure that the area receives maximum light and heat.

Skylights work where windows may be a problem. For example, a skylight will bring in light and a view of the sky while maintaining your privacy. A skylight is also an option worth considering if obstructions on your site won't allow much light in through a window, or if you live in a row house where the only way to light the middle rooms is from the top.

Natural light is difficult to focus and control, so you won't be able to create very specific lighting effects. But there are some principles of good lighting that you should keep in mind when planning your window or skylight. If you want to use a window for task lighting (for writing, sewing, or other concentrated activities), try to plan so that light comes from the right or the left of the viewer; you'll find reading and writing much easier if you sit with your side to the window, not facing it.

Area lighting—the less concentrated, less intense lighting required for a hallway or living room—depends on light reflected from the walls or ceiling. This is the kind of lighting your window or skylight is most likely to provide. Using a light-colored paint on the walls and ceiling—as well as the light shaft of a skylight, if you have one—will enhance the effect by spreading the light evenly over the area. A large clear or translucent north-facing skylight is especially good for reliable, even light.

Dramatic lighting effects depend on a beam of direct light focusing on art objects, plants, or a certain area of a room. Although dramatic lighting is easiest to achieve with artificial light, natural light can also have dramatic effects. For example, a long, narrow, diffusing skylight positioned close to a wall can illuminate art objects on that wall.

The best way to ventilate and cool a room is by placing windows opposite one another at heights that let the incoming breeze wash around the occupants of the room. The combination of a window and a venting or opening skylight works well. Because hot air rises, the skylight opening in the roof lets out warm air, while the cool breeze enters through the window. For more information, turn to the sections on window considerations, beginning on the next page, and on skylight considerations, beginning on page 21.

SEASONAL VARIATIONS IN SUN ANGLES

In winter, the sun travels in a low arc across the sky; during the summer months, the arc is much higher. This allows the winter sun to penetrate deeper into a room through a south-facing window (a north-facing one in the Southern Hemisphere) than the summer sun. The amount of sunlight entering a skylight during the winter months depends on the angle of the skylight, the shape of the light shaft, and the latitude of your home.

You can place a skylight so light reaches areas of a room that light from a window may not reach; an opening in the roof can give almost five times more light than an equivalent opening in the wall. A skylight can give you a better distribution of light as well. In the summer, though, a south-facing skylight, unless shaded, may bring in more direct light and heat than you want. Misplaced skylights can also cause glare, so plan carefully. For south-facing walls, a window with an overhang is the best option for keeping cool in the summer because the degree of penetration of the sun into your home is reduced *(page 29)*.

WINDOW CONSIDERATIONS

Windows provide light, view, and ventilation, but they also create a sense of space and act as passive solar devices to heat our homes. Whatever your primary goal, you'll want to be familiar with the basic principles that apply to each window function.

WINDOWS FOR LIGHT

The orientation, placement, size, shape, and number of windows, as well as the colors in the room, will affect the intensity, distribution, and quality of the room's natural light. Though you'll want all areas of the room to be lighted, it's wise to avoid absolutely uniform lighting—it will make the room look sterile and uninteresting. Also, keep in mind that people tend to gravitate from darker to lighter areas.

Wherever your windows are placed, if you mount draperies, shades, or other coverings so that they clear the glass completely when they're open, then you won't lose any light from those windows. Because screens can absorb as much as 50% of available light, use them sparingly, and then only over the opening parts of the window.

Orientation and size of windows: The orientation of your windows will have a significant effect on the amount of light they bring into your room. A south-facing window (north-facing in the Southern Hemisphere) will let in the most light and is desirable in all but hot climates; a window oriented north provides soft, diffuse light. Light from east- and west-facing windows is very intense during the summer, because of the low angle of the sun in the morning and late afternoon, and requires careful management.

When you're choosing the size of the window, remember that useful light from a window penetrates not more than $2^1/_2$ times the height of the window. The only way to overcome this limitation is with clerestory windows deep in the room (*page 27*), a skylight, or additional windows on other walls.

Number and shape of windows: The number of windows, and whether they are on the same wall or different walls, affects light distribution. One large window, or several small ones grouped together, may give more even, glare-free light than separate small windows in the same wall. Windows in more than one wall provide more pleasant and uniform distribution of light than windows in a single wall. You'll also have good illumination over a larger portion of the day.

The window's shape also has an effect on light distribution, as shown in the illustrations at right. Short, wide windows create a broad, shallow distribution of light; tall, narrow windows provide a thin, deep distribution. If a tall, narrow window is situated near a light-colored wall, its effectiveness is enhanced because the wall reflects the light, becoming a secondary light source.

Reflected light: Exterior surfaces adjacent to a window reflect light to varying degrees, and can affect the amount of light entering a window. Likewise, reflections from interior surfaces affect the intensity and distribution of light within the room. A white wall reflects as much as 90% of the light. Medium tones, such as tan, rose, light blue, green, and gray, reflect 30% to 50%. Dark colors and dark woods reflect less than 15% of the light.

LIGHT DISTRIBUTION PATTERNS

Wide window creates broad pattern.

Narrow window creates thin pattern.

Wall adjoining window reflects light.

High window creates deep pattern.

WINDOWS FOR VIEW

Being able to look out of a window is as important to us as receiving light and air through it. Windows connect us to the environment, enhance our sense of space, and satisfy our curiosity. The placement and size of your window should be at least partly determined by what you'll see from it. Just as the framing brings out the best in a painting, so it is with a view, whether it's a dramatic panorama or a glimpse into an intimate garden.

Selecting the right window: If a spectacular view demands a large picture window, you may want to consider breaking up the expanse of glass with muntins, vertical and horizontal dividers that separate a large pane of glass into many small panes called lights or lites *(page 26)*.

The small panes serve to create a multitude of framed views, and to provide a greater sense of enclosure. Some architects recommend several smaller windows instead of a single large one; this allows people to catch glimpses of the view as they move around the house. The view becomes a little less overwhelming and doesn't lose its attraction, as it might if it could be seen in its entirety from a sitting area.

Try to avoid or minimize large obstructions in the line of sight. Horizontal divisions, especially more than 4 inches wide, are undesirable, although vertical ones don't create so much of a problem. Remember that screens can interfere with a clear view; if you don't need ventilation, consider fixed glass.

TYPICAL WINDOW HEIGHTS

Dining room — 6'8", 2'6", 4'3", 3'11"

Living room — 6'8", 4'1", 3'9", 10"

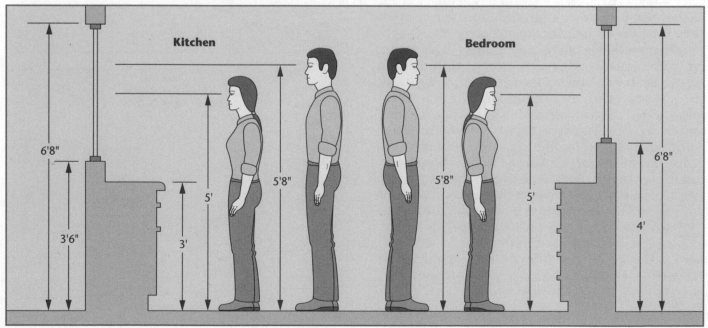

Kitchen — 6'8", 3'6", 3', 5', 5'8"

Bedroom — 5'8", 5', 4', 6'8"

Window placement: Situate windows where they'll provide the best possible view of the outside; try to avoid windows that look out on a wall or a fence. Even if your home fronts on a busy street, you can design a second-story window or a high first-floor window so you can look out but passersby can't look in.

When planning the height of a windowsill, consider not only the view, but also the room's function and furniture arrangement. The illustrations on the previous page show you typical window heights. Ideally, the sill should be below eye level. In a kitchen, however, you may want the sill to be above the level of the counter; in a dining room, at about the level of the table; and in a bedroom, at about 4 feet from the floor. In a living room, consider placing the sill 10 to 14 inches from the floor so you can view the outdoors from a sitting position. If you have a private patio, deck, or garden outside your bedroom, consider this low sill height; you'll be able to see outside without craning your neck above a high sill. NOTE: Building codes may require the use of tempered glass within 18 inches of the floor.

WINDOWS FOR VENTILATION

Air moves because of a difference in temperature or pressure. Warm air rises; in a single-story house, warm air venting through an open skylight creates an air flow and pulls air in through an open window.

It's the pressure difference, though, that mainly influences air flow—from high pressure to low. When wind hits the wall of a house, air pressure rises along that wall; on the opposite side of the house, where there is protection from the wind, air pressure drops. Windows in these two walls optimize air movement; air coming in through one window and exiting through the window on the opposite wall creates cross ventilation, a relief on warm nights. Study seasonal wind patterns around your house, and, if you can, place windows to take advantage of the prevailing breezes. As shown at right *(above)* opening the top sash allows cool air to flow over the heads of a room's occupants.

In summer, some of the cooling effect of air depends on its speed. To accelerate the flow of air through an area, make the opening of the windows through which air exits larger than the ones through which it enters *(right, below)*. Take a look inside and outside for any obstructions that can slow the movement of air; room partitions and even furniture can reduce air flow.

Air currents through a house provide the greatest comfort when they flow at the level of the occupants; if possible, place windows low in the wall, and keep windows away from corners to maximize air movement.

All windows, except the swinging type, open only 50% and can't change air direction. Place them in front of the area through which you want air to move. Casements, awnings, and other swinging windows open more fully and can direct air sideways, upward, or downward.

WINDOWS FOR APPEARANCE

If you're adding or replacing windows in an existing structure, you can add architectural interest by making the new windows a focal point. Geometrically shaped windows are especially good for this. A triangular window in the end wall of an A-frame, for example, can highlight the house's shape. Be sure to select windows that match your home's general style. Before adding or replacing a window, study the arrangement of the existing ones. Draw plans to see how the new addition will affect the building's appearance. If the new window will be a different size or shape than the existing ones, plan it so the house has a balanced appearance.

WINDOWS AND SOLAR HEATING

In the Northern Hemisphere, windows must face south or within 20° east or west of true south to admit the maximum amount of the sun's heat; this orientation is essential for catching the winter sun.

When the sun's direct rays enter a house, their radiant energy or heat is trapped inside, but only for the time the

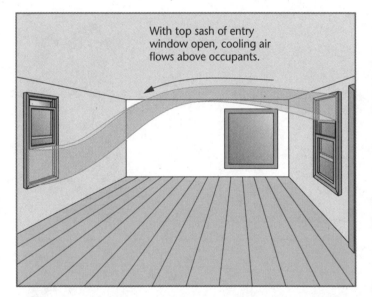

With top sash of entry window open, cooling air flows above occupants.

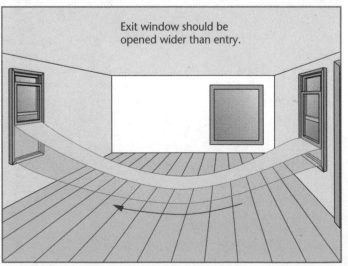

Exit window should be opened wider than entry.

sunlight is present. When the sun goes down, interior heat is transmitted out through the glass to the colder environment. To retard this heat loss, there are various options: You can install windows with high performance glazing (sealed windows with at least two panes of glass, specifically designed to reduce heat loss); you can install storm windows (to add a layer of air, which does not conduct heat well); or you can use an insulating material (such as an insulating shade). In very cold climates, you may want more than one of these options. You can also absorb and store the sun's heat by letting the sunlight fall on a material, such as brick, masonry, concrete, or water, that will slowly release heat into the surrounding environment after sundown, keeping the interior of the house warm. For maximum efficiency in passive solar heating (using the sun to help heat your house), keep in mind that south-facing windows can provide a net positive energy balance, if they are both properly glazed and insulated; they should not be obstructed between 9:00 in the morning and 3:00 in the afternoon, because almost 95% of the low winter sun is intercepted between those hours. By recessing windows back from the outside wall, you'll reduce air movement against them, thereby reducing air infiltration. A recessed opening that is splayed (sloped outward) will increase the amount of direct sunlight coming through in winter, but it will also reduce shading in summer. You'll find more information on controlling heat beginning on page 29.

SKYLIGHT CONSIDERATIONS

A skylight adds light, view, and, in some cases, ventilation, without affecting privacy or taking up any wall space. With a skylight, you can create an indoor garden and enhance the interior design of your room. If you're planning to install a unit in a ceiling that you can reach (such as a sloping ceiling in a renovated attic), you can install a roof window instead of a skylight. The difference between a roof window and a skylight depends on accessibility. If you can reach it directly from the floor, it's called a roof window, whereas if it's inaccessible (in a cathedral ceiling, or at the top of a light shaft) it's called a skylight. Most roof windows can be opened and many skylights cannot, but sometimes the same window unit may be installed as either a roof window or a skylight.

Whatever your goal, there are certain issues to consider when you're planning a skylight. If your house has an attic or crawl space between the ceiling and the roof, you must install a light shaft to direct the light through the attic to the room below. Even if the shaft is light-colored, some light will be lost. The longer the light shaft, the larger the skylight must be to achieve the same level of lighting on a given area; splaying the light shaft will help with this problem (page 22). Structural limitations, such as roof members or proximity to a load-bearing wall, may prevent you from placing the skylight where you want it. If you have easy access to your attic, check for potential problems in placement (page 81).

SKYLIGHTS FOR LIGHT
All skylights bring in light, but the quality and quantity of illumination are affected by orientation and glazing. In the Northern Hemisphere, a south-facing skylight with clear glazing brings in a great amount of light and heat, but it may produce glare; you can use a relatively small skylight to create a mood or provide visual interest. For uniform, soft lighting, use a north-facing skylight, or one with translucent or tinted glazing. Or, you can install a diffusing panel at the ceiling level (page 92).

If you want a skylight for an indoor garden, your choice will depend on the kind of plants you want to grow. A clear unit is best for plants that need direct sunlight. But remember that sunbeams keep moving throughout the day—track the sun's motion and plant accordingly. For most plants that don't require direct light, a skylight with translucent glazing works well.

SKYLIGHTS FOR VIEW
Skylights with clear, translucent, or tinted glazing allow you to enjoy the view overhead. Bronze- or gray-tinted glazing produces less glare and heat than a clear unit; white translucent glazing cuts out glare altogether.

When you're considering skylight placement, remember that though a view of the trees might be pleasant, putting your unit directly under a tree can present problems, since dirt and debris will collect on it.

In placing a roof window, remember that you'll want to be able to see out from a sitting or standing position; the exact height of the sill from the floor will depend on the size of the window and the slope of the roof.

SKYLIGHTS FOR VENTILATION
For ventilation purposes, you'll obviously select a unit that opens. These units are especially practical in bathrooms and kitchens. You'll also appreciate a venting unit if you live in a warm climate or have a flat-roofed house; when combined with a few open windows, opening the skylight at night will allow hot air to escape, cooling down your house.

SKYLIGHTS AND SOLAR HEATING
In the Northern Hemisphere, skylights, like windows, will admit the maximum amount of the sunlight in winter when oriented south or within 20° east or west of true south; ideally, the skylight should be tilted toward the

south at an angle of the area's latitude plus 15°. In many cases, the roof will be sufficiently steep to provide this angle.

In climates where heating is the priority, skylights are not effective for passive solar heating. Even when properly insulated, and used in conjunction with a material that will store the sun's heat during the day (such as a masonry floor), a roof with a skylight will generally show a net energy loss, as compared with a plain roof. However, a skylight may still be a good choice in such a climate, since it adds natural light and a sense of space to a room, and may allow you to use space which is otherwise unusable. You can minimize the heat loss by choosing an energy-efficient glazing material, and insulating properly.

Clear glazing admits the maximum amount of light and heat for the area covered. Translucent glazing reduces glare and also reduces solar gain. So does tinted glazing; it cuts down both light transmission and solar radiation to a considerable degree. You may also want to shade your skylight, either from the inside or from the outside, to reduce unwanted solar gain in summer (*page 34*).

SKYLIGHT SIZING CONSIDERATIONS

The size of the skylight you get will depend not only on the size of the area you want to light and the reflection of the surfaces in that area, but also on the depth and shape of the light shaft.

Sizing principles: A general rule of thumb for determining skylight area is to figure on 1 square foot of skylight area for every 20 square feet of floor space. For example, if your room area is 100 square feet, your skylight area will be 5 square feet. Light-colored ceiling, walls, light shaft, and furnishings reflect more light, requiring a smaller glazing area for a given lighting requirement. Though you can use any size skylight with any rafter spacing, many prefabricated units are designed to fit standard rafter spacing; this makes installation easier and more economical.

If your home has trusses rather than rafters, then the maximum size single skylight that you can install is one that will fit between two trusses. Trusses are part of the supporting structure of your house and cannot be cut. However, if you want a larger expanse of glass, you can install two skylights side by side or end to end. You can get the special flashing required for this from your skylight manufacturer.

Light shafts: You'll need a light shaft—either straight, angled, or splayed—if there's a space between the roof and the ceiling. These three types are illustrated at right. In a straight light shaft the skylight sits directly above the ceiling opening. The skylight is positioned off to one side of the ceiling opening in an angled light shaft. In a splayed light shaft, the ceiling opening is larger than the roof opening.

If you use a straight light shaft, then the deeper your light shaft and the higher your ceiling, the larger your skylight will have to be to provide the desired amount of light. But if you use a light shaft splayed between 30° and 60°, you can bring in the same amount of light with a smaller skylight.

If you need a fairly long light shaft, then a splayed shaft is usually the best option. Not only does it allow more light to reach the room below, it also ensures better air circulation in the light shaft itself. This helps reduce the chances of condensation on the inside of the skylight.

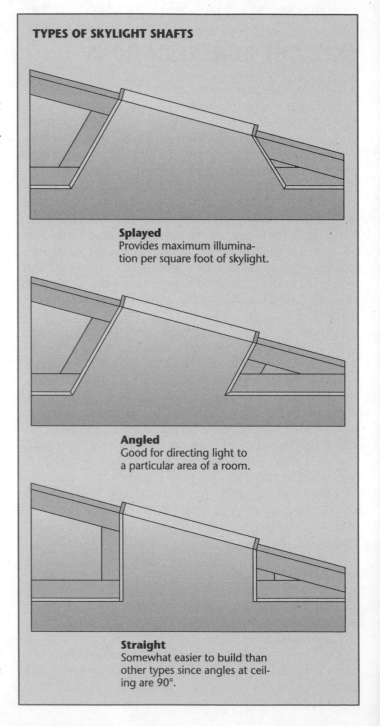

TYPES OF SKYLIGHT SHAFTS

Splayed
Provides maximum illumination per square foot of skylight.

Angled
Good for directing light to a particular area of a room.

Straight
Somewhat easier to build than other types since angles at ceiling are 90°.

When you're planning to add a window or skylight, a scale model of the room (or your whole home) is an invaluable design tool. Without actually cutting any holes in the walls or roof of your home, you can check the light and view from a proposed window or analyze the quality and amount of light that you'll gain from a skylight. Building a model that is adequate for studying the placement and size of a proposed window or skylight is simple and requires only several hours of time and a few dollars for materials.

Materials and tools for the model: Before buying any materials, you'll have to measure your room's floor, walls, and ceiling, and note the size and location of existing windows and skylights. Unless the roof is flat, you'll also need to measure the roof and its slope. To keep track of your measurements, make a sketch of each area, marking all of the dimensions; use a scale of ½ or 1 inch per foot. You'll also need to know the dimensions of the window or skylight you're planning to install. Estimate the amount of material you'll need for the model, and buy enough extra material so you'll be able to make several versions of the wall or ceiling where you intend to put the window or skylight.

Construct your model from corrugated cardboard, cardboard or plastic-foam mounting board (available at art supply stores), or balsa wood (available at hobby stores). Using plastic-foam mounting board or balsa wood allows you to glue the cutouts back into the walls or ceiling if you change your mind. You'll also need common white glue, straight pins, a ruler, a square, a pencil, and a sharp knife.

Building the model: Work on a flat surface (protect it from damage by using a panel of plywood or hardboard). Using the scale that you've chosen, draw the floor plan, walls, ceiling, and roof on the building material. Mark all existing and proposed openings. Cut the floor, walls, ceiling, and roof; then cut the window, door, and skylight openings.

With the floor plan as your guide, glue or pin walls to the floor and to each other; then attach the ceiling and roof. You may want to cut and glue light shaft walls to the opening edges of the skylight before attaching the roof to the walls. If you want to be able to make changes, use the glue sparingly so you can remove and replace walls easily.

How to use the model: To see how your new skylight or window will alter the light in your home, place your model in direct sunlight, facing in the same direction as your house. Use small plants to simulate any trees that cast shadows on your house.

Observe the model at different times of day, and study the quality and intensity of the changing light. To study the effect of sunlight at different times of the year, you can tilt the model to simulate the change in the height of the sun during the year. Place the model on a table outside the room, and consider the view through the proposed window.

Move, reduce, or enlarge the opening for the proposed window or skylight until you get the effect you want; you may even want to change an existing window. Once you're satisfied, you'll be much more confident about cutting holes in the walls or roof of your home.

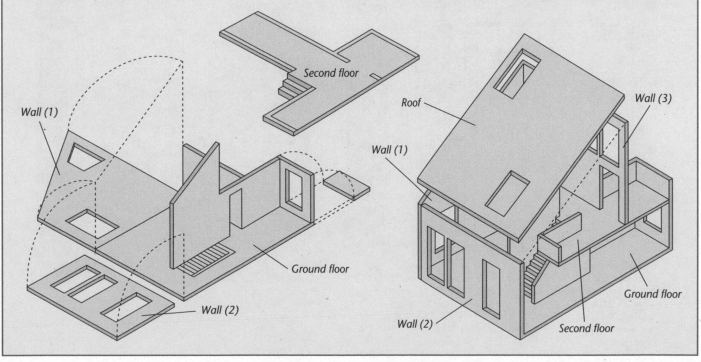

Second floor

Wall (1)

Roof

Wall (3)

Wall (1)

Ground floor

Wall (2)

Ground floor

Wall (2)

Second floor

THE CHOICES IN WINDOWS

Windows come in all shapes, sizes, and designs, with different kinds of framing materials, glazing, and weather stripping. How do you select the window that's right for you? There are several criteria to consider—your budget, the architectural style of your home and its existing windows, and your needs. Does the window give you the light, ventilation, or view that you want? Is it well insulated and weatherproof? Will it be easy to operate and maintain? Can you install it yourself? In the following pages, you'll find information on the basic window styles, situations that call for special designs, as well as the different glazings and window materials you can choose from.

Study the windows in your home and in the houses in your neighborhood. At first glance, the windows may all look very different because of the variety of sizes, shapes, and muntin arrangements. But it's likely that all the windows fall into three basic categories—sliding, swinging, or fixed.

Sliding windows: Windows that have movable sash that slide in either horizontal or vertical tracks are known as sliding windows *(below)*. With this type of window—examples are double-hung, vertical sliding, and horizontal sliding—only half the window can be opened at a time and it's impossible to direct a breeze to different areas of the room.

Swinging windows: Casements with sash that swing out, awning windows (outward-swinging), and hoppers (inward-swinging) are all examples of swinging windows *(opposite)*. Because swinging windows are usually easy to operate, you can place them in hard-to-reach areas. But you may not want to install casements or awnings in areas where people passing outside might bump into the open sash.

Some types of swinging windows can be power-operated—opened and closed by means of a remote control, a switch mounted on the wall, or an outdoor rain sensor. Look for a system that will also lock the windows.

SLIDING WINDOWS

Double-hung
Both sash slide in grooves in the frame. Sash movements and positions are controlled by springs, weights, or friction devices. With certain models, the sash can be removed, rotated, or tilted for cleaning. If only one sash slides, the window is called vertical sliding or single-hung.

Horizontal sliding
One or both sash slide horizontally in tracks. Sometimes the sash are removable for easy cleaning.

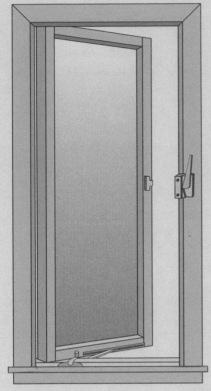

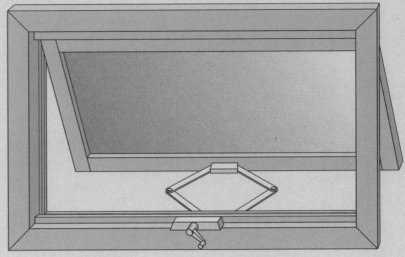

Awning
Sash pivots at the top, opening out; usually operated with a crank. Hinges must be sturdy and allow both sides of the sash to move equally to prevent twisting.

Casement
Sash swings out, usually operated with a crank. Good for ventilation because the open sash can scoop in air not blowing directly into the window.

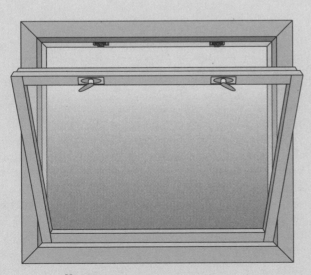

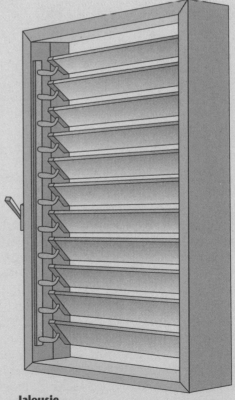

Hopper
Pivoting at the bottom and opening inward, these windows direct air upward; they should be placed low in the wall. The space directly in front of them is unusable, but they are easy to operate and wash.

Jalousie
Similar to awning windows, but made of a number of horizontal glass slats set in metal clips, which can be opened and closed in unison with a crank. Best for warm climates and for areas which don't need to be heated or air-conditioned, because the slats don't seal completely when closed.

Fixed windows: These windows *(below)*, also called picture windows, cannot be opened. They can be used alone or in combination with windows with movable sash. Fixed windows may be glazed with a single large pane of glass or with divided lights (small panes of glass separated by muntins). You can also get simulated divided lights (muntins affixed to a single pane of glass), or removable grilles for easy cleaning. Fixed windows come in a variety of shapes, such as those shown on page 27. The corner window below, which has one fixed pane of glass bent in the middle, could be installed alone or together with windows on one or both of the adjacent walls.

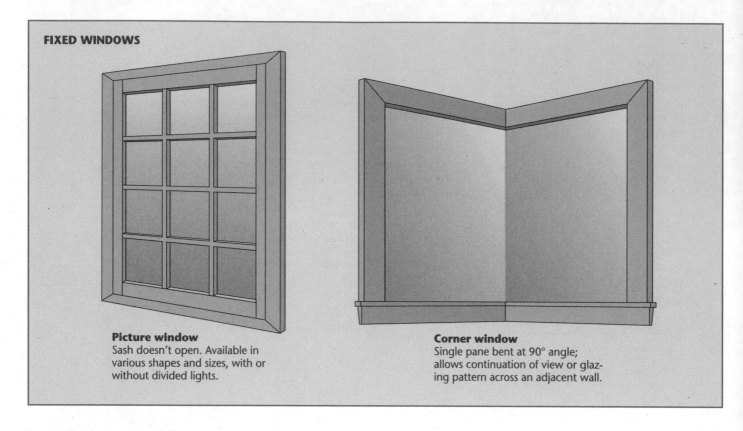

FIXED WINDOWS

Picture window
Sash doesn't open. Available in various shapes and sizes, with or without divided lights.

Corner window
Single pane bent at 90° angle; allows continuation of view or glazing pattern across an adjacent wall.

SPECIAL SITUATIONS

Specially designed windows can brighten a dark interior, provide light and warmth for an indoor garden, or create an intimate seat where you can curl up with a book.

In any room where you spend time during the day, try to have an area where you can see out comfortably; ideally, the windows should open so that fresh air will flow into the room and you can enjoy the sights and sounds outside. A large window with a low sill, or an alcove or bay window with a window seat can be an attractive addition. Window seats are great for relaxing or reading, but only if they're comfortable. Before you build one, put a comfortable armchair or sofa where you want the window seat, and try it out; then build the seat as wide and as well padded as the chair or sofa, for built-in comfort.

Projecting windows, such as angle bays, box bays, and bows *(page 28)*, add space to the interior, providing a place to enjoy the outside, and enhancing the view. Greenhouse windows (or garden windows) made of metal or wood are relatively small projecting windows designed for growing plants. They come with shelves for pots and planters and are often made to fit standard-size window openings; opening sides or tops help prevent fogging.

Solariums and sunrooms both have walls of glass and may also have a glass roof. Greenhouse sections are especially good for growing plants and flowers all year long. They're all designed to take advantage of the warmth of the sun, and can provide a bright and cheery addition to your home. In severely cold climates, ventilation is important because condensation may be a problem. Ideally, you should be able to close the greenhouse section off from the rest of the house.

Cathedral and multistory windows both have large expanses of glass. Cathedral windows, which have fixed glass, are used in rooms with very high ceilings. Admitting extra light and permitting a better view, the window generally follows the slope of the roof and may have vertical divisions. Multistory windows, as the name implies, extend from the ground floor to the floors above; the glass can be fixed or opening. In homes with cathedral or multistory windows, the rooms on the upper floors often have doors or interior windows placed in such a way that they can share the light and view. Interior windows are openings on inside walls that allow rooms to share light and view, add a sense of space, and let the occupants of the house communicate with each other.

Clerestory windows, also known as "ribbon windows," are a set of windows, often with fixed glass, running along the top of a wall near the ceiling. They often project into the room, so they're ideal for admitting light and heat deep into a space without sacrificing privacy, as shown at right.

If your turn-of-the-century home demands a special fixed window, or your A-frame in the country requires a triangular window, you may need to have it custom-made. But you'll find an impressive collection of window styles that you can obtain ready-made. Custom-made or ready-made, windows come in a variety of shapes, such as circle, oval, half-circle, quarter-circle, ellipse, eyebrow, polygon, or triangle; some of these are shown below.

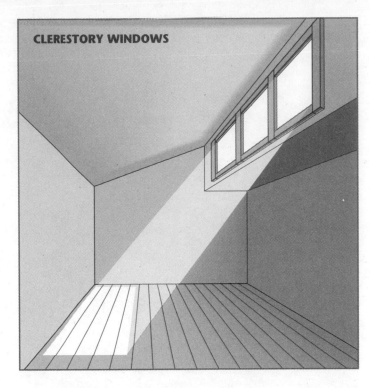

CLERESTORY WINDOWS

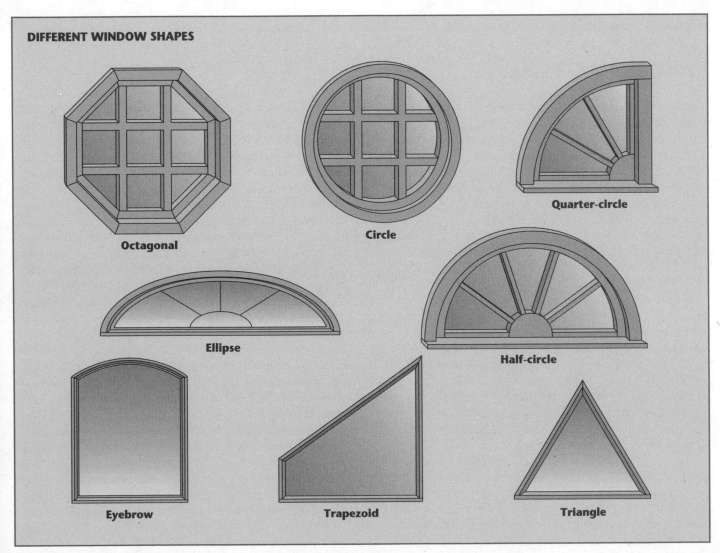

DIFFERENT WINDOW SHAPES

Octagonal

Circle

Quarter-circle

Ellipse

Half-circle

Eyebrow

Trapezoid

Triangle

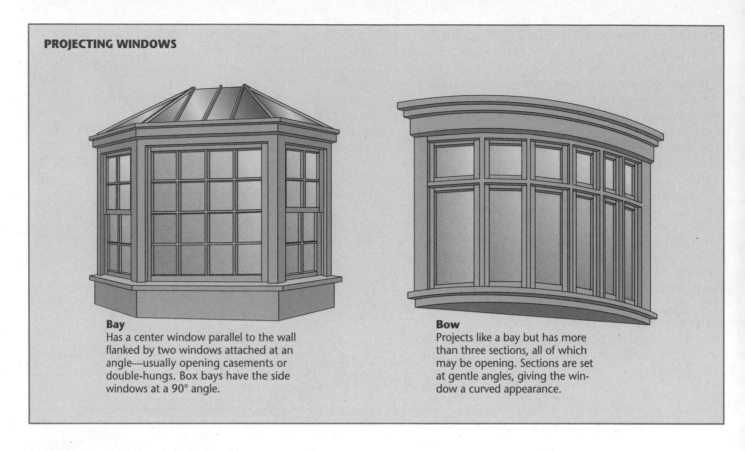

Bay
Has a center window parallel to the wall flanked by two windows attached at an angle—usually opening casements or double-hungs. Box bays have the side windows at a 90° angle.

Bow
Projects like a bay but has more than three sections, all of which may be opening. Sections are set at gentle angles, giving the window a curved appearance.

WINDOW MATERIALS

Window manufacturers offer a wide range of products, made of wood, aluminum, steel, vinyl, or fiberglass. Windows with better weather protection are more expensive, but can pay off in energy savings.

Wood is a very good insulator. It doesn't become as cold as other materials, so that the moisture in the warm interior air is less likely to condense on it. However, wood is subject to shrinkage and swelling, so it will warp and rot over time unless it is protected, either by paint or by a covering (or cladding) of a more weather-resistant material such as vinyl, aluminum, or fiberglass.

Aluminum windows, more durable than bare wood, are also thinner, lighter, and easier to handle. Aluminum windows sold today are insulated with a thermal break of extruded vinyl, and sometimes also foam, which reduces heat loss and condensation on the inside. Aluminum windows are available with finishes that protect the aluminum from corrosion and eliminate the need for maintenance, but they're not recommended for use in coastal areas, where the salt spray can be highly corrosive.

Steel is stronger than both aluminum and wood, so steel windows have very thin frame members, which look quite attractive. However, they are not generally used in homes because they're more expensive; they may be used as replacement windows to match older existing ones.

Vinyl windows have members extruded from impact-resistant, rigid polyvinyl chloride (PVC), with hollow spaces inside to make them resistant to heat loss and condensation. Some vinyl windows have a tendency to distort when exposed to extremes of heat and cold; they may become harder to operate and allow more air infiltration. Vinyl windows can't be painted—the color is integral to the vinyl—so pick a color you can live with, and keep in mind that they may discolor over time.

The energy-efficiency of windows has increased greatly, in large part due to improvements in glazing. When shopping for energy-efficient windows, the two most important terms to look for are the window's overall R-value, and its overall U-value. The R-value is a material's resistance to heat transfer. The higher the R-value, the better the insulating property of the window. The U-value is the best indicator of a window's energy-efficiency. It tells you the rate of heat flow through the window; a lower U-value means the window is more energy-efficient. However, keep in mind that the U-value of the glazing material may be different from the U-value of the entire unit; the U-value of the entire unit tells you how it will perform when installed in your home. The U-value you need will, of course, depend on where you live: An average U-value is fine for warm climates, but in cold climates, a lower U-value is more important.

Insulating windows typically have two—sometimes more—panes of glass sealed together with either air or argon gas trapped inside to act as an insulator. If the unit is properly sealed, there should be no moisture between the panes, but sometimes a drying agent is used in the spacer (the strip inside the panes, which helps keep them apart) as added insurance.

Low-emissivity (or low-e) glass has a coating applied to one of the glass surfaces. Sometimes a low-e coating is suspended between the panes of an insulating window. A low-emissivity coating allows light in but prevents some solar rays from being transmitted through the glass. A low-e coating for warm climates helps keep your home cool by blocking longer-wave radiant heat from entering, while low-e for colder climates helps to prevent the radiant heat in your home from escaping through the glass; there are some low-e coatings that combine these two functions. Low-e coatings also block ultraviolet rays, which helps reduce the fading of carpets and fabrics.

Tinted glass, usually either bronze or gray, reduces glare and limits the amount of light and heat from the sun (solar gain) in your home. The color in tinted glass runs through the material. Reflective glass, which also reduces solar gain, obscures the view from inside; it is mainly used in commercial applications.

Safety glass may be required by local building codes for certain situations and is always a good choice where a person could walk into a window. Safety glass is available tempered, laminated, or wire-reinforced.

Tempered glass is heat-treated during the manufacturing process after it has been cut to size to increase its strength and resistance to shattering. Laminated glass consists of a sheet of plastic laminated between two panes of glass. Wire-reinforced glass is seldom used in homes, because it's not very attractive. Some manufacturers offer windows glazed with plastic (such as acrylic) as an alternative to safety glass.

STAINED GLASS

Elegant, nostalgic, and colorful, stained glass can turn a window into a work of art. Depending on its design, a stained glass window can also provide privacy both at night and during the day.

The glass used in stained glass panels can be mineral-hued, painted, clear, sandblasted, or mirrored. Textures can vary from smooth to rough, rippled, or knobbly, and edges may be beveled. To learn to build your own stained glass panel, look for classes given by schools, museums, or private studios; materials are available from art supply centers.

Whether you intend to make a panel yourself or buy one, consider the effect you want the stained glass to have, the size and color scheme of the room, the direction the panel will face, and the amount of outdoor view you'd like. A rectangular or curved stained glass frame around a clear pane can focus attention on the view, while a stained glass panel the size of the window will

block out an undesirable view. For an example of a stained glass window, see page 13.

Stained glass can also be lovely around doors, but check if this is permitted in your local building code, and don't use stained glass where people could walk or fall into it.

You can permanently install small stained glass panels in the same way that you install ordinary clear panes (page 69). Large panels need additional support for permanent installation; fit them into their own routed wood frames, or block their edges on both sides with wood strips nailed to the sill and window frame. Be sure to set the panel in glazing putty and caulk all outside joints. You can also install a panel so it can be removed easily; that way, you can take the panel with you if you move. To install a panel temporarily, secure it $1/2$ to $3/4$ inch away from the inside of the clear pane; use wood strips between the panel and the sash, and brads, stops, or molding to hold the panel in place.

CONTROLLING LIGHT AND HEAT

Heat flows from warmer areas to cooler ones. If the air outside is cooler than the air inside, your inside heat will seek to flow to the cold air outside. Conversely, hot air from outside will flow into the house's cooler interior when it's hotter outside than inside.

Windows make up less total surface area than the walls or roof, but lose or gain much more heat per square foot, because they're less resistant to heat flow; this is especially true of single-glazed windows. Heat flows through the glazing, through the muntins and

sash frames, and through the fixed frame. If the window is poorly fitted or sealed, heat can escape or enter through cracks and gaps. A poorly fitted, single-glazed window may lose twice as much heat through gaps and cracks in the frame as through the glass.

In winter, you'll lose heat through your windows at night. You can reduce this heat loss by adding a layer of glazing (installing insulating windows or using storm windows) or by covering the glass with an insulating material, or both.

Traditionally, storm windows consisted of a single pane of glass set in a wood or aluminum frame, and were installed seasonally on the outside of a window. Today, storm windows may be removable or permanent; set in wood, aluminum, or plastic frames; and installed on the outside or inside of a window. Some permanent units are designed on a double- or triple-track system with glass and insect-screening panels for year-round use. An easy and inexpensive option for insulation in winter is to apply a layer of thin plastic film to the inside of the window; you can buy a kit that contains the film and the tape used to attach it. The film is heated with a blow-dryer so that it shrinks and fits tightly. If it's properly applied, the film is unobtrusive and very effective. However, many new windows have insulating properties built in, such as low-e coating on the glass, or argon gas sealed between the panes (argon is a better insulator than air), so that storm windows aren't required.

Shutters, shades, and other insulating devices can be put on at night and removed during the day to expose the glazing. They come in a variety of forms and materials. You can install these movable devices either inside or outside your house.

Exterior shutters must be strong enough to withstand the effects of wind, rain, snow, and sun. Rolling shutters are made from interlocking vinyl, or aluminum slats that slide in rigid tracks; the slats may be filled with polyurethane. They're operated from the inside either by a hand crank or a motor. Rolling shutters reduce heat loss and provide both privacy and security. Hinged or folding shutters are also available for exterior application.

Windows can be insulated from the inside with thermally lined draperies, hinged or rolling shutters, or shades. Draperies lined with insulating fabrics can reduce heat loss; the lining can also be hung separately behind the draperies. Interior shutters, either wood or synthetic, can also help insulate by trapping an extra layer of air between the room and the window. Interior shades can be made from quilted fabric, layers of plastic or nylon, or layers of vinyl around a fiberglass core. Quilted shades generally have a core layer of reflective vapor barrier fabric sandwiched between polyester fiberfill and outer fabric coverings. The bottom of the shade is weighted; to reduce air infiltration, the sides may slide in tracks attached to the window frame. Vinyl-coated fiberglass shades may have a chain roller system, or a spring, and may be in tracks at the sides. Some roll-down shutters can also be installed inside the window; they're operated either mechanically or automatically.

In summer, shading devices can prevent unwanted heat from penetrating the interior of your home. Any shading device—an overhang, an awning, or even trees and vines—that keeps the sun off your window altogether works to keep down indoor temperatures. Overhangs (usually planned as part of the original construction) and awnings (either fabric or metal) are most effective on south-facing windows, but give little protection against the low-angle sun on the east and west sides of a house.

Screening devices (shutters, blinds, and shades) can be used either inside or outside your window. Some rolling shutters used for reducing winter heat loss can also be used for summer sun control. Shutters with horizontal louvers are also good for summer shading; they're usually installed on the inside of the window. Screens may be inside or outside. Outside screens may be louvered aluminum, or woven fiberglass; inside screens are woven fiberglass. They cut light without entirely blocking the view.

Blinds can also be used inside or outside. The outdoor type are made from wood or aluminum slats. The slats can be tilted to allow some light, view, and ventilation, or they can be closed; they can be operated either manually or automatically. Indoor blinds are made of various materials, including aluminum and PVC. Conventional horizontal louvers (venetian blinds) and vertical blinds can reduce heat gain by between 20% and 70%. Several manufacturers supply double-glazed windows with louvered blinds between the two panes (below); you can adjust the angle of the louvers with a crank. Indoor shades come in a variety of fabrics, which block light to varying degrees; blackout shades are designed to block light entirely.

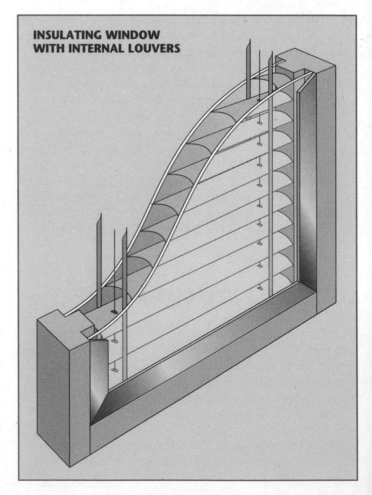

INSULATING WINDOW WITH INTERNAL LOUVERS

You can use glass blocks wherever you don't need ventilation but want to bring in light—both on the exterior and the interior of your home; think of them as translucent or transparent bricks that soften light by diffusing it, eliminating glare.

Glass blocks are made by fusing two halves of pressed glass together, creating a partial vacuum inside; they have approximately the same insulating value as a double-glazed insulating window. Because glass blocks can transmit up to 80% of the available daylight, they're ideal for bathrooms where you want both light and privacy, and for house plants, which thrive in the filtered light. Glass block windows in an entry or over a kitchen counter can provide natural light, yet preserve security. The blocks are thick and virtually impenetrable: They form a barrier to intruders, reduce noise by an average of 40 decibels, and prevent dust and dirt from entering your home. In a room that is heated to 70°F with 40% humidity, glass blocks will remain free of obscuring condensation until the outside temperature drops to -24°F; under similar conditions, condensation would form at 30°F on a single-glazed window.

Blocks made of acrylic are also available, although the range of sizes and patterns is not as great as with glass blocks. Acrylic blocks have many of the same advantages as glass blocks, and are lighter. In both cases, cleaning is simple: Just wipe the inside surface with a damp cloth and wash the outside surface with a hose. No regular maintenance is required.

You can buy 3- or 4-inch-thick square or rectangular glass blocks in many sizes; specially shaped blocks are available for corners, curves, and finishing edges. Textures range from smooth to rippled, wavy, or gridded. For sun control, you can use solar-reflective glass.

Acrylic blocks are available in 3-inch-thick squares or triangles, in various sizes; they may be colored or clear. Both glass and acrylic blocks can be purchased in pre-assembled panels, which makes installation easier.

Glass blocks may be laid in mortar, like bricks. They may also be installed using a system of spacer strips and silicone sealant available from the manufacturer. For detailed installation instructions, consult a manufacturer or supplier. You'll also need to check your local building code for construction requirements for glass blocks. Once you know what's involved, you'll be able to decide whether or not you can do the work yourself.

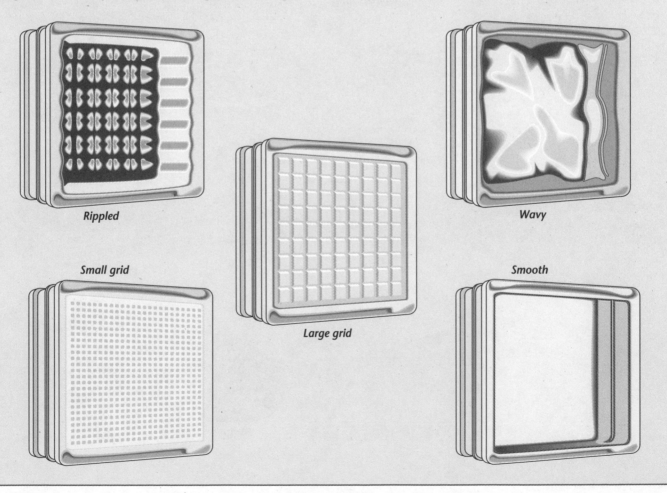

Rippled

Wavy

Small grid

Large grid

Smooth

THE CHOICES IN SKYLIGHTS

You can buy a prefabricated skylight or have one specially made for your needs. Manufacturers offer skylights in a variety of shapes, sizes, and glazings, and in both fixed and opening designs. Skylights may be flat, domed, or pyramidal, and can vary in size from one small enough to fit between two rafters to a skylight large enough to roof a small room; you can also combine several skylights to cover a large area of roof.

Skylights with flat surfaces are glass. Domed skylights have some type of plastic glazing; plastic molds easily into complex shapes. Opening skylights generally open at the bottom, with hinges at the top. Both types may be power-operated; some can be operated with a manual or motorized rod. Fixed skylights are available with a vent, which helps increase air circulation and reduce condensation on the skylight. Many manufacturers also make shading devices designed to go with their skylights, which can be operated either manually or electrically.

There are three basic skylight designs: step-flashed, curb-mounted, and self-flashing; all three types are available with different glazing materials. The installation method that you use depends to some extent on your roofing material. Some manufacturers require a minimum roof pitch for installation of their skylights or roof-windows; however, they often have a mounting curb available for flat or low-angle roofs, which will provide the pitch required for installation.

Whatever skylight design you choose, proper installation is of crucial importance. Failure to properly install the skylight can allow wind-driven rain, and

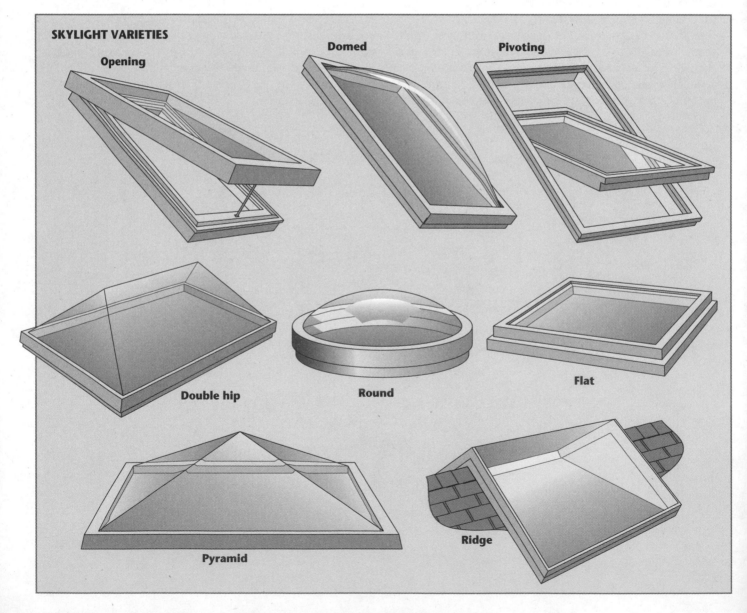

SKYLIGHT VARIETIES

Opening

Domed

Pivoting

Double hip

Round

Flat

Pyramid

Ridge

melting ice to damage your walls and drip down into the interior of your home. Condensation may occur on the interior of the pane, even with a skylight that has been properly installed. To deal with this problem, some manufacturers install condensation gutters; others make skylights with vent flaps, which allow air to circulate in front of the pane. A splayed light shaft also helps reduce the possibility of condensation, because it allows for better air circulation.

Step-flashed skylights come with an integral curb *(right, above)*. These skylights are usually fastened in place with mounting brackets that are screwed through the roof deck. They are flashed around the outside, and the flashing is interleaved with the roofing material. Step-flashed skylights can be used with any type of roofing material, but thick roofing materials (such as Spanish tile or concrete tile) and thin roofing materials (such as asphalt shingle) require different flashing kits. A step-flashed skylight may require a minimum roof pitch.

Curb-mounted skylights are attached to a site-built curb *(right, middle)*. They can be used on roofs with any roofing material, and are especially recommended for roofs with thick roofing materials, such as wood shakes or Spanish tile. Step flashing is added around the curb.

Self-flashing skylights may or may not have an integral curb. They're mounted directly on the roof *(below)*, nailed through a flange, and are intended for use with thin roofing materials. To ensure leak-free installation, some manufacturers make a special sealing kit for use with their self-flashing skylights.

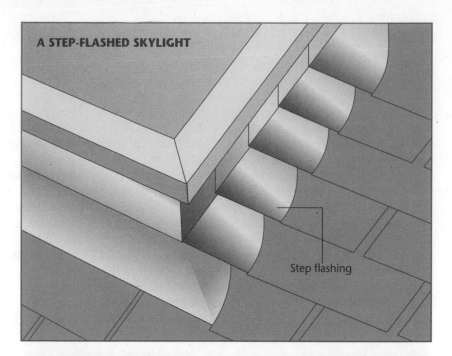

A STEP-FLASHED SKYLIGHT

Step flashing

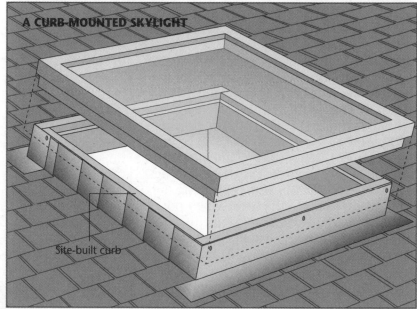

A CURB-MOUNTED SKYLIGHT

Site-built curb

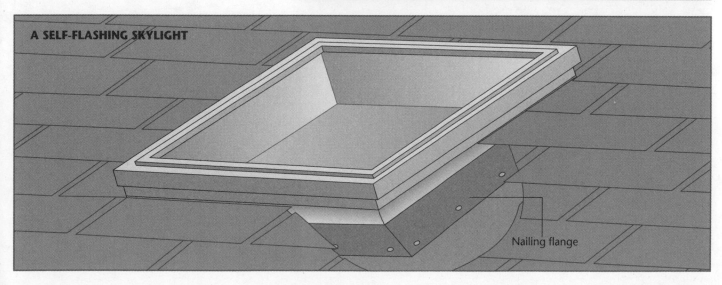

A SELF-FLASHING SKYLIGHT

Nailing flange

SKYLIGHT MATERIALS

Skylights are available in vinyl, aluminum, or clad wood. Wood and vinyl are both poor conductors of heat, so skylights that are made of these materials have insulating properties built in. Some aluminum skylights have insulating frames; they have a thermal break of vinyl, with or without insulating foam. If you live in a warm climate, where controlling heat loss is not a problem, you may prefer a standard aluminum frame.

Skylights may have glass or plastic (acrylic or polycarbonate) glazing. The differences between acrylic and polycarbonate domes are subtle, so you'll probably base your choice on factors such as color or availability. Acrylic and polycarbonate skylights are usually domed; they are available clear, tinted (to reduce glare and heat gain), or translucent white (good for diffusing light).

For skylights with glass panes, you have the same glazing options as for windows. Insulating glass, which is two or more panes of glass sealed together in an insulated frame, is also available with argon gas between the panes. Skylights are available with low-e coated glass, for energy efficiency. Low-e coatings prevent energy of certain wavelengths from passing through the glass. There are low-e coatings for warm climates and for cold climates; they're designed to either help keep your inside heat from escaping, or help keep the heat outside from entering your house. Low-e coatings also block ultraviolet rays, helping to reduce fading of fabrics and carpeting. Safety glass (either tempered or laminated) is available for skylights; check your local building code to determine whether safety glass is required for skylights in your area. Check your local building code for other safety regulation for skylights (such as requiring that they be surrounded by a curb of a certain height, to minimize risk of firefighters falling through them). CAUTION: Skylights are not designed to support your weight; do not walk or stand on them.

CONTROLLING HEAT AND LIGHT

Skylight manufacturers, as well as companies that produce shutters, shades, and blinds for windows, offer a variety of standard or custom-made shading devices for skylights, both for summer shading and winter insulation. Among the items available are exterior awnings, interior shades, and blinds.

Some skylights come with exterior awnings that reduce heat gain without blocking the view and retract into the frame when not in use. Blinds and shades for skylights are available for interior or exterior application. Exterior shades may be movable or fixed. Vinyl coated fiberglass mesh is used outside to cut glare, and reduce heat gain and heat loss, without completely obstructing the view. Solid fabric shades may be used outside as well, but you can't see through them. Interior blinds and shades for skylights are similar to those discussed on page 30 for windows. You can get horizontal louvered blinds (venetian blinds) in aluminum and vinyl, as well as insulating quilted shades or pleated shades backed with a coating designed to reflect the sun's heat in summer, and to retain interior heat in winter. Shades designed simply to block sunlight are also available, both as roller shades or pleated shades.

HOW TO REACH YOUR PIECE OF THE SKY

Manufacturers offer various options for opening and closing your skylight and its shading devices. You can use a simple manually operated extension pole, which may hook into a crank mechanism or onto a cord, to open either the skylight or the shade. You can get a motorized extension pole, which does the same thing, but which you don't have to turn by hand.

Some companies offer a fully motorized system, which comes with a motor drive to open and close your skylight and shading devices. It may be connected to a wall switch, or be operated by a remote control. You can even get a rain sensor for your skylight, which will close the skylight when it starts to rain.

WORKING WITH PROFESSIONALS

The effort that you can contribute to any home remodeling project depends on your knowledge, your abilities, your patience, and your health. Some jobs you can do yourself; for others, you may require some professional help. For example, you may prefer to do only the nonspecialized work, such as clearing the site for construction and cleaning up afterward, but hire experts for everything else.

If you decide to consult a professional, be as precise as possible about what you want. Collect pertinent photographs from magazines, manufacturers' brochures, and advertisements. Describe the types of windows or skylights that you want to use, and where you want to put them. If you have questions, write them down before the interview. It's a good idea to choose a professional who belongs to a trade association, because membership indicates a willingness to comply with the code of ethics adopted by the association. Also, if you do have a complaint, there is an established body that you can turn to with the problem.

Acquiring building permits: You probably will not need a building permit for simple jobs such as replacing glass in a window or even replacing the entire unit. But for more substantial changes, like adding a window or skylight, you may need to apply for one or more permits: a structural permit and other permits for plumbing, mechanical heating or cooling, reroofing, or electrical work. Your local building department can inform you about any permits you may need. For your permit, you'll be charged a flat rate or a percentage of the estimated cost of materials and labor; you may also need to pay a plan-checking fee.

 ASK A PRO

ARE THERE ANY COMPUTER TOOLS I CAN USE TO DEVELOP MY DESIGN IDEAS?
There are software packages available for home computers to help you draft plans and test your design ideas. A computer program will help you visualize what a new window or skylight will look like in your existing wall or roof, and you can try out different sizes or shapes, and different types of windows, so that you can find a design you're satisfied with before you do any remodeling. If you don't have a computer at home, you may be able to find a computer and the appropriate software at your local public library.

Before you obtain permits, a building department official—a plan checker or building inspector—may need to see drawings to ensure that your remodeling concept conforms to local zoning ordinances and building codes. If the project is simple, written specifications or sketches may suffice. More complicated projects may require that the design and the working drawings be executed by an architect or design-build contractor with the appropriate license for that state.

If you plan to do all the work yourself, you should still hire a professional when building codes are involved—especially for plumbing and electrical systems. In fact, it is usually better not to obtain permits yourself, since the person who obtains the permits is generally considered the contractor, and therefore responsible if the work does not conform to building codes. If you do decide to act as your own contractor, you must ask the building department to inspect the work as it progresses. Adding a window usually requires only two inspections: one after the framing is completed, and another one after the job is finished. More complicated jobs require more inspections. Failure to obtain a permit or an inspection may result in your having to dismantle completed work. You may also have to sign an owner-builder release exempting you from worker's compensation insurance before receiving the permits (you don't need the insurance if a state-licensed contractor retained by you applies for the permits and does the work).

Choosing an architect or designer: Architects can, of course, draw up plans acceptable to building department officials. Some will also send out bids, help you select a contractor, specify materials for the contractor to order, and supervise the contractor's performance to ensure that your plans and time schedule are being followed. Designers (or design-build contractors, as they're often called) provide both design and construction services; they can see your project through to completion, from drawing up the plans to the finishing details.

Licensing requirements vary from state to state. Some states that do require architects to be licensed do not require the same of design-build contractors; many design-build contractors charge less for their labor. If stress calculations must be made, design-build contractors may need state-licensed engineers to design the structure and sign the working drawings; architects can do their own calculations. Some architects and design-build contractors don't charge for time spent in an exploratory interview. For plans, you'll probably be charged on an hourly basis. If you want an architect to select the contractor and keep an eye on construction, or if you hire a design-build contractor for the project, try to negotiate a fixed fee. If your project is very small, you may be able to entice an apprentice or drafter working in an architect or designer's office to draw plans for you; expect to pay by the hour.

Choosing a contractor: When you're looking for a contractor, ask architects, designers, and friends for recommendations. Contact one or more of the various trade associations of the remodeling industry, such as the National Association of the Remodeling Industry, or the National Association of Home Builders Remodelors™ Council *(right)*, and ask for their recommendations. It's a good idea to meet with several contractors to discuss your project, and then call back those whom you feel comfortable with. To compare bids for the actual construction, give each contractor you're considering either an exact description and sketches of the desired remodeling or plans and specifications prepared by a professional. Include a detailed account of who will be responsible for what work.

Ask each contractor for the names and phone numbers of customers who've had projects similar to yours. Call several of these references, and discuss their level of satisfaction with the contractor; be sure to ask specific questions about whether the work was done on schedule, whether the site was well maintained, and whether they would hire the same contractor again; if you can, inspect the contractor's work. You can also contact the Better Business Bureau, to find out whether there are existing complaints about the contractor you're considering.

Most contractors will bid a fixed price for a remodeling job, to be paid in installments based on the amount of work completed. Many states limit the amount of money that contractors can request before work begins. Though some contractors may want a fee based on a percentage of the cost of materials and labor, it's usually wiser to insist on a fixed-price bid. This protects you both against an unexpected rise in the cost of materials (assuming the contractor does the buying) and against the chance that the work will take more time, adding to your labor costs. Don't be tempted to make price your only criterion for selection; reliability, quality of work, and on-time performance are also important.

Make sure your agreement with the contractor you've selected includes the following items in writing (include brand names and model numbers where appropriate): plans and material specifications, services to be supplied, cost, method and schedule of payment, time schedule, and warranty against defects. You can get a model contract from the American Homeowners Foundation, which covers these elements in straightforward terms; see the box at right for their address.

The contract is binding to both parties, and it minimizes problems by defining responsibilities. You can change your mind once construction starts, but remember that this usually requires a contract modification, and will probably involve both additional expense and delays.

Hiring workers: Even if you decide to do the work on your own, you may also want to hire workers on an hourly basis. As an employer, you're expected to withhold state and federal income taxes; to withhold, remit, and contribute to Social Security; and to pay state unemployment insurance. For more information about your responsibilities as an employer, talk to a building department official, or look under the subheading "Taxes" under your state in the white pages of your telephone directory.

FOR MORE INFORMATION...

Various trade associations will provide information about how to find and hire a contractor or other remodeling professional. The National Association of Home Builders Remodelors™ Council will send you a brochure called "How to choose a remodelor who's on the level," if you include a self-addressed stamped envelope. Their address is: 1201 15th Street NW, Washington, DC 20005.

The National Association of the Remodeling Industry also publishes a brochure about how to select a remodeling contractor. Contact them at 1-800-440-NARI for a free copy of the brochure and a list of NARI members in your area.

The American Institute of Building Design will also supply an information brochure as well as a list of designers working in your area; you can call them at 1-800-366-2423.

To purchase a copy of the model home-improvement contractor agreement or other literature, contact the American Homeowners Foundation at 6776 Little Falls Road, Arlington, VA, 22213; their telephone number is 1-703-536-7776. For credit card orders, you can call them at 1-800-489-7776.

WINDOWS

Few do-it-yourselfers question their ability to replace an existing window with another window of the same size. But many may wonder whether they have the skills to cut a hole in the side of their house to add a window where there's never been one.

Actually, installing a window in a house with wood siding is fairly straightforward. It usually requires only a knowledge of basic carpentry. However, depending on the project you choose, you may need some skills in other areas, such as siding and roofing. If your siding is masonry, masonry veneer, or aluminum, you'll probably require assistance from professionals. Sometimes you'll have to get professional help for your window project even if your house has wood siding; for example, if you're installing a large expanse of glass; if the work involves moving pipes, wires, or ducts; if the new window is located within 4 feet of a corner of the house; if a bearing wall is involved; or if the job requires major structural changes. Information about dealing with professionals begins on page 35.

Most windows sold at home centers are ready-to-install, prehung (prefabricated) units that come with frame, sash, glazing, weather stripping, and hardware. Once you've prepared the opening, you can install one of these windows in a few hours.

In this chapter, you'll find step-by-step instructions for installing several different types of windows in a frame house. You'll learn how to use an existing opening, enlarge or reduce an existing opening, cut a new opening, and close an old one that's no longer needed. Beginning on page 63, you'll find information on repairs and maintenance for your existing windows. On page 62, you'll find out how to make your windows and skylights more secure. And on page 76, we'll tell you how to weather-strip your windows to keep out the cold.

Installing a bay window increases the sense of space in a room and can also provide a cozy seat.

TOOLS AND SUPPLIES

As well as standard tools—claw hammer, tape measure, putty knife, and utility knife—the tools shown below will help you install or repair a window. You'll also need a ladder, common nails for framing, finishing nails for applying trim, lumber to frame the opening, molding, nails or screws (as specified by the manufacturer) to attach the window, wallboard screws or nails, and finishing materials, caulk, and wood shims.

Always follow basic safety guidelines. Wear work gloves when handling rough or sharp materials, and eye protection when using a striking tool. When working on projects that create a lot of dust (such as cutting through walls), wear a dust mask or respirator, and if your project requires you to be on the roof or to work high off the ground, do it safely; read the section on safe working practices found on page 79.

Be aware of hidden dangers, such as lead paint and asbestos-cement siding. Paint produced before 1978 may contain lead; consult your local housing department before removing such paint. Asbestos-cement shingle siding releases hazardous particles when cut or crushed. Consult your health and safety office for information on removing it.

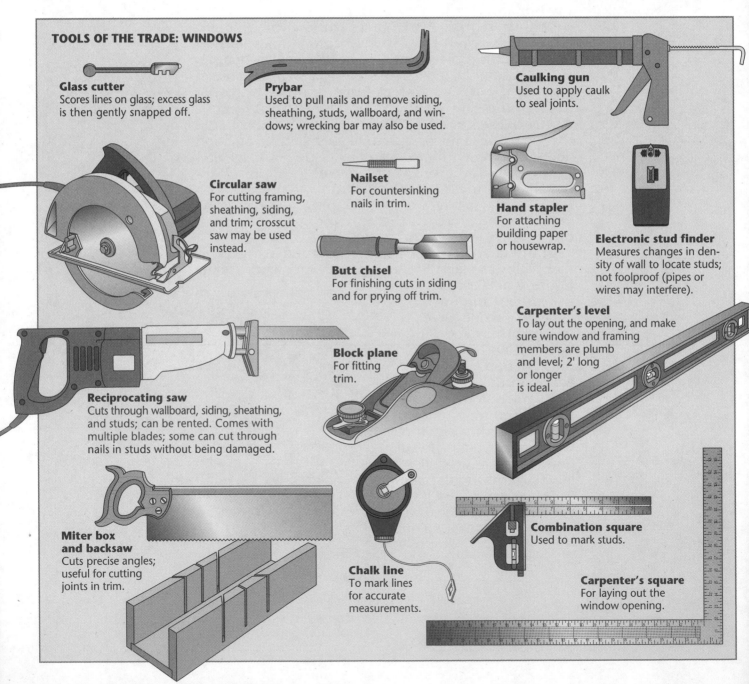

TOOLS OF THE TRADE: WINDOWS

Glass cutter
Scores lines on glass; excess glass is then gently snapped off.

Prybar
Used to pull nails and remove siding, sheathing, studs, wallboard, and windows; wrecking bar may also be used.

Caulking gun
Used to apply caulk to seal joints.

Circular saw
For cutting framing, sheathing, siding, and trim; crosscut saw may be used instead.

Nailset
For countersinking nails in trim.

Hand stapler
For attaching building paper or housewrap.

Electronic stud finder
Measures changes in density of wall to locate studs; not foolproof (pipes or wires may interfere).

Butt chisel
For finishing cuts in siding and for prying off trim.

Reciprocating saw
Cuts through wallboard, siding, sheathing, and studs; can be rented. Comes with multiple blades; some can cut through nails in studs without being damaged.

Block plane
For fitting trim.

Carpenter's level
To lay out the opening, and make sure window and framing members are plumb and level; 2' long or longer is ideal.

Miter box and backsaw
Cuts precise angles; useful for cutting joints in trim.

Chalk line
To mark lines for accurate measurements.

Combination square
Used to mark studs.

Carpenter's square
For laying out the window opening.

BEFORE YOU BEGIN

Taking a close look now at the wall you want to open will help you avoid problems—and perhaps additional expense—later on. You'll want to consider the following questions: Will work involve just one wall or will it require more extensive remodeling or redecorating? What type of framing was used in the original construction of your house? Does cutting an opening into the wall require any rewiring or rerouting of wires, pipes, or ducts *(page 41)*?

Are you required to have a building permit or conform to any building codes or regulations? Be sure to call your local building department and find out before you even begin planning.

TYPES OF FRAMING

How you'll shore up the ceiling before cutting the opening and how you'll frame it depend on the type of wood framing used in your house—either balloon or platform (also called Western).

Balloon framing: Standard until about 1930, this framing is still used in some houses veneered with stucco, brick, or other masonry material. In balloon framing, the studs in bearing walls extend from the sill on top of the foundation to the sill supporting the rafters *(below)*.

From your basement or crawl space, examine the framing on top of the foundation. If the studs (usually

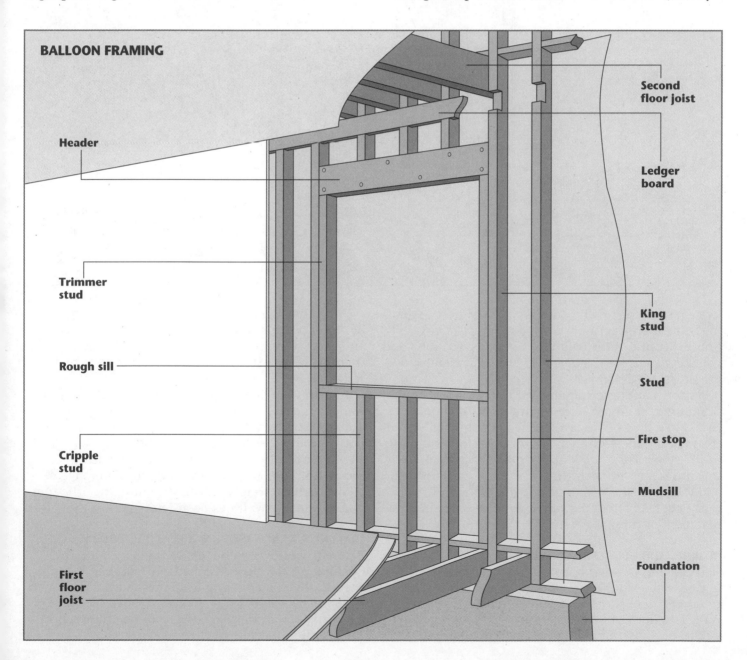

BALLOON FRAMING

Header

Trimmer stud

Rough sill

Cripple stud

First floor joist

Second floor joist

Ledger board

King stud

Stud

Fire stop

Mudsill

Foundation

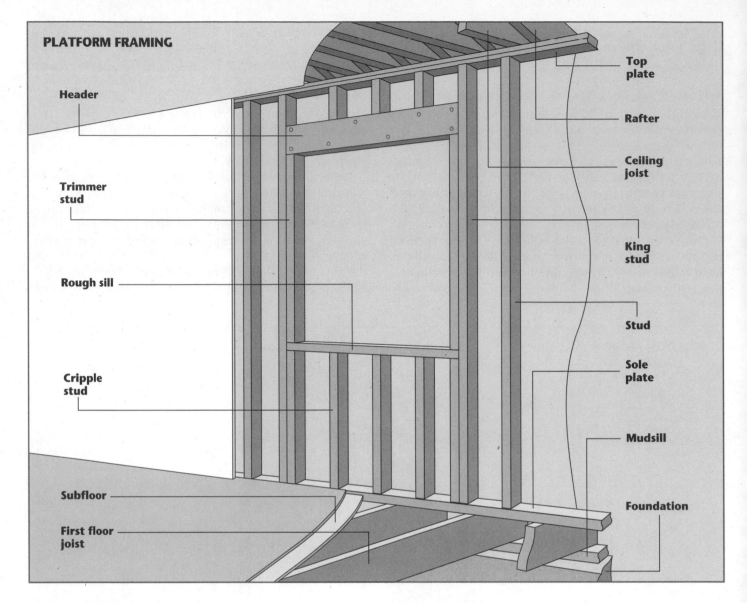

Header

Trimmer stud

Rough sill

Cripple stud

Subfloor

First floor joist

Top plate

Rafter

Ceiling joist

King stud

Stud

Sole plate

Mudsill

Foundation

2x4s) rest on the sill and are nailed to the sides of the joists, balloon framing was used in constructing your house. Because of the length of the studs, you can't add new king studs for the opening; instead, you must use existing studs as king studs.

Platform or Western framing: Homes using this type of framing, common in residential construction since the 1930's, are built in layers. The floor structure sits on the foundation, and the first-floor walls follow on top of the floor. These walls support the ceiling and roof structures *(above)*. In a two-story house, another floor and wall structure is built on the first-floor walls. In this type of construction, the studs are not visible from the basement or crawl space.

BEARING AND NONBEARING WALLS
You can add window openings to either bearing or nonbearing walls. Any wall that runs at a right angle to rafters, floor joists, and ceiling joists is a bearing wall. The studs in such walls support the weight of the structure above, including the major load of the roof.

Walls that run parallel to the rafters and joists may be either bearing or nonbearing walls. In some cases, end walls support the weight of the roof. And if there's a second story in the house, they bear that weight as well.

To be on the safe side, it's best to treat all exterior walls as bearing walls. This means that before you cut any openings in an exterior wall, you'll have to support its weight with a temporary shoring wall *(page 44)*. The opening itself should be surrounded with heavy framing, as described beginning on page 42, to support the weight of the structure once the temporary shoring wall has been removed.

FRAMING A ROUGH OPENING AND SIZING YOUR WINDOW
Before a window can be installed in any wall, the opening for it must be framed with lumber to support the window. In a bearing wall, the framing must also support the weight of the structure above the window and transfer that weight to the studs on either side of the opening.

The rough opening size—the height and width of the opening for the window—is the measurement that you'll work with in framing the opening with trimmer studs, header, and rough sill. Generally, these dimensions are 1/2 to 1 inch larger than the actual size specified for the window. If you want to replace a window with a new one of the same size, you'll need to determine the size of the existing rough opening. To do this, remove the trim from the inside of the window *(page 48)*, and measure both height and width. Select a window that calls for the same rough opening size.

In manufacturer's catalogs, at least three sizes are given for the width and height of each window—rough opening size, actual or unit size, and nominal or sash size. A window's rough opening size tells you the dimensions of the rough opening required to install that particular window. Actual or unit size includes the frame around the window; it is the measurement from the outside of one jamb to the outside of the other, and from the top of the head jamb to the bottom of the sill. Nominal or sash size tells you the width and height of the sash inside the frame.

Don't make any final decisions on window size until you've located the wall studs; see the section on finding the studs on page 43. You may be able to simplify your project by selecting a window slightly larger or smaller, or by moving the window to one side or the other. After you've determined the size of the proposed opening and the window size, you're ready to purchase the window. But don't begin preparing the opening until you've taken delivery of the window, because you'll need to check your measurements against the actual window.

LOCATING OBSTRUCTIONS

Your walls and ceiling conceal wires, pipes, and heating or air-conditioning ducts that may be just where you want to place a new window or skylight. You'll need to do some investigating to determine where these obstructions are, before you decide where your new opening should go; you might prefer to hire a specialist in pipe locating. If you find wiring, pipes, or ducts in the way, the easiest and least expensive option is to change your plan for the location of the window. If you decide to reroute the offending wire, pipe, or duct, it's best to hire a professional, who will have the specialized skills and tools for the job; some rerouting work may be regulated by your local building code.

Even if you have a set of architect's drawings for your home, you'll have to search for clues to obstructions in the walls. First, make a sketch of the wall; be sure to show the position of the nearest side wall. As you find clues to what lies behind the wall, you can mark them on the sketch.

Look outside for any pipes coming through the roof directly above the proposed window opening. Pipes projecting above the roof indicate drain pipes in the wall directly below; you may find hot and cold water pipes, as well. Check the second story above the proposed opening; is there a radiator against the wall? If so, there may be a hot water or steam heating pipe in the window area. Is there a hot-air register in the wall under the proposed opening or above it on the second floor? If so, a heating duct may be in the wall. Remove the register's grille and reach into the duct to determine if it leads to the proposed window area.

On your sketch, mark the locations of receptacles, switches, and wall lights. Connect them to reach each other with vertical and horizontal lines. Since electricians usually install wiring in these directions, the lines on your sketch show possible locations of wires. Go up to the attic with a light, tape measure, pencil, and your sketch. Locate the top plate of the wall you propose to open. Measuring from the nearest side wall (you should be able to see the top of it), mark on your sketch the locations of any wires, pipes, or ducts coming through the top plate. If your house has a basement or crawl space, repeat the process. When you've marked all this information on your sketch, you should have a good idea of the locations of wires, pipes, and ducts hiding in the wall.

PLAY IT SAFE

DON'T CUT BLINDLY INTO A WALL
Turning off the electrical power to a room may not disable all circuits; some circuits, such as for central air-conditioning, may still be active. To open walls easily and safely, use a saber saw fitted with an old blade broken off so that it extends only about 1/2 inch beyond the saw's base plate on the downstroke (below). The blade will retract above the base plate on the upstroke so that the blade will have to punch through the wallboard on each stroke. This should not be a problem since wallboard is relatively soft. Using this technique, you can cut through only the wallboard without risk of cutting into anything behind the wall.

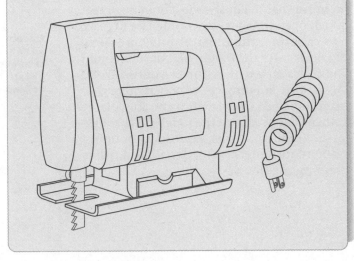

FRAMING A NEW WINDOW OPENING

A professional can install a window where none existed before in one day, but it will probably take you longer. Plan to spread the work over several days, or even several weekends. The procedure described below allows you to keep the exterior of your house intact until you're ready to put the new window in place. The installation instructions beginning on page 51 are typical, but if they're different in any way from the manufacturer's instructions, follow the directions that come with your window.

The frame you construct around the opening supports both your new window and, if it's a bearing wall, the ceiling above it. If your house was built with balloon framing, you'll have to provide additional support for the studs above the opening. Illustrated at right are three different possibilities for framing a standard window. You'll find instructions for framing the opening for special windows, such as octagons or other shapes, on page 47. Our instructions use an existing stud for one king stud and a new stud for the other; adjust the procedures to meet your situation. If your house has balloon framing *(page 39)*, you'll have to use two existing studs as king studs. After you've installed the header, you can use as many trimmer studs as necessary to reduce the opening width to the correct size.

Before you begin framing, gather all the materials you'll need for the job. Be sure to have on hand enough lumber for the king stud (if needed), the rough sill, the header, and the trimmer studs; use 2-by lumber the same width as the studs in your walls. Keep in mind that building code requirements for rough openings may vary from place to place. For example, the illustrations here show single 2x4s for the rough sill, but some building codes may require the use of two 2x4s. Also, some building codes may require the trimmer studs to extend to the sole plate, rather than resting on the rough sill as shown here. Be sure to check your local building code requirements for the sill and other framing members.

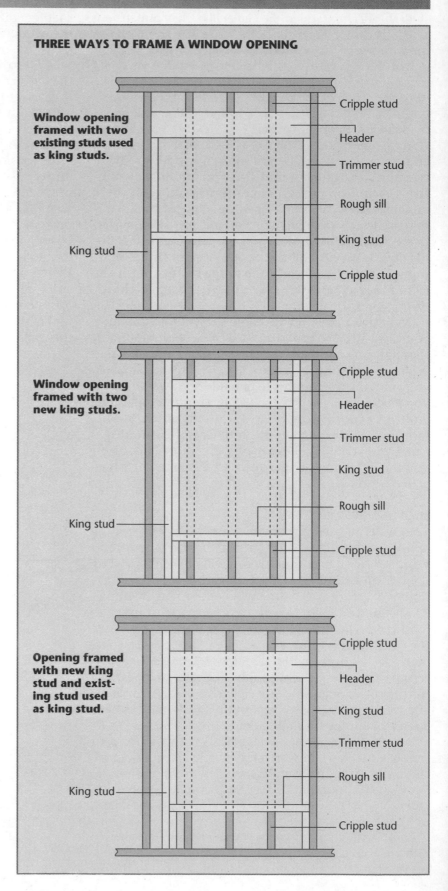

THREE WAYS TO FRAME A WINDOW OPENING

Window opening framed with two existing studs used as king studs.

- Cripple stud
- Header
- Trimmer stud
- Rough sill
- King stud
- Cripple stud

King stud

Window opening framed with two new king studs.

- Cripple stud
- Header
- Trimmer stud
- King stud
- Rough sill
- Cripple stud

King stud

Opening framed with new king stud and existing stud used as king stud.

- Cripple stud
- Header
- King stud
- Trimmer stud
- Rough sill
- Cripple stud

King stud

TOOLKIT
- Tape measure
- Electronic stud finder (optional)
- Carpenter's level
- Reciprocating saw or saber saw
- Claw hammer
- Wrecking bar
- Combination square

1 Finding the studs

To locate the studs on both sides of the opening, measure the actual width of the window (width over the outside of the jambs) and mark this width on the wall where you want the window. Tap along the wall away from each mark and parallel to the floor; when the hollow sound changes to a dull thud, mark that spot. You can use an electronic stud finder instead, which locates studs by measuring changes in a wall's density. Once you've found the inside edges of the two studs, make a vertical pencil line on the wall to mark the edge of the stud; use a level to ensure the line is straight. Repeat for the stud on the other side.

Having found the studs, reevaluate the position of the window; if you can move it a couple of inches to use one of the existing studs as a king stud, you'll save considerable work.

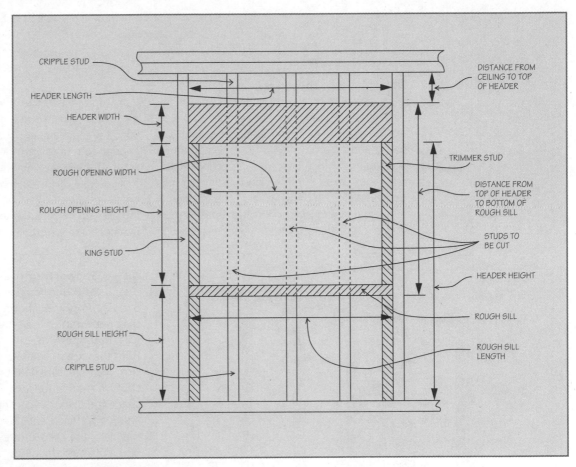

CRIPPLE STUD

HEADER LENGTH

HEADER WIDTH

ROUGH OPENING WIDTH

ROUGH OPENING HEIGHT

KING STUD

ROUGH SILL HEIGHT

CRIPPLE STUD

DISTANCE FROM CEILING TO TOP OF HEADER

TRIMMER STUD

DISTANCE FROM TOP OF HEADER TO BOTTOM OF ROUGH SILL

STUDS TO BE CUT

HEADER HEIGHT

ROUGH SILL

ROUGH SILL LENGTH

2 Making a drawing and marking the opening

Once you've found the studs, make a drawing of the existing framing. Then, using shading or a pencil of a different color, so you can keep the marks straight, sketch in the outline of the rough opening and the new framing; mark all dimensions *(above)*. Check them carefully and recheck them often as you work.

Next, mark the wall area that you'll be removing. If you're using an existing stud for one king stud and installing a new stud for the other, you'll need to remove the wall covering from floor to ceiling between the king studs so you can nail the new stud to the sole plate and top plate. Using a level and a pencil, extend the line marking the edge of the stud (the one you're using for the king stud) up to the ceiling and down to the floor. Make sure it's plumb. Mark the location of the new king stud (as shown on your drawing) on the top and bottom of the wall by measuring from the line; connect the two points on the top and the two on the bottom with straight, perpendicular lines, and check them with your level. Crosshatch the areas of the wall you need to remove.

If you're using two existing studs as king studs, you'll need to remove the wall covering to the floor below the window and above the window so you'll have room to cut the studs and toenail the header to them.

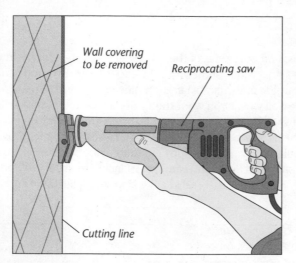

Wall covering to be removed

Reciprocating saw

Cutting line

3 Cutting away the wall covering

First, remember that there may be pipes or electrical wiring behind the wall *(page 41)* and shutting off the power to the room may not disable all circuits. The safest way to cut into a wall is to use a saber saw with a shortened blade. You can also use a reciprocating saw, but be very sure you won't cut any wiring or into a pipe.

Cut along the vertical lines or the vertical and horizontal lines, as appropriate. Use a hammer and wrecking bar to remove the wall covering. Wearing work gloves and a dust mask, remove any insulation in the wall. If any wires or pipes cross the opening, you'll have to have them rerouted.

4 Marking the studs

Referring to your drawing and measuring from the floor, mark the height of the bottom of the rough sill on each stud. Using a combination square and a pencil, mark horizontal lines through these points on two adjacent sides of each stud. On any stud you'll use as a king stud, mark a horizontal line on the side facing the opening.

Again referring to your drawing, similarly mark the height of the top of the header on each stud.

If the top of the header is within 3" of the top plate, you can remove the studs from the rough sill to the top plate, and make the header wide enough to rest against the bottom of the top plate. This will save quite a bit of work.

If you're working on a bearing wall, don't begin cutting until you've supported the ceiling and structure above the marked opening, as described in the next step.

5 Supporting the ceiling of a bearing wall

Build a temporary shoring wall slightly longer than the width of the opening and parallel to the wall, to support the ceiling, and place it about 4' from the existing wall, so you have room to work. First, measure from floor to ceiling and cut 2x4s for studs to this dimension, minus 4$\frac{1}{2}$". You'll space the 2x4s 16" on center, and you'll need another for each end. For the sole plate and the top plate, use 2x4s about 2' longer than the width of the planned opening.

Using a combination square, mark the location for the studs on the sole plate and top plate. Lay the studs on the floor, and face-nail the sole plate and top plate to each end, using two 3$\frac{1}{2}$" nails for each stud.

Position a 12" wide strip of $\frac{3}{4}$" plywood where you want the wall to be. Have your helpers raise the wall, then lift it onto the plywood. While a helper uses a level to make sure the shoring wall is plumb on the side and the end, drive shims under each stud between the sole plate and the plywood, so that the top plate is tight against the ceiling *(left)*. Toenail the sole plate to the plywood through each shim.

Carpenter's level

Top plate

2x4 stud

Plywood strip

Sole plate

Shim

HOW DO I SUPPORT BALLOON-FRAME STUDS?

You'll need to support the studs above the opening as well as the ceiling (step 5) by placing a waler, a horizontal board, against the ceiling and bolting it to the studs (right). The waler must be long enough to span the opening and reach the studs beyond the king studs. For the waler, cut a 2x8 at least 3 feet longer than the width of the rough opening if your studs are spaced 16 inches on center, or about 5 feet longer if they're 24 inches on center.

You'll need a helper to place the waler on edge and hold it tight against the ceiling. Make sure the center is over the center of the rough opening. Drive a few 3-inch nails through the waler into the ledger board to hold the waler temporarily. Drill a pilot hole for a $^1/_2$- or $^3/_8$-inch lag screw at least $4^1/_2$ inches long, through the waler and ledger board and into each stud. Placing a flat washer under the head of each screw, secure the waler to the studs with the lag screws.

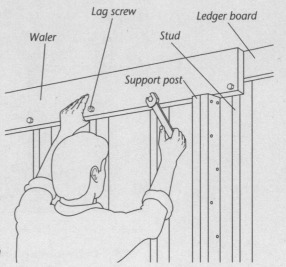

For support posts, cut four 2x4s or two 4x4s long enough to wedge between the waler and the floor; if you're using 2x4s, nail two of them together with 3-inch nails to make one 4x4 post. Wedge a post under the end of the waler; pad the end, if necessary, to protect the floor.

Framing the opening

TOOLKIT
- Reciprocating saw
- Claw hammer
- Tape measure
- Carpenter's square
- Circular saw or crosscut saw

1 ► **Cutting the studs**

With a reciprocating saw, cut the studs to be removed at the lines marking the bottom of the rough sill; be sure to cut exactly along the lines so the rough sill will fit tightly against the cripple studs. Next, cut on the lines marking the position of the header. Keep the cutoff pieces of lumber; you may be able to use them to build the framing.

If your header fits tightly against the top plate, remove the upper part of each stud completely. Remove any nails protruding from the top plate.

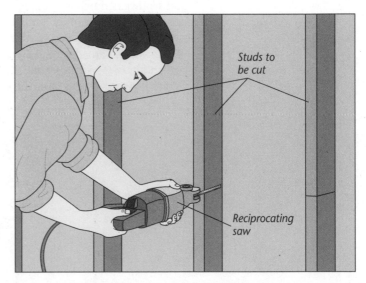

2 **Installing a king stud**

If you need to install a king stud, measure and mark the required distance from the existing king stud on the top of the sole plate and on the underside of the top plate. Using a carpenter's square and a pencil, draw a line through each point. On these lines, you'll place the edge of the new king stud that faces the opening.

Carefully measure the distance between the lines you just marked to determine the length of the new king stud. Cut lumber to this length, making sure both ends are square. To set the stud in place, line up the face on the opening side with the top and bottom lines. Toenail the stud to the sole plate and top plate with 2½" nails.

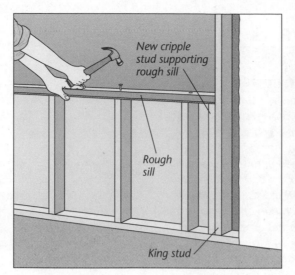

New cripple stud supporting rough sill

Rough sill

King stud

3 Installing the rough sill

Mark the height of the bottom of the rough sill on the sides of the king studs facing the opening. Measure down from these marks to the top of the sole plate and cut two cripple studs to this length. Use 3" nails to fasten these cripple studs to the facing edges of the king studs. Make sure the ends of the cripple studs fit tightly against the sole plate. The tops of these new cripple studs should be the same height above the floor as the cripple studs you created by cutting the studs to make the opening.

Measure the distance between the king studs across the cripple studs; cut a stud to this length for the rough sill. Place it on top of the cripple studs, and toenail it to the king studs with 2½" nails. Face-nail it to the cripple studs with 3½" nails (left).

4 Determining the size of lumber for the header

Requirements for the header vary, depending on the width of the opening and whether the wall is bearing or not. For headers in nonbearing walls, you can use a 2x4 placed flat, just like a rough sill, unless a heavier header is required by your building code. For a bearing wall, if your wall is framed with 2x4s, you'll need either two pieces of 2-by lumber, with ½" thick plywood sandwiched between them, or a single piece of 4-by lumber (4-by lumber may be difficult to find in the required width).

If your wall is framed with 2x6s, you'll need three lengths of 2-by lumber and 2 pieces of ½" thick plywood. In any case, the width of the lumber depends on your local building code requirements, and the length is determined by the distance between the king stud.

If the top of the header will be within 3" of the ceiling plate, you can eliminate the cripple studs by making your header wider; the lumber will cost a little more, but you'll have less work to do. If the span above the window is long, the space may not be wide enough for a header of the required width. In this case, you'll have to use a steel girder ordered from a structural steel company. Measure the required length accurately: Once the girder is cut, you can't adjust the length with your tools.

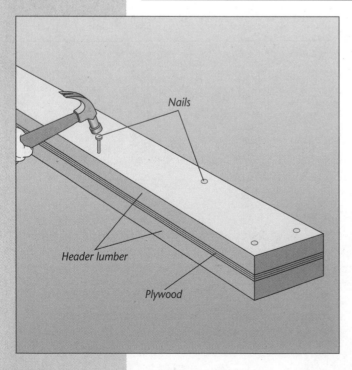

Nails

Header lumber

Plywood

5 Assembling the header

Sight along the edges of the lumber to see if the pieces are curved. If so, assemble the header with the two crowned or convex edges on the same side; then install that side on top. Square up one end of each header piece and the plywood piece by marking them with your square and cutting them off with a saw. Measure the space between the king studs where the header will be installed and check the measurement against your drawing. Make sure the measurements agree before you cut the lumber. Starting from the squared-off end of each piece, measure to length and mark the point; draw a cutting line at that point with a combination square. Using a circular saw or crosscut saw, cut each piece along the line.

Lay one of the pieces of 2-by lumber on a flat surface; note the position of the crowned edge, if any. Place the plywood on top, cover it with the other piece of lumber—make sure its crowned edge is on the same side as the first piece of lumber—and line up the edges. Square the stack and nail the pieces together with 3½" nails (left); place two nails at each end about 2" from the cut edge and stagger them about 12" apart along the length. If the ends protrude through the other side, clinch them over.

6 Installing the header and trimmer studs

Measure along one king stud from the floor to the top of the header; check that the mark is level with the mark on the other king stud. Measure the distance from the top of the rough sill to these marks and cut stud material for trimmer studs to fit. Have your helper position the top of the header, crown side up, against the cripple studs or top plate while you place the trimmer studs against the king studs. Use a hammer, if necessary, to drive them into position against the king studs. Nail the trimmer studs to the king studs with 3" nails. Be sure that the distance between the trimmer studs is the same as the width of the rough opening on your drawing.

The header should fit tightly against the sheathing on the outside and the cripple studs or top plate above it. If necessary, drive shims between the tops of the trimmer studs and the header until it fits tightly. Measure the distance between the bottom of the header and the top of the sill at each end, and make sure it matches the height of the rough opening on your drawing. Using 2½" nails, toenail the ends of the header to the king studs and the cripples to the header. If the header rests against the top plate, toenail the header to it.

You can patch the interior wall now, as described on page 50, or wait until you install the window (*page 51*).

SPECIAL WINDOWS

Bays or oriels, bows, greenhouse sections, and most other special windows require rectangular openings framed in the same manner as described above. Be sure to study the manufacturer's instructions for any special requirements. Some bay windows, for example, extend from floor to ceiling and require substantial structural changes that are best left to a contractor.

The most difficult windows to frame are those special windows with nonrectangular shapes, such as circular, semicircular, quarter-circle, hexagonal, or octagonal. With these windows, you'll first have to frame a square or rectangular opening with header, trimmer studs, and rough sill, as described above. Then you'll have to add additional framing to support the window, as shown in the illustration below. Framing should not be closer than ½ inch to the outside of the window frame. Detailed instructions for installing nonrectangular windows are given on page 54.

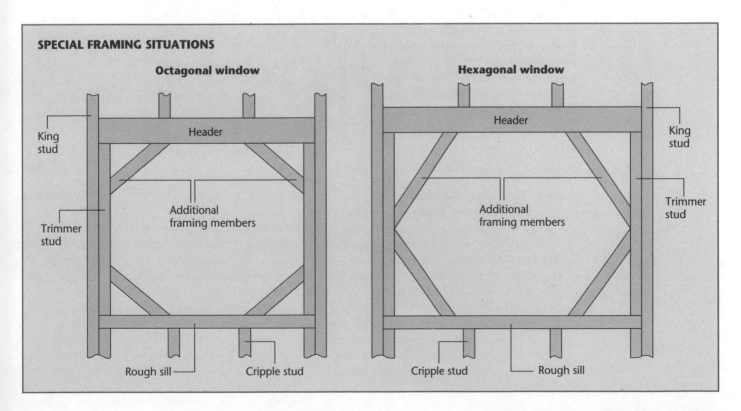

SPECIAL FRAMING SITUATIONS

Octagonal window — King stud, Header, Trimmer stud, Additional framing members, Rough sill, Cripple stud

Hexagonal window — Header, King stud, Trimmer stud, Additional framing members, Cripple stud, Rough sill

ALTERING AN EXISTING OPENING

Replacing an old window and frame with one of the same size is not very difficult, but you must remove the existing window and frame to expose the rough opening. Measure the size of the rough opening and order a window that calls for the same rough opening size. When you have the new window, check to be sure it's the correct size.

You may want to enlarge an existing opening, but often there's as much work involved in this job as in cutting a new hole in a wall; you have to remove not only the old window but also much of the rough framing, including the header and the sill. And before you rip out the header, you must build a temporary wall to support the ceiling. The methods used to enlarge an opening are similar to those for making a new opening, so before you start, read the section on opening up the interior wall beginning on page 43.

Installing a window that's smaller than the existing window is a fairly easy task. After removing the old window, you simply frame in from the sides of the existing opening. The hardest part of the job is finishing the framed area to match the siding outside and the wall covering inside.

Removing an existing window and closing the old opening is also easy. As with installing a smaller window, what's difficult about closing an opening is matching the new surfaces to the old ones. On the following pages, you'll find instructions for all of these ways of altering an existing opening.

Taking out a window

TOOLKIT
- Butt chisel
- Claw hammer
- Screwdriver (optional)
- Utility knife
- Prybar
- Reciprocating saw with metal-cutting blade, or hacksaw (optional)

1 ▷ Removing the interior trim and the sash

Before you remove the existing window, carefully pry off the trim from the inside of the window, using a butt chisel and a hammer (*right*).

Take out the sash, if possible, before removing the frame. For casement or awning windows, remove the operator (*page 73*) and unscrew the hinges. For a sliding window, lift the sash and pull it out from the bottom. Removing the sash of a double-hung window is a little more complicated. Pry off the interior stop (*page 64*), and then remove the lower sash and disconnect the sash balances. Remove the parting strip (*page 65*) and repeat with the upper sash.

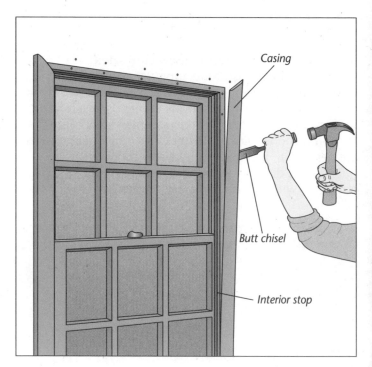

Casing

Butt chisel

Interior stop

2 Removing the exterior trim and the frame

Using a utility knife, cut through the caulking between the outside of the window and the siding. Use a prybar, butt chisel, and hammer to pry off the trim. If your new window includes trim, you don't need to save the old trim.

Determine how the window frame is fastened to the house. If the frame is nailed directly into the framing around the opening, either pry out the nails with a prybar, or cut through them with a reciprocating saw fitted with a metal-cutting blade, or a hacksaw. If the frame is nailed through a flange to the sheathing, pry the nails out; place the claw of your prybar under the nailhead, and pry against the frame.

If you want to reuse the frame, carefully remove it from the opening and pry out any exposed nails. If you're not planning to reuse the frame, saw through the rough sill and pry off the two pieces, then remove the side jambs and head jamb. Clear away the debris.

Enlarging an opening

TOOLKIT
- Tape measure
- Saber saw with shortened blade
- Wrecking bar or prybar
- Reciprocating saw with metal-cutting blade
- Claw hammer
- Combination square
- Circular saw

1 ▶ **Planning the opening**
Remove the trim from around the inside of the window *(opposite)* so you can study the framing. Make a drawing of the existing opening, showing all the existing framing pieces. Mark the rough opening for the new window on the drawing using shading or a pencil of a different color to help you keep the measurements straight *(right)*; draw in the new framing pieces. It's helpful to mark the rough opening size and the measurements for the header, rough sill, trimmer studs, and cripple studs. From your drawing, determine how much wall covering you need to remove to build the new framing. Mark the outline of this area on the wall and add crosshatched pencil lines, as shown on page 44.

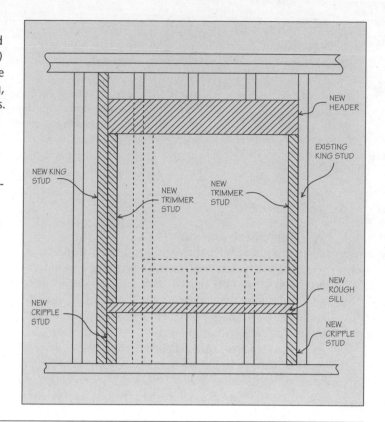

NEW HEADER

EXISTING KING STUD

NEW KING STUD

NEW TRIMMER STUD

NEW TRIMMER STUD

NEW ROUGH SILL

NEW CRIPPLE STUD

NEW CRIPPLE STUD

2 **Removing the old framing**
CAUTION: There may be pipes or electrical wiring behind the wall you need to cut *(page 41)*. To avoid them, use a saber saw with a shortened blade. Cut along the lines you marked on the wall. Pry off the wall covering and remove any insulation behind it; wear protective gloves and a dust mask or respirator when handling insulation. Have any wiring or pipes rerouted, if necessary.

Build a temporary shoring wall to prevent the ceiling from sagging or collapsing *(page 44)*. If your house was built with balloon framing, you'll also need to build a support for the studs above the enlarged opening *(page 45)*. Turn to the section beginning on page 39 to determine the type of framing used in your house. Remove the window as described opposite. Pry the trimmer studs away from the sides of the opening with a wrecking bar or prybar, remove the nails, and set the studs aside. Pry out the header with a wrecking bar. If it doesn't come away easily, put a metal-cutting blade in a reciprocating saw, and cut through the nails holding it. Since the sheathing on the outside is nailed to the header, you may have to remove some of the siding and sheathing to free the header.

Using a combination square and a pencil, mark cutting lines on all the studs within the opening at the height of the bottom of the rough sill and the top of the header *(page 44)*. Using a reciprocating saw with a blade that cuts through nails, cut the studs along these lines and remove the cutoff pieces and the rough sill.

Remove any exposed nails from the remaining framing and clear away the debris.

3 **Framing the enlarged opening**
The procedure for framing the opening is basically the same as that for framing a new opening *(page 45)*. Be sure to check the lengths of the cripple studs before installing them. Install the new king stud; then cut and nail a cripple stud to it, to support the end of the rough sill. Install the new rough sill. Build the new header and cut the trimmer studs to length. Install the header as described on page 47. Nail the trimmer studs to the king studs; then toenail the header to the king studs and the cripple studs to the header with 2¹/₂" nails.

If any sheathing or siding overlaps the rough opening, cut it back to the opening's edges.

Reducing an opening

TOOLKIT
- Tape measure
- Combination square
- Circular saw or crosscut saw
- Claw hammer

1 Planning the opening

First, remove the trim from the inside of the window, as described on page 48. Then, make a drawing of the existing opening and mark its width and height. Determine exactly where you'll position the new window in the opening. Because the tops of the windows in a house are usually all at the same height, you can use the bottom of the header as the top of the new opening. Although you can center the window in the opening, you'll have less work to do if you use an existing trimmer stud for one side of the opening.

2 Framing the opening

Measuring from the existing trimmer stud you plan to use, mark the width of the new opening on the top of the rough sill and the bottom of the header. Using a combination square, draw a line across the rough sill and the header through these points. On these lines, you'll place the side of the new trimmer stud that faces the opening.

Cut a new trimmer stud to fit between the header and the rough sill. If the new stud will be close to the old trimmer stud, use several small pieces of 2-by lumber as blocking to close the space. Face-nail these pieces to the top, middle, and bottom of the old trimmer, then face-nail the new trimmer to them. Toenail the new trimmer to the header and rough sill with 3" nails.

Measure the distance between the two trimmer studs at the top and bottom of the opening; check that it's the same as the width of the rough opening on your drawing. If the distance between the new trimmer stud and the old one will be more than $14^{1}/_{2}$", install additional studs between header and rough sill to fill that space; they should be 16" on center.

To install a new rough sill that is 3" or less above the existing one, nail layers of lumber to the old rough sill to form the bottom of the new opening. If the new rough sill is considerably higher than the old, don't try to build it up. Instead, use 3" nails to toenail another set of cripple studs to the existing rough sill. The length of the new cripple studs should be the same as the distance between the top of the old rough sill and the bottom of the new one. For the rough sill, cut a piece of 2-by lumber the same length as the width of the rough opening and nail it to the top of the new cripple studs with $3^{1}/_{2}$" nails.

Measure the distance between the header and the new rough sill on both sides of the opening. It must be the same as the height of the rough opening on your drawing.

3 Finishing the opening

Patch the sheathing on the outside. If necessary, use $2^{1}/_{2}$" nails to fasten studs to the existing framing to support the edges of the new sheathing. Don't patch the siding until after you install the new window. Fill the spaces between the new and old framing with insulation, vapor-barrier side facing in. Replace the interior wall covering around the opening.

ASK A PRO

HOW DO I CLOSE UP AN OPENING IN THE WALL?

After you remove the window (page 48), measure the distance between the sill and the header. Cut enough studs to enclose the opening: one on each side of the opening and one every 16 inches on center ($14^{1}/_{2}$ inches apart) within the opening.

Nail one stud to each existing trimmer stud with $2^{1}/_{2}$-inch nails. Space the remaining studs 16 inches on center and toenail them to the header and sill with $2^{1}/_{2}$-inch nails.

Cover the outside with sheathing; use $2^{1}/_{2}$-inch nails to fasten studs to the existing framing to support the edges of the new sheathing, if necessary. Apply siding or other material to the sheathing to match the existing material, and finish the siding so it blends with the existing finish.

Inside, fill the open spaces between the framing members with insulation, vapor-barrier side facing in. Apply wallboard, paneling, or other material to the framing to match existing material.

INSTALLING A WINDOW

Whether you cut a new opening, enlarge or reduce an existing one, or use an old opening, the directions for installing a prehung window are the same. There are three common methods for installing a prehung window: nailing it through a flange that surrounds the window and sets against the sheathing; nailing it through the exterior trim; or screwing it through the jambs to the trimmer studs and the header. Installation methods vary from one manufacturer to another; follow the instructions for the window you buy. For windows with factory-finished exterior trim, you may need to use masonry clips even on a house with wood siding; nailing through the trim may void the warranty.

Some manufacturers make replacement sash to be installed in an existing frame: You remove the existing sash and the old stops, attach new jamb liners (which come with the kit), and install the new sash.

The installation instructions on the following pages are for wood siding. To cut aluminum or vinyl siding, use a utility knife or tin snips. For stucco, you'll need a circular saw fitted with a masonry-cutting blade.

If you're installing a window in a brick or masonry wall, which you can't nail the trim into, you can use metal masonry clips; the clips allow you to attach the window to the trimmer and king studs rather than to the exterior of the house. The window comes with grooves on the jamb which the clips fit into; you then fasten them to the jamb with screws. Once the window is positioned properly, you bend the clips around the framing studs and fasten them with screws on the inside.

In this section, you'll also find typical methods for installing a bay or bow window, a greenhouse window, and a nonrectangular window.

STANDARD PREHUNG WINDOWS

A prehung window comes complete with sash, frame, sill, hardware, and all the trim, except for the casing, stool, and apron, which you must supply. All the different types of windows (double-hung, casement, awning, hopper, and fixed) are available prehung. It's best to install a window from the outside, though you can maneuver it through the opening from the inside and lean through the window to fasten it. If you want to install the window from the inside, make sure you're safely attached and won't fall out.

Putting in a prehung window

TOOLKIT
- Electric drill
- Carpenter's level
- Straightedge or chalk line (optional)
- Circular saw
- Hammer and butt chisel
- Tape measure
- Hand stapler
- Claw hammer
- Crosscut saw
- Screwdriver (optional)
- Caulking gun

To cut flashing:
- Tin snips

1▶ Cutting the opening in the exterior wall

If you're putting a window in a new opening, first cut away the sheathing and siding. From the inside, drill a hole at each corner of the rough opening through the sheathing and siding. Stick a nail through each hole so you can find them on the outside.

On the outside, mark the outline of the rough opening on the siding with a pencil and carpenter's level *(right)* or straightedge (a long 1x4 or 1x6). Or stretch a chalk line around the four nails and snap it between each pair.

Using a circular saw, cut through the siding and sheathing along the lines; lay the cut material aside.

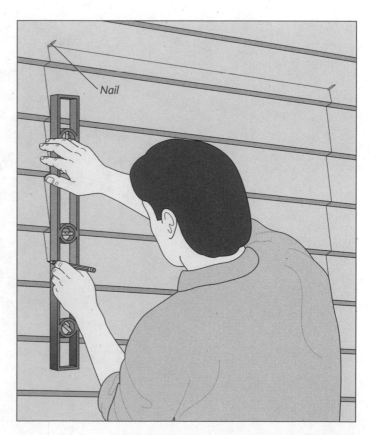

Nail

Carpenter's level

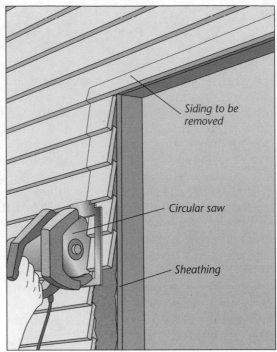

Siding to be removed

Circular saw

Sheathing

2 Cutting away the siding

If necessary, assemble the mounting flanges and flashing of your window according to the manufacturer's instructions. From outside the house, center the window in the opening and have your helper hold it in place. While one person checks for level and plumb with a carpenter's level *(above, left)*, the other person should be inside, placing shims between the bottom jamb and the rough sill, until the window is level. Next, have the person outside mark the outline of the flange or trim on the siding, and remove the window. Using a circular saw, cut along the pencil line on the siding *(above, right)*; don't cut through the sheathing. Finish the cuts with a hammer and chisel.

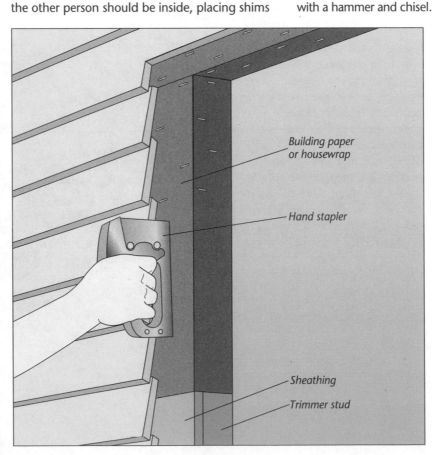

Building paper or housewrap

Hand stapler

Sheathing

Trimmer stud

3 Adding building paper or housewrap

Cut building paper or housewrap into strips about 8" wide. Slide the strips between the siding and the sheathing on all sides of the window. Curl each strip around the frame, toward the interior of the house, and staple it to the sheathing and the trimmer stud *(left)*. The strips should stop just before the inside edge of the rough opening.

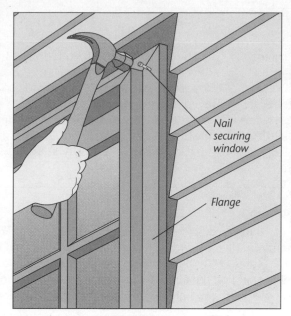

Nail securing window

Flange

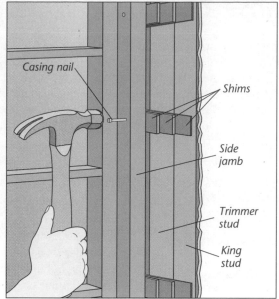

Casing nail

Shims

Side jamb

Trimmer stud

King stud

4 **Fastening the window**
Center the window in the opening again. While your helper holds it in place, drive a nail through the flange or trim at one of the top corners *(above, left)*. Check that the window is level. If it is, nail through the flange or trim at the other corners. If it isn't, have your helper adjust the shims inside until the window is level, before you nail through the other corners. To maintain a constant width at the top, center, and bottom of the window, use shims between the jambs and trimmer studs, spaced about 12" apart; make sure that they are not so tight that they push the jamb out of plumb.

Nail through the jamb and each set of shims to the trimmer stud, using 2$^1/_2$" casing nails

(above, right); drill pilot holes for the nails first. Wearing gloves and a dust mask or respirator, push insulation into the gaps between the frame and the window. Trim off the shims flush with the jambs using a crosscut saw. Outside, nail the flange or trim to the sheathing, using 1$^1/_2$" roofing nails for a flange and 2$^1/_2$" galvanized finishing nails for trim.

For windows that are attached through the jambs, with a helper, insert shims from both inside and outside the window until it's level and plumb. Drill pilot holes, and screw through the jambs and the shims to the trimmer studs and header. Insulate, and trim off the shims.

5 **Finishing the outside**
Unless your roof has a pronounced over-hang, it's a good idea to install flashing, also known as a drip cap, over the top of the window.

Thoroughly caulk the joints between the siding and the new window *(left)*. If you attached the window by nailing through flanges, you'll have to add exterior trim before caulking.

Drip cap

Trim

Caulking gun

ASK A PRO

WHEN SHOULD I REMOVE THE BRACING?
It's best not to remove any blocking or bracing installed to prevent damage during shipment until after the window is fastened in place. Check that the sash operate freely before you install the interior trim or caulk the exterior and make any necessary adjustments.

NONRECTANGULAR WINDOWS

Installing an octagonal or other nonrectangular window (*page 27*) is basically not a difficult job—once you've framed the rough opening. What is difficult is adding the trim around the window on the inside. If you're not an experienced woodworker, you may want to have a cabinetmaker or finish carpenter make the trim for you.

The method described below is for an octagonal window but is applicable to round, hexagonal, and other shapes. If the outside is exposed to the weather, you'll need flashing for the upper half. You can use flexible vinyl drip cap or have a sheet metal shop make the flashing for you. Some manufacturers make a drip cap to go with their specially shaped windows.

Installing an octagonal window

TOOLKIT
- Electric drill
- Straightedge
- Circular saw
- Butt chisel
- Claw hammer
- Compass saw (optional)
- Caulking gun

For cutting flashing:
- Tin snips

1 **Preparing the opening**

Frame the rough opening as described on page 47. At each corner of the opening, drill holes through the sheathing and siding. Mark the outline of the opening on the outside by connecting the holes with a straightedge and a pencil. Cut along the lines with a circular saw; use a chisel to finish the cuts. For a circular opening, locate the center of the opening and use it to mark the circle. Use a compass saw to cut along the lines.

2 **Fastening the window**

If the siding is flat and smooth, the exterior trim can fit against the flat surface. If the siding is not flat, set the window in the opening and mark the outline of the exterior trim on the siding. Using a circular saw set to cut only through the siding, saw around the lines and remove the siding (*page 52*). Fasten the flashing to the window, setting it in a bed of caulk. Apply a bead of caulk on the back of the trim and on the flashing.

Put the window back in the opening and center it with shims between the jamb and the framing. Drive 2½" galvanized finishing nails through the exterior trim and sheathing into the rough frame. If your window is nailed through a flange, use 1½" roofing nails to attach it, then apply exterior trim. Carefully caulk all joints between the window and the siding. Finally, trim the window (*page 59*).

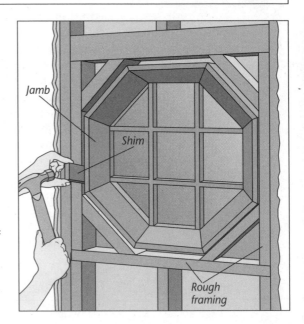

Jamb

Shim

Rough framing

PROJECTING WINDOWS

Cantilevered bay windows (also known as oriels), box bay windows, and bow windows (*page 28*) can be built in the same type of opening as conventional windows. The job involves a little more work, but it's no more difficult than installing a conventional window. The building code requirements for the rough sill for a bay window may be different than for a conventional window, because it must support considerably more weight; check your local building code.

You can buy a bay window as a kit with the windows, head board, and seat board, plus various trim pieces you must assemble, or as a completely assembled unit ready to install. Then, all you need to do is build the roof over the window (unless it reaches the soffit), install support brackets, and finish the inside. Some manufacturers supply a precut roof or roof framing and will also supply the support brackets or cable support system that they recommend. The installation method described on the following pages is for a bay, but it's applicable to a bow or box window as well. Be sure you have all the necessary materials before you start.

You'll find out how to install a greenhouse window on page 58. These windows, designed to fit common window sizes, are fastened to an exterior wall, with the bottom of the window below the sill or resting on it. If you're installing a greenhouse window in a new opening, you'll have to frame a rough opening (*page 42*); follow any manufacturer's instructions. Greenhouse windows need less support than other projecting windows because they don't have to support people's weight.

Installing a bay window

TOOLKIT
- Tape measure
- Circular saw
- Hand stapler
- Claw hammer
- Wrench
- Screwdriver
- Carpenter's level
- Utility knife
- Electric drill
- Caulking gun

1 Preparing the window and opening

If necessary, assemble your window according to the manufacturer's instructions. Check the outside dimensions of the window against the rough opening. The height and width of the window should be about 1/2" less than the opening's height and width. Make any necessary adjustments. You may need to cut back the siding to clear the trim on the window (consult the manufacturer's instructions). Mark the outline and cut along the lines with a circular saw, as described in step 2 on page 52. Set the blade to cut through the siding only. Slide pieces of building paper or housewrap under the siding, wrap it into the opening and staple it in place.

To set the window in place, you'll need helpers, one for every 3' of window width. You'll also need a sawhorse every 3' to support the window once it's installed in the opening. An assembled window is heavy and unwieldy. Installing one on the second floor requires strong scaffolding for a working platform; unless you have installation experience, have a professional do this job and finish the interior yourself.

To install support brackets, toenail a cripple stud to the rough sill and the sole plate under each mullion, if there isn't already one there. Position one of the support brackets under one of the mullions with the long leg against the siding; the short leg goes against the underside of the window. Use 3/8" lag screws to fasten the long leg through the siding into the cripple stud. The other leg is fastened to the underside with wood screws. Install the other bracket. For very large windows, more support brackets are required.

Some manufacturers suggest installing the brackets first, before the window is lifted into the rough opening, others suggest raising the window into the frame first, and adding the brackets afterward; follow the instructions that came with your window. If your window requires a cable support system instead of (or in combination with) support brackets, or any brackets or supports between the head board and the studs above the window, follow the manufacturer's instructions to install them.

2 Placing the window in the opening

Pick up the window and rest the bottom platform on the rough sill (right). Then tilt the unit up so the trim around the outside butts against the sheathing. Center the jambs between the trimmer studs. While your helpers hold the window against the siding, support it with sawhorses. Don't let your helpers leave; they'll come in handy when you level and plumb the window.

Rough opening

Sawhorse

Seat board

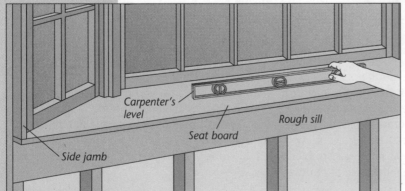

Carpenter's level

Seat board

Rough sill

Side jamb

3 Shimming the window bottom

Use a level (left) to determine which end of the seat board is the highest. Nail that end to the rough sill, placing the nail 2" to 3" from the jamb. Leave the level on the seat board. With a helper, drive shims from both inside and outside between the sill and the seat board, placing shims over each cripple stud, until the seat board is level. When the seat board is level, nail it through the shims to the rough sill.

4 ▶ Shimming the window sides

To check that the jambs are plumb in both directions, first put the level on the front edge of the side jamb *(right)*. While helpers move the window as needed (have one hold the level for you), drive shims between the jamb and the trimmer stud until the jamb is plumb. Space the shims about 12" apart and make sure the jamb is absolutely straight. Then, placing the level on the interior edge of the side jamb, move the top of the window in and out until the jamb is plumb.

Check the side jamb again to make sure it's still plumb. Drive nails through the jamb and shims into the trimmer stud; drill pilot holes for them first. Be sure not to drive nails through any part of the window mechanism. Repeat the process at the other side.

Side jamb

Trimmer stud

King stud

Header

Head board

Shim

◀ 5 Shimming the window top

Install shims from inside and outside between the head board and header until the head board is straight *(left)*. Measure at several places between the head board and seat board; the measurements should be exactly the same. Secure the head board by driving nails through it and the shims into header. Fill any spaces between the jambs and the framing with insulation; wear protective gloves and a dust mask or respirator when handling insulation.

6 Installing cables

Some manufacturers recommend using cable support systems with their bay windows. The cables are generally anchored to platform boards mounted above and below the window. They go up the corner mullions, where the middle window meets the side windows, and are attached above to rafter tails, to blocking added between the rafter tails, or to other structural members (such as the second floor wall studs). The seat board and head board are notched to accommodate the cables, which are hidden by the interior trim.

Different manufacturers have different installation methods; follow the instructions that come with the cable support system that you're using.

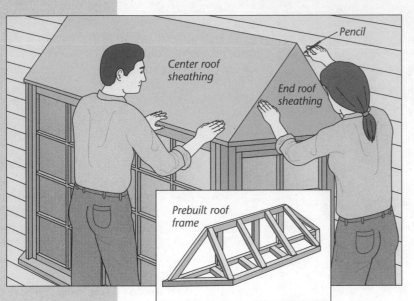

Center roof sheathing

End roof sheathing

Pencil

Prebuilt roof frame

7 Cutting the siding

Unless there's a soffit right above the window, you'll have to build a roof; design it to reflect the architectural style of your home. If you're using a prebuilt frame (*inset*), set it on top of the window, and rest the center piece of roof sheathing on it so it's touching the siding; draw a pencil line where the sheathing touches the siding. Repeat with the end pieces. If you're not using a frame, simply rest the center piece of roof sheathing against the top edge of the window, and against the siding; mark where the sheathing touches the siding. Repeat with the end pieces. Remove sheathing and the frame, if you're using one, and saw along the pencil lines with a circular saw. Remove the siding.

End rafter

Hip rafter

Head board

8 Building the roof

Staple a plastic vapor barrier over the top of the window, and trim it around the edge of the window with a utility knife. If you're installing a roof with a prebuilt frame, position the roof frame on top of the window, and fasten it to the cripple studs in the wall, and to the top of the window. If you're building your roof without a frame, you'll have to install rafters. Cut and nail hip and end rafters at each end, as shown at left. Nail the end pieces of sheathing to the rafters and to the top of the windows, using 2" nails spaced 6" apart.

Cover the top of the head board with insulation, packing it loosely inside the frame, if you're using one; wear protective gloves and a respirator or dust mask. If you haven't already attached the end pieces of sheathing, attach them now. Then, attach the center piece of sheathing.

You can shingle the roof of the bay to match your house or have a professional cover it with copper; from some manufacturers you can order a copper-covered roof when you order your window. If you shingle the roof, you'll need flashing between the shingles and siding, and a drip edge at the bottom of the roof, around the top edge of window. You can order the flashing from your window manufacturer, or have it made by a sheet metal shop.

 ASK A PRO

WHAT IF THERE'S A SOFFIT RIGHT ABOVE THE WINDOW?

If there's a soffit above the window, just fill in the space between the frame on the outside of the window and the soffit above with a piece of wood or molding. You may need to add a wood spacer under the piece of molding you're adding, so that it is flush with the window frame.

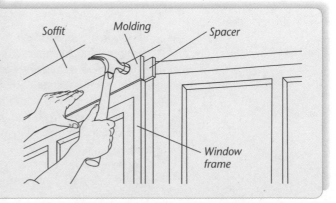

Soffit

Molding

Spacer

Window frame

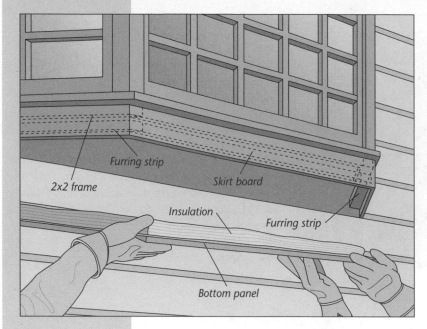

2x2 frame

Furring strip

Skirt board

Insulation

Furring strip

Bottom panel

9 Finishing the exterior

Install any exterior trim, then caulk around all sides of the window. You may also need to install a skirt and bottom panel; some manufacturers sell a kit with the required materials.

Cover the bottom of the window with a plastic vapor barrier. Then install a frame of 2x2 strips near the outer edges. Nail furring strips to the skirt boards, and attach the boards to the 2x2s by screwing through the 2x2s into the backs of the skirt boards —drill pilot holes first. Wearing protective gloves and a dust mask or respirator, cover the bottom panel with insulation and attach it to the furring strips *(left)*.

There are other ways to finish the bottom of a bay window—to hide support brackets, you may need to install a frame and sheathing panels on a diagonal. Or you can build a wall under the window, extending it to the ground, and covering it with siding to match the house wall.

Installing a greenhouse window

TOOLKIT
• Caulking gun
• Carpenter's level
• Screwdriver

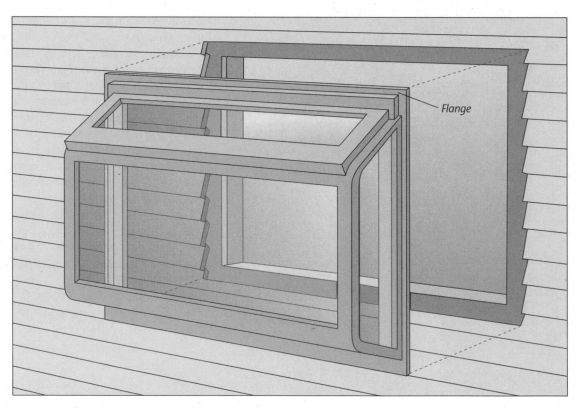

Flange

1 Fastening the window

If you're using an existing window opening, remove the window as described on page 48. You'll need to cut back the siding to accommodate the nailing flange or trim; follow the procedure outlined on page 52. If you're putting the window in a new opening, frame the opening as described beginning on page 42.

Run a generous bead of caulk around the flange or trim where it will touch the sheathing. Have your helpers raise the window into place. Check that the interior sill is level, then attach the flange or trim with wood screws long enough to bite into the house frame at least $2\frac{1}{2}$"; some manufacturers may recommend shorter screws. Install a drip cap at the top of the window. Run a neat bead of caulk around all sides. If you've attached the window through flanges, you may need to add exterior trim. To finish the inside, read the information on trimming a window, beginning on the opposite page.

TRIMMING A WINDOW

To complete your window project, you'll need to install wallboard to fill the gap around the edges of the window; fit the new pieces as close as possible to the jambs on all sides. You'll also need to finish the inside edges of the window with molding. On a single- or double-hung window, this involves fastening a stool to the windowsill, attaching an apron to the wall underneath the sill, and fastening casings to the sides and top to cover the joints between the wall and window. Other types of windows—casement, awning, and hopper—are usually finished with casings on all four sides, though sometimes a stool and apron are used.

You'll need some common tools (such as a tape measure, combination square, nailset, and hammer), tools for installing casing, a fine-toothed backsaw and miter box to cut the casings accurately, and perhaps a block plane for trimming them.

In modern houses, the jambs on the window tend to be flush with the inside wall of the house. In older homes, though, the edge of the jambs may be below the surface of the wall. If so, you'll have to add extension jambs, to build the jambs out flush with the wall before you can put moldings on the window.

Generally, casings are not installed flush to the edge of the jambs because they can't be aligned well enough.

A setback, or reveal, of 1/8 to 1/4 inch is common. The stool usually extends 1/2 inch past the casing on both sides.

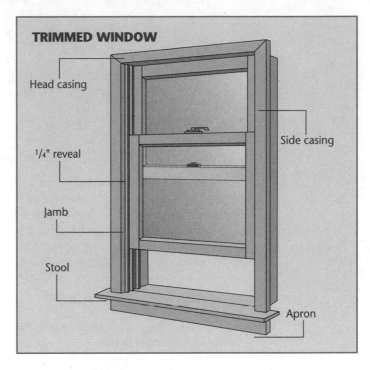

TRIMMED WINDOW

Head casing

1/4" reveal

Jamb

Stool

Side casing

Apron

Adding extension jambs

TOOLKIT
- Tape measure
- Circular saw
- Straightedge
- Claw hammer
- Nailset (optional)
- Plane or sanding block
- Putty knife

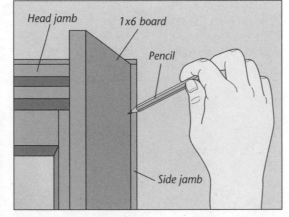

Head jamb   1x6 board

Pencil

Side jamb

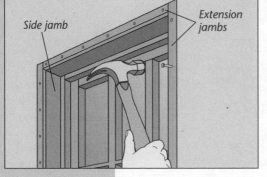

Side jamb   Extension jambs

1 Marking the extension
You'll need a piece of 1-by lumber at least wide enough to fill the space between the jambs and the wall; 1x6 clear pine is usually a good choice. If possible, cut all the required extension strips from the same piece. Measure the length of the longest dimension of your window and cut the lumber to this length. Set the edge of the board on the edge of one of the long jambs. At each end, mark the side of the board where it's flush with the wall *(left)*.

Remove the board and draw a straight line between the two points. Saw the board along the side of the line away from the jamb.

2 Fastening the piece
Use finishing nails to attach the cutoff strip, sawed edge out, to the edge of the jamb *(left)*. The nails should be three times longer than the sawed thickness of the strip. Repeat for the other jambs, starting with the other jamb of the same length, then cut the board to the length of the shorter jamb; it should fit inside the extension jambs. If you're installing casing instead of a sill at the bottom of the window, add an extension jamb there; it should fit inside the extensions for the side jambs. If the extension jambs project or aren't flush with each other at the corners, countersink the nails in that area, then plane or sand the jamb flush. Finally, plane or sand the extension flush with the inside edge of the jamb, then fill the joint with wood putty and sand it smooth.

TOOLKIT
- Tape measure
- Straightedge
- Circular saw or crosscut saw
- Combination square
- Claw hammer
- Backsaw and miter box
- Block plane or sanding block (optional)
- Nailset
- Putty knife

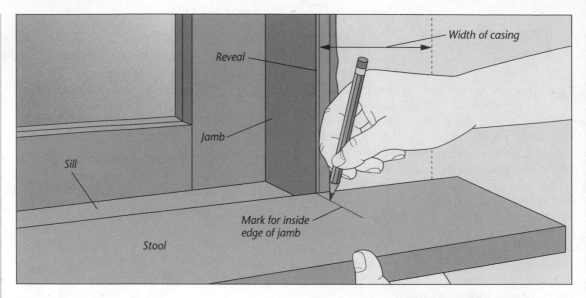

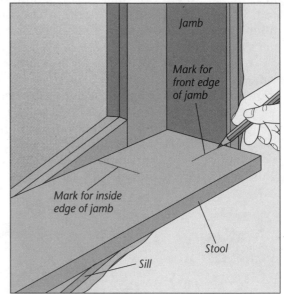

1 Marking the stool

First measure and mark with a straightedge and pencil a $1/8$" or $1/4$" reveal at the side and head jambs. To determine the length of the stool, measure the width of your casings, add the width of the reveal plus $1/2$". Double this figure, and add the width of your window. Cut the stool to this length. For the stool, use either a flat piece of lumber, or a preformed rabbeted stool.

Center the stool in the opening, marking the center point on both the stool and the sill. Mark the inside of each side jamb on the edge of the stool *(above)*. Place the back edge of the stool against the window, with one edge against a side jamb; mark the front edge of the jamb on the stool *(right)*. Mark the other side of the stool in the same way. At each end, extend the two lines until they cross, using a combination square.

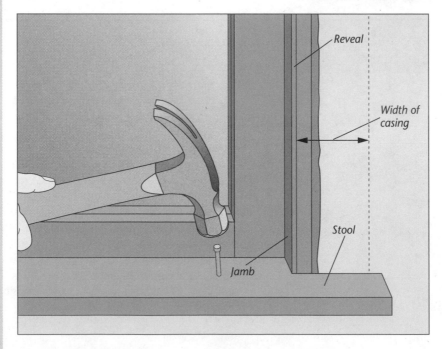

2 Fastening the stool

Cut the stool along the lines. Set the stool in place and fasten it to the sill with 2" finishing nails *(left)*.

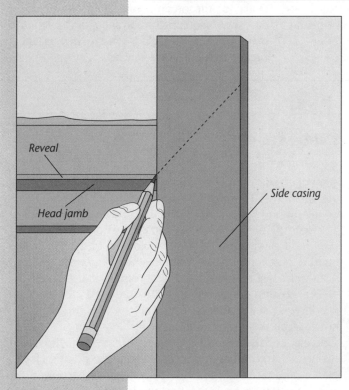

3 Installing the apron

For the apron, mark a piece of molding 1" shorter than the stool *(left)* and cut it. Center it under the stool; the ends will line up with the outside edges of the casings. Nail the apron through the wallboard to the rough framing with 2" finishing nails.

Width of casing

Stool

Molding for apron

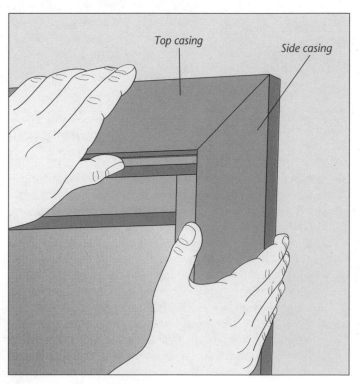

Reveal

Head jamb

Side casing

Top casing

Side casing

4 Installing the side and top casings

Square off one end of a piece of casing. Set that end on the stool, aligning it with the reveal line. Mark the inside edge of the casing where it crosses the reveal line of the head jamb *(above, left)*. Using a backsaw and miter box, cut that end at a 45° angle. Repeat for the other side casing. Line up the inside of the side casings with the reveal lines, and tack them so they stay in place while you fit the top casing. Measure the distance between the side casings at the longest point, and cut the top casing to this length. Miter both ends of the top casing to 45°. Align the three pieces of casing *(above, right)*, making adjustments where necessary, before attaching them permanently. You may need to plane or sand them so they fit well. Apply carpenter's glue to the mitered edges of each piece before you fasten it to the jamb and rough framing.

Fasten the side casings to the side jambs using 1$\frac{1}{2}$" finishing nails spaced about 8" apart. Then fasten them through the wallboard to the trimmer studs with 2" finishing nails; fasten the top casing to the head jamb and through the wallboard to the header. Once the casings are all in place, toe-nail the mitered edges together, using 2" finishing nails. Set the nails with a nailset and fill the holes with putty. Sand any rough areas before finishing the trim.

Trimming other types of windows

Casement

If a stool is required, trim a casement window in the same way as a double-hung window *(page 60)*. For windows without stools, apply casings to all four sides of the window, mitering the ends of the casings at 45°. Fit the casings as described on page 60.

Bay or bow

A bay or bow window, whether double-hung or casement, is usually trimmed with casings on all four sides. If the seat and head boards are not included by the manufacturer, you'll have to cut and install them before applying the casings.

Nonrectangular

These windows are trimmed with casing on all sides; there's no stool or apron.

Making the corner miter joint of a rectangular window is straightforward. For other shapes, you need to understand a little geometry. The angle at which you cut the casings must be half the desired angle of the corner. For an equilateral triangle, the angle you cut is 30°; for a pentagon, 54°; for a hexagon, 60°; and for an octagon, $67\frac{1}{2}°$ (or $22\frac{1}{2}°$).

After you've cut the casing pieces and checked their fit, nail them to the jamb with $1\frac{1}{2}$" finishing nails and to the rough frame with 2" finishing nails. Set the nails with a nailset, fill the holes with putty, and finish the trim with paint or stain.

Trimming a circular window can be quite a challenge for the do-it-yourselfer; unless you have a well-equipped wood shop, ask a cabinetmaker to make the casing. You can then nail the circular casing in place yourself.

SECURING WINDOWS AND SKYLIGHTS

To make your home more secure, you can add locking devices to make windows difficult to pry open; replace ordinary glass with much stronger tempered, laminated, or wire-reinforced glass; attach grilles to windows; or install an alarm system. But remember, windows must be easy to open quickly in an emergency, and there must always be a second way to exit a bedroom, in addition to the door.

Locking tips: Many devices are available to make prying open a window more difficult; the type you choose depends on the type of window—sliding, double-hung, or casement. Homemade devices can also be effective.

Sliding panels present a security problem because they can be lifted off their tracks. To prevent this, drive three evenly spaced sheet metal screws into the groove of the upper track; adjust them so they just fill the space between the groove and the top of the sash. To keep an inside panel from sliding, drop a dowel or a 1x2 into the empty portion of the lower track. Cut the piece ¼ inch shorter than the distance between the panel and the jamb.

Manufactured track grips, tightened by a thumb screw or key, are metal stops that straddle the lower track and secure inside sliding panels. A spring bolt lock has a pin that snaps through a hole drilled in the edge of the lower track and bottom of the sash. Use this lock on either inside or outside panels.

You can buy various types of sash locks to secure double-hung windows. Some locks are designed to lock the sash in an open position, to allow for ventilation and security at the same time. To make your own secure lock for a wooden double-hung window, drill holes that angle slightly downward completely through the top corners of the bottom sash and halfway into the bottom corners of the top sash. Insert a loosely fitting eye bolt into the holes to secure the sashes; the eye makes a handle for removing the bolt.

The existing hardware on crank-operated casement windows is usually adequate to keep the windows closed, but you can buy cranks that lock.

Break-resistant panes: Tempered glass is five times stronger than ordinary glass. Laminated glass (which has plastic laminate between two panes) is even stronger, and harder to cut, as is the steel mesh embedded in wire-reinforced glass. Or you can use glass blocks *(page 31)* instead of panes.

Window guards: A window grille allows a secured window to remain open for ventilation. A model with a quick-release mechanism is recommended, for easy escape in case of fire.

Perimeter alarm systems: An alarm system linking windows and doors to a central bell or horn can also be effective. In one system that's commonly used, two-part magnetic contacts placed on windows and doors are wired into the household electrical system. When an opening is forced, the two parts separate, breaking the current and sounding the alarm.

REPAIRING A DOUBLE-HUNG WINDOW

Wooden double-hung windows *(right)* generally have one of three types of opening mechanisms. In a tension-spring balance system *(page 66)*, a balance unit with a spring-loaded drum inside fits into the frame; a flexible metal tape hooks onto a bracket screwed to the sash. A spiral-lift balance *(page 67)* has a spring-loaded spiral rod encased in a metal or plastic tube, which rests in a channel in the side of the stile. The rod holds the sash in any position; the spring tension can be adjusted by rotating the rod, which assures that the sash is properly balanced. A weight and pulley system has weights attached to the sash with cords or chains *(page 67)*. Whatever system you have, if parts are broken, your windows may not stay open or may jam partway. If your windows have sash cords, it's a good idea to replace the cords with longer-lasting chains.

Even if your sash mechanism is in good order, your window may not work properly for other reasons. It may be painted shut or the sash channels may need cleaning. The stop moldings may need to be repositioned to make the sash channel wider or narrower; to reposition a stop, see page 64. Glued mortise-and-tenon joints at the corners of a sash can loosen, making the sash jam. On the following pages, you'll find detailed instructions for repairing double-hung windows and for fixing problems associated with older wooden windows. For most repairs, you'll need only the basic tools shown on page 38. Occasionally, you may need more specialized tools, such as clamps or a block plane.

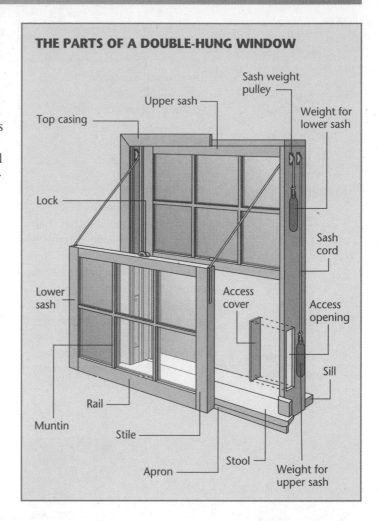

THE PARTS OF A DOUBLE-HUNG WINDOW

Top casing · Upper sash · Sash weight pulley · Weight for lower sash · Lock · Sash cord · Lower sash · Access cover · Access opening · Sill · Rail · Muntin · Stile · Stool · Apron · Weight for upper sash

---

Freeing a stuck sash

TOOLKIT
• Utility knife
• Putty knife
• Mallet (optional)
OR
• Prybar
OR
• Claw hammer

Putty knife

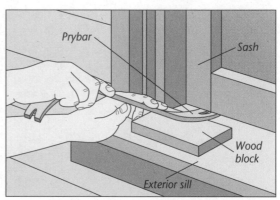

Prybar · Sash · Wood block · Exterior sill

Moving the sash
To free a paint-stuck sash, try one of the following three methods. Score the paint by running a sharp utility knife between the sash and the stop molding on both sides of the window, and along the bottom between the sash and both the sill and the stool. Then use a wide putty knife to loosen the sash; tap the end of the knife with a mallet, if necessary *(above, left)*.

Pry up the sash from the outside by wedging a prybar between the sill and sash; work first at one end and then at the other to move the sash up evenly. Use a wood block to protect the sill.

If the window is stuck open and can't be pried, place a block of wood on top of the sash at one side and tap down on it with a hammer. Alternate sides until the sash moves freely.

Easing a binding sash

Cleaning the sash channel

Using a butt chisel, scrape off any paint or dirt that has accumulated in the channels and sand all scraped surfaces. Clean metal or plastic channels with steel wool. Lubricate the channels with household paraffin or commercial silicone lubricant; silicone spray works best for metal and plastic.

Widening the channel

If the stops are nailed rather than screwed, you can widen the channel of a sticking sash fairly easily. Place a wood block slightly larger than the channel at the point of binding and use a hammer to tap the wood against the stop *(right)* until the channel is wide enough to let the sash move easily. If this doesn't work, you'll have to reposition the stop *(below)*.

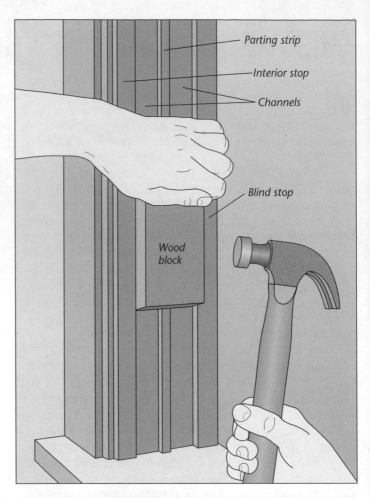

Repositioning the stop moldings

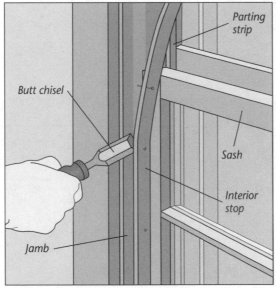

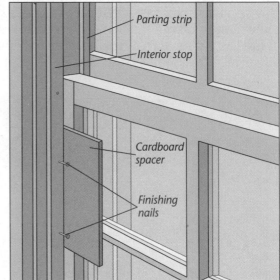

If the stop is fastened with screws instead of nails, remove the screws. Otherwise, to remove the stop molding, first use a putty knife and then a chisel to pry it away from the window frame *(above, left)*. Minimize paint chipping by scoring the paint between the jamb and the molding with a utility knife. If the old molding breaks during removal, save it to use as a sample when buying new molding.

Before repositioning the molding, chisel any built-up paint off the edge facing the sash. Sand the stop and sash smooth, and apply paraffin. To give the sash added clearance, use a thin cardboard spacer between the stop molding and the sash as shown *(above, right)*. Fasten the molding to the frame with finishing nails; use new nail holes, so that the stop does not return to its original position.

Fixing a loose sash

TOOLKIT
- Utility knife
- Claw hammer
- Nailset
- Putty knife

Moving the stop molding

Score the paint between the stop and the sash with a utility knife to prevent chipping. Then place a thin cardboard spacer between the stop and the sash. Position a block of wood against the outer surface of the stop, and hammer toward the sash along the entire length of the stop molding until the paint breaks and the stop rests against the spacer. If the stop springs back to its original position, secure it in the desired position with finishing nails. Set the nails with a nailset, fill the holes with putty, and touch up the paint.

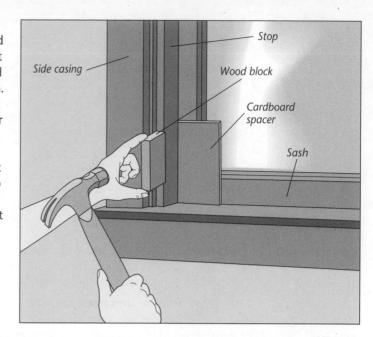

Repairing loose sash parts

TOOLKIT
- Needle-nose pliers to remove nails from weather stripping (optional)
- Slip-joint pliers
- Screwdriver and butt chisel (optional)
- Bar clamp

For inserting dowels:
- Electric drill
- Crosscut saw
- Mallet
- Backsaw (optional)
- Sanding block

For attaching brackets:
- Screwdriver

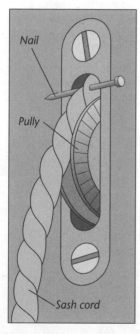
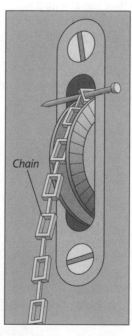

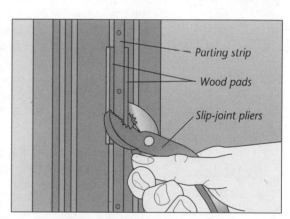

1 Removing the lower sash
Pry off the stop molding (*opposite page*). Raise the sash and slide it out, angling it toward yourself. Draw up the cords or chains until the weights touch the pulleys on both sides. To keep the cords or chains from feeding back through the pulleys, push a nail through each cord (*above, left*) or through a chain link (*above, right*). Untie the cords and slip them from the sash grooves, or remove the screws or nails that hold the chains to the sash.

If your window has interlocking weather stripping that fits into a groove in the sash, take it off before you remove the sash from the frame. Remove the interior stop, raise the sash to the top, and remove the nails that hold the weather stripping to the channel. Lower the sash and angle it out of the frame.

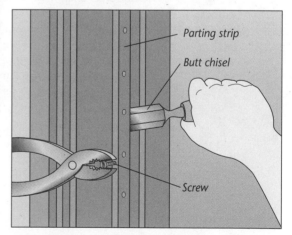

2 Removing the upper sash
After you remove the lower sash, use slip-joint pliers to pry out the parting strip between the two sash; protect the parting strip from the pliers by placing wood pads on both sides of the strip (*above, top*). Or you can fasten a screw to the parting strip and use the pliers to pull on it while you pry against the strip with a butt chisel (*above, bottom*). Ease the upper sash out of the frame.

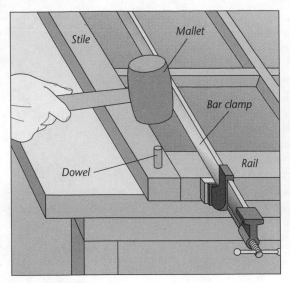

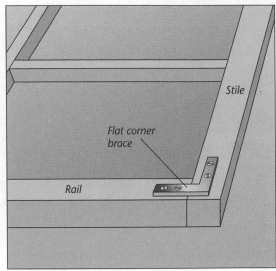

3 Reinforcing loose corners

Lay the sash on a flat surface and clean out the gap in the joint between the stile and the rail. If the sash is in good condition and the joint is clean and open, you can add waterproof glue to the joint; clamp it until the glue dries. Or you can drill holes and tap in glue-coated dowels. Clamp the sash rails together, then drill a 5/16" wide hole into the stile about 1/4" shorter than the thickness of the stile, about 1/2" from the center of the adjoining rail. Cut a length of 5/16" diameter dowel, coat it with glue, and tap it into the hole with a mallet (above, left). After the glue has set, trim the dowel with a crosscut saw or backsaw and sand it flush with the stile.

Another possibility is to clamp the rails together and screw flat corner braces in place. Position the braces so they don't interfere with the movement of the window.

Replacing a tension-spring balance

TOOLKIT
• Screwdriver
• Slip-joint pliers

Installing a new balance

Remove the stop (page 64) on the side of the window where the spring balance is broken, and ease the sash out of its channel. Unhook the tape and let it wind back on the drum. Remove the screws from the drum plate and pry the unit out. Insert the new spring-balance drum into the jamb pocket and secure it with woodscrews. Using slip-joint pliers, pull the tape down and hook the end to the bracket on the sash. Ease the sash back into its channel, check its operation, and reseat the stop (page 64).

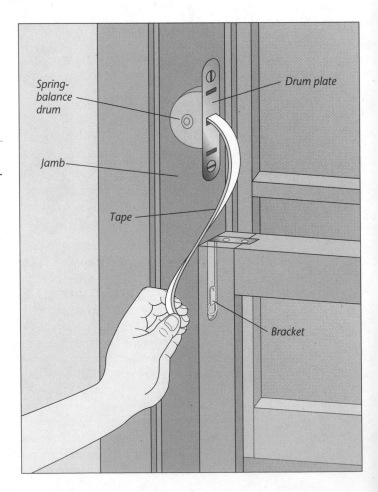

Replacing a spiral-lift balance

TOOLKIT
• Screwdriver

1 ▶ Removing the broken balance

Pry out the stop *(page 64)* on the affected side and unscrew the tube where it's fastened to the top of the jamb *(right)*. Let the spring unwind; then angle the sash out of the frame. If the rod is attached to the bottom of the sash with a detachable hook, unhook it; support the sash in a raised position with a wooden block, and unscrew and remove the mounting bracket.

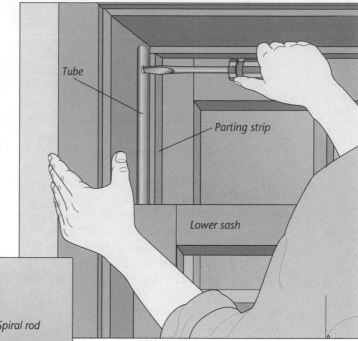

Tube

Parting strip

Lower sash

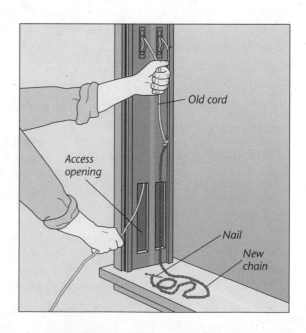

Spiral rod

Mounting bracket

2 ◀ Installing the new balance

Position a new tube in the channel, and screw it into the top of the jamb. Pull the spiral rod down as far as it will go, and turn the rod clockwise four complete turns to tighten the spring *(left)*. Let the rod retract into the tube far enough so you can fasten the mounting bracket to the bottom of the sash. Ease the sash back into the frame.

Slide the sash up and down; if it moves up when you release it, loosen the spring by detaching the tube from the top of the jamb and letting the spring unwind a bit. If the sash slides down, you need to tighten the spring by turning the rod clockwise a few times. Replace the stop *(page 64)*.

Replacing a sash cord or chain

TOOLKIT
• Screwdriver
• Claw hammer (optional)
• Slip-joint pliers

1 ▶ Removing the cord or chain

To get to the weights, remove the stop molding and ease out the lower sash *(page 65)*; unscrew and pry out the access plates. If a plate has been painted over, tap the area with a hammer until cracks reveal the plate's outline. If your window has no access plates, remove the side casings to reach the weights.

Tie one end of the new chain to the end of the old cord or chain; insert a nail in the other end of the new chain. Remove the weight from the old cord or chain, and pull the old cord or chain through the access opening *(right)* until the nail in the end of the new chain reaches the pulley. If your old cord or chain is broken, simply thread the new chain over the pulley.

Old cord

Access opening

Nail

New chain

2 ▶ Attaching the chain

Untie the chain from the cord and loop the chain through the hole in the weight; using slip-joint pliers, secure the chain with wire *(inset)*. Before putting the weight back into its pocket, clear the opening of any debris or protruding nails. Adjust the chain so the weight will be about 2" above the stool when the sash is open. Secure the chain in the sash groove by inserting wood screws through two of its links into the sash *(right)*.

Make sure that the sash moves properly, then replace the pieces you've removed. If you've removed both windows, replace the parts in the following order: upper sash, parting strips, access plates, lower sash, and then the interior stops.

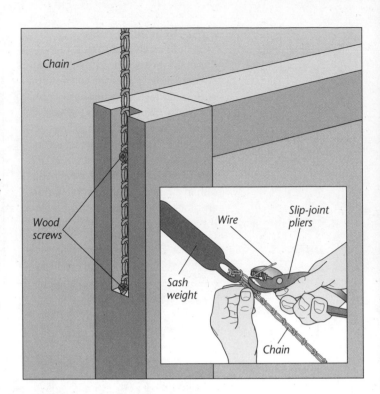

Chain

Wood screws

Wire

Slip-joint pliers

Sash weight

Chain

Restoring a damaged sill

TOOLKIT
- Putty knife
- Sanding block
- Paintbrush

For restoring a rotted sill:
- Electric drill

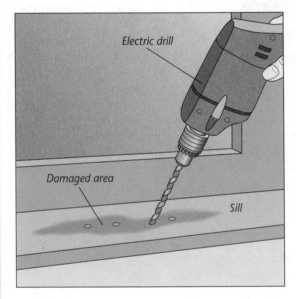

Electric drill

Damaged area

Sill

 ASK A PRO

ARE THERE OTHER WAYS TO REPAIR A SILL?

You can cover a sill that's deteriorated with a piece of aluminum. Using heavy paper, make a pattern that covers the top, sides, and front: Cut a piece of aluminum sheet to match. Caulk the joints between the sill and the house, form the aluminum around the sill, and nail it into place. Caulk any open joints and paint the sill to match the trim.

Building up the sill

You can restore a rotted sill by drilling holes and filling them with a liquid consolidant to reinforce the wood, and then covering the sill with a putty-like mixture of resin and hardener, which can be painted to match the trim; the required products come in a kit. First drill holes in the damaged area of the sill, using a 3/16" bit; angle the drill slightly *(left)* and don't drill all the way through the sill. Cover the damaged area with the liquid consolidant and allow it to dry. Wearing vinyl gloves, use a putty knife to apply the two-part mixture of resin and hardener to build up the surface of the sill; apply enough to allow for sanding. When the sill is dry, you can paint it; sand and prime it first.

Prolong the life of a sill by filling cracks in the wood with linseed oil and putty. Clean the surface, then soak the sill with a wood preservative. When the preservative dries (in about 24 hours), pour boiled linseed oil over the sill, and work it into the wood and the cracks with a paintbrush. Repeat the linseed oil application the next day. Let the wood dry, then fill any cracks or holes with putty. Wait a few days for a skin to form over the putty; then sand, prime and paint the sill.

Badly damaged sills that must be built up require an application of wood putty, epoxy filler, or a wood filler made of fine sawdust and a waterproof glue. For jobs requiring more than a 1/4" buildup, apply two or more coatings of wood filler; let each coat dry completely before applying the next. Sand, prime, and paint the sill after the last layer of filler has dried.

REPLACING A BROKEN PANE

At some point, you'll probably have to replace a cracked or shattered pane in a window; replacing a pane, especially one smaller than 2 by 3 feet, is easier than you may imagine. Larger panes, though, are best left to a professional.

To determine what size pane you'll need, measure the opening in the sash at its widest point after removing all broken glass and old putty, and subtract 1/8 inch from each dimension. With an old wood sash, be sure to measure at several points in case the sash is out of square. You can usually have the glass cut to size where you buy it; if you can't, you'll have to cut it yourself.

Replacing glass in a wood sash is relatively easy. However, you may have a little trouble beveling the putty; if so, just remove it and try again. In some metal sash, the glass is held in place with clips and glazing compound; in others, rubber seals, rubber gaskets, or metal or plastic moldings secure the glass.

PLAY IT SAFE

WORKING WITH GLASS
Wear heavy work gloves whenever you're removing broken glass or when you're handling or cutting loose panes; wear safety goggles when you're prying out glass shards or cutting glass. Pad glass with several layers of paper or other padded material when transporting it and dispose of glass slivers immediately.

Make sure you have enough helpers inside and out to handle large panes, and don't work on a windy day.

Reglazing a wooden sash

TOOLKIT
- Butt chisel
- Paintbrushes
- Heat gun (optional)
- Putty knife
- Long-nose pliers
- Tape measure
- Glass cutter
- Straightedge
- Slip-joint pliers (optional)

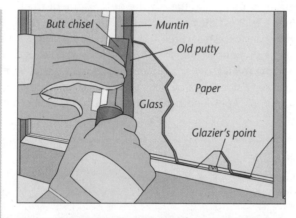

1 Removing the broken glass
Tape paper to the inside of the sash to catch any fragments. Working from the outside, wiggle the shards back and forth to free them from the putty. Working from the top of the sash, remove bits of glass and old putty with a butt chisel *(left)*. If the putty is hard, brush it with linseed oil and let it soak for half an hour, or heat it gently with a heat gun; pry off the softened putty with a putty knife. Use long-nose pliers to extract glazier's points from the sash. Clean and sand the wood, then coat it with linseed oil or wood sealer.

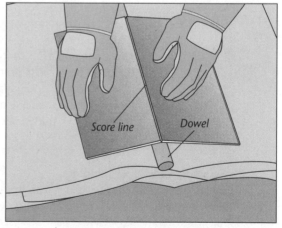

2 Cutting a new piece of glass
Ideally, have the glass cut to size when you buy it. If you must cut it yourself, measure the size you need and mark it on the pane with a grease pencil; lay the glass on several sheets of paper to protect it. Score the glass deeply with a glass cutter dipped in kerosene; use a straightedge to guide your cut *(above, left)*. Score the glass only once; don't try to go over your score line. Center the score line over a dowel and press down on both sides *(above, right)* or tap along the underside of the score with the ball end of the glass cutter.

If the break is uneven, nibble off the extra pieces using the notches on the cutter, or use slip-joint pliers with a twisting motion.

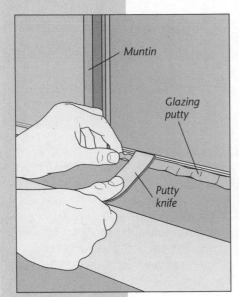

Muntin

Glazing putty

Putty knife

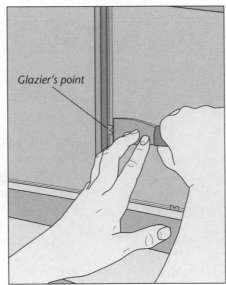

Glazier's point

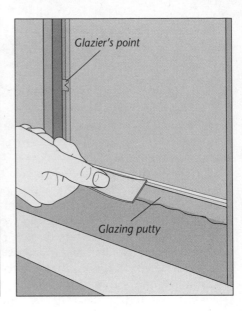

Glazier's point

Glazing putty

3 Installing the new pane

Warm the putty in a pan of hot water to make it easier to work with. With a putty knife, press a ¼" thick rope of glazing putty around the edges of the opening *(above, left)*. Press the new pane into the putty, and remove any excess. Secure the pane with glazier's points; use a putty knife to push the points into the frame *(above, center)*. For small panes, use two points to a side; for larger panes, use one point every 4" to 6". Apply another rope of putty about ¼" thick around the outside edges; the bead of putty should be flush with the outer edge of the frame and even with the wood frame visible through the window. Press it down to form a tight seal, beveling the edge with a putty knife *(above, right)*. When the putty is dry, paint it to match the wood. Instead of putty, you can use glazing compound, which is applied the same way but is easier to work with.

Reglazing a metal sash

TOOLKIT
• Putty knife or screwdriver

Using clips and putty

To replace a pane held with clips, remove the clips by pinching them together and pulling them from their holes. Clean and prepare the sash as explained above for wooden windows. Lay a thin rope of glazing compound in the channel, and press the new pane of glass into it. To secure the glass, push clips into the holes in the sash *(right)*; apply glazing compound around the pane and bevel it smooth with a putty knife.

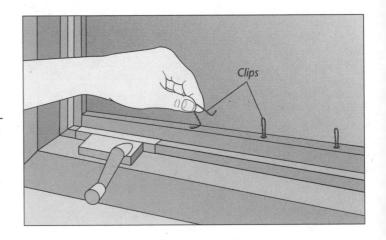

Clips

Using seals, gaskets, or moldings

To replace glass secured with rubber seals from the inside, unscrew the sash halves and remove the inside one. Brush out any glass fragments, set a new pane against one sash half, replace the other half of the sash, and secure it with screws.

If the glass sits on a continuous rubber gasket (or four separate ones), remove the screws from a vertical end of the sash and pull the end away from the sash. Clean the old glass from the gasket, and pull the gasket around the new pane; slide the pane into the sash and secure the end.

To replace glass in a sash with snap-out moldings, remove any broken glass and loosen one end of a piece of molding from the sash by inserting the tip of a putty knife where two ends meet. Pull out the loosened strip of molding and remove the remaining strips in the same manner. Clean the frame and position the new pane. Replace the moldings, starting with the short pieces, by pushing each piece into place with your hands. If the moldings look even slightly damaged, you'll have to replace them.

REPAIRING A CASEMENT OR AWNING WINDOW

A CASEMENT WINDOW

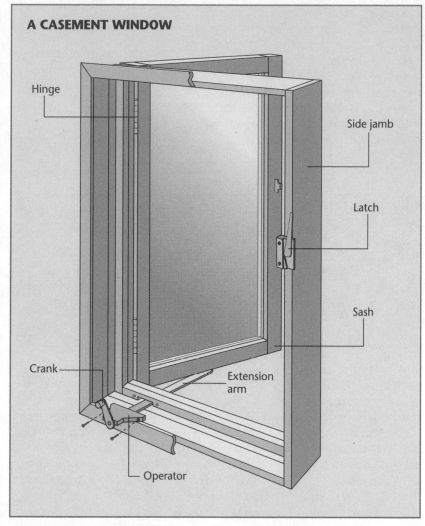

Hinge

Side jamb

Latch

Sash

Crank

Extension arm

Operator

AN AWNING WINDOW

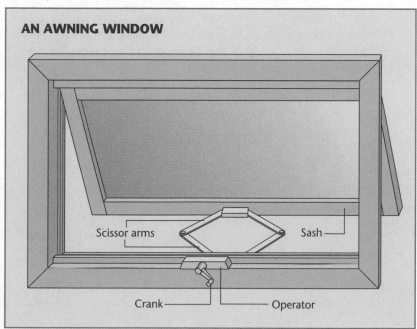

Scissor arms

Sash

Crank

Operator

The operation and care of casement and awning windows, as well as the inverted awnings called hoppers, are similar. In both window types, the sash is hinged at the side, top, or bottom, and is operated either by a sliding rod (in older versions) or by a crank and gear mechanism, as shown at left; the extension arm slides in a track on the underside or along the bottom rail of the sash.

To keep casement and awning windows working smoothly, you'll need to lubricate the hardware occasionally with a few drops of a light household oil or silicone spray. On a casement window, apply the lubricant to the hinges, the pivot of the latch, the extension-arm track, and the base of the crank. On an awning window, oil or spray the hinges, the joints where the scissor arms of the operator are fastened to the sash, the pivots in the middle of each scissor arm, and the base of the crank.

If a casement or awning sash sags or sticks in its frame, its hinges probably need adjusting or replacing. If it resists opening and closing, look for hardened grease or paint on the sliding rod or in the tracks and gears of the crank. Cleaning and lubricating the channel and the crank and gear assembly usually solves the problem. Details of these repairs are found on the following pages.

If the gears are worn, you'll probably have to replace the entire unit: To remove the operator, open the window slightly and unscrew the operator from the frame. Pull it toward you until the extension arm slips free of the track, and through the hole in the window frame. Then, buy a replacement operator and reverse these steps to install it.

Solving sash problems

TOOLKIT
- Butt chisel for scraping excess paint
OR
- Sanding block or block plane
- Paintbrush (optional)
OR
- Sanding block

Fixing a binding or warped sash

If paint is preventing the sash from closing, scrape away any excess and sand the surface smooth.

If the sash is swollen, sand the part that rubs against the stop with rough sandpaper, or plane it lightly, then smooth it with fine sandpaper. If you expose bare wood, coat it with sealer to prevent future swelling, and repaint it.

If the stop has swollen, remove, sand, and replace it; refer to the information on removing and repositioning a stop molding on page 64. You can compensate for a mild warp in a wood sash by removing the stop molding on the side that is warped and repositioning it; move any weather stripping.

Adjusting hinges

TOOLKIT
To tighten a hinge:
- Screwdriver
- Crosscut saw
- Claw hammer
- Butt chisel
- Electric drill
To shim a hinge:
- Claw hammer
- Punch (optional)
- Screwdriver
- Utility knife or scissors

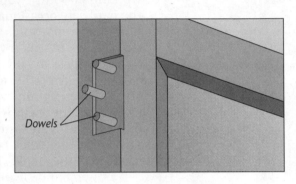

Dowels

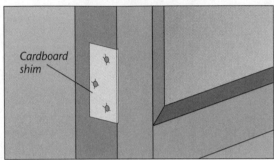

Cardboard shim

Tightening or shimming the hinges

If a hinge pin is loose in its guides, you'll have to replace the entire hinge with an identical model. But if the screws have worked loose or the hinge is recessed too deeply in the jamb, tightening or shimming should solve the problem. Work on only one hinge at a time, so you can check fit; support the sash in an open position, as described below.

If the screws can't be tightened, the screw holes may have become enlarged. Open the window fully while supporting the sash; cut wooden dowels to size, coat them with glue, and hammer them into the holes *(above, left)*. After the glue dries, trim the dowels flush with a butt chisel; drill pilot holes into them and replace the hinges.

A hinge that is recessed too deeply in the jamb or sash will cause the sash to bind on the latch side at the diagonally opposite end; a simple cure is to shim the hinge *(above, right)*. Support the sash in the open position, and free the hinge pin by hammering from below on a nail or punch. Remove the hinge leaf on the sash or jamb side.

Using the hinge leaf as a template, cut a shim, complete with screw holes, from noncompressible cardboard (the type used for file folders). Make the shim slightly smaller in all dimensions. Place the shim between the hinge leaf and the sash or jamb, and screw on the hinge. If the sash is still binding, use an extra shim.

 ASK A PRO

HOW DO I HOLD THE WINDOW OPEN TO WORK ON THE HINGES?

To support the window in an open position, you'll need to build a support from a piece of 2x4 and a 1x6 board; the 2x4 must be long enough to reach from the window to the ground. Face-nail the board and the 2x4 together to make a T. Lay the board on the ground with the 2x4 pointing up toward the window, and position it next to the window.

Open the window and attach the sash to the 2x4 with a C-clamp. Make sure that the support is properly positioned to hold the window securely, before you unscrew the hinges. If you're working on a window on the second floor, you may need to have a helper stand on a ladder and hold the window while you work on the hinges.

TOOLKIT
- Wire brush for extension-arm track
- Screwdriver
- Butt chisel (optional)
- Sanding block (optional)

Fixing an operator

To clean the extension-arm track, open the window fully and scrape out any caked grease, dirt, or paint with a wire brush. Take care to clean out the lip of the track as well. Lubricate the inside of the track lightly with petroleum jelly or silicone spray; remove any excess lubricant. Open and close the window several times.

To check the gear assembly, open the window partially and remove the screws that fasten the operator to the frame, as illustrated on page 71. To disengage the extension arm from its track on a casement, slide the arm along until it slips free. On an awning window, release the arms from the mounting bracket fastened to the bottom of the sash, then pull the operator toward yourself until the arms slide through the hole in the window frame. Inspect the gears carefully; if the teeth are damaged or worn, replace the unit with a new one. If you have a casement window, be sure the new unit cranks in the same direction as the old one.

If the gear teeth are sharp, but clogged with dirt or grease, remove the dirt with a piece of coat hanger wire or clean the assembly with a solvent, such as mineral spirits, and let it dry. Lubricate the metal gears with powdered graphite, silicone spray, or petroleum jelly; then turn the crank several times to spread the lubricant. Use silicone spray on nylon gears; if they still malfunction, replace the entire assembly.

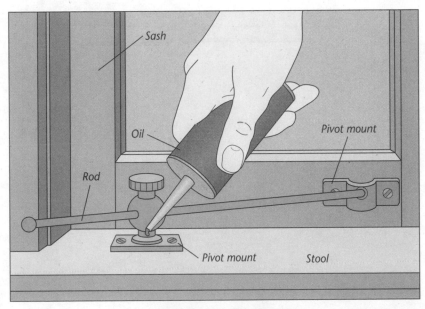

Sash

Oil

Rod

Pivot mount

Pivot mount

Stool

Fixing a pivot-mount rod

Remove paint or dirt from the rod with steel wool and lubricate the rod with paraffin. Oil all the pivot points *(left)*. Check the screws holding the mounts to the sash and stool; tighten them if necessary.

Fixing a sliding-shoe rod

Unscrew the channel from the sill. Clean the channel with steel wool and lubricate it with paraffin. If necessary, scrape any layered paint off the stool with a butt chisel and sand lightly. Replace the channel.

Tighten the screws on the pivot mount fastened to the sash and oil the pivot points on the stool and the sash.

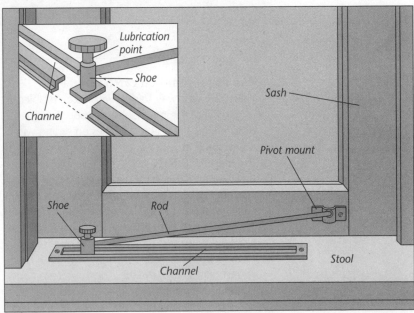

Lubrication point

Shoe

Channel

Sash

Pivot mount

Shoe

Rod

Stool

Channel

REPAIRING A SLIDING WINDOW

The sash in sliding windows move along metal or vinyl tracks fitted into the window frame at the top and bottom. Sometimes plastic rollers are attached at the top and bottom, or at the bottom alone, to ease the movement of the sash.

A sliding sash may stick or bind because its track is dirty or bent, or because paint has sealed the sash to the frame. The window may jam or not close properly if catches bend or become loose or damaged. To free a paint-clogged sash, score the paint with a sharp utility knife and rock the sash from side to side. If the sash is sticking because of dirt, clean the track and the sides of the sash with a wire brush; use the blade of a screwdriver for stubborn spots. Lubricate the track with paraffin. If the rollers are sticking, lubricate them lightly with powdered graphite or silicone lubricant until they move freely. If the rollers are broken, you'll have to take the sash to a glazier to have them replaced. If the problem is with the track or the catch, you'll have to remove the sash to fix it, as described opposite.

A SLIDING WINDOW

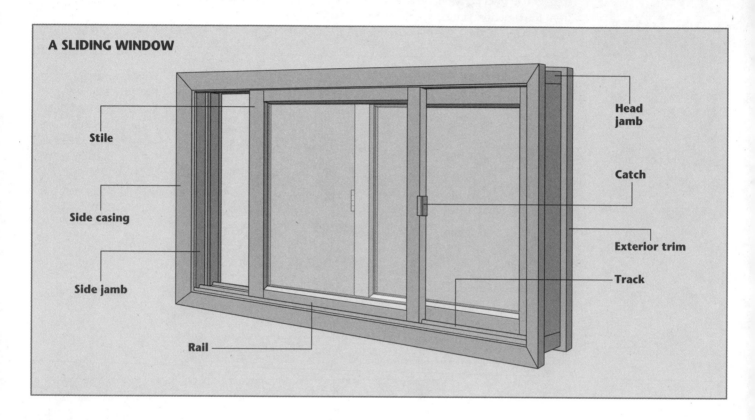

Stile

Side casing

Side jamb

Rail

Head jamb

Catch

Exterior trim

Track

Fixing a catch

TOOLKIT
• Screwdriver
• Vise
• Slip-joint pliers or claw hammer

Repairing common catch problems

Often the best way to deal with catch problems is to replace the mechanism, although sometimes repair is possible. Catches on sliding windows come in a variety of styles, depending on the manufacturer and the material of the window frame. If you have a catch-plate and dog mechanism, you may be able to reshape a bent catch-plate, or secure or replace a malfunctioning dog. You'll have to remove a catch-plate to reshape it, but first determine how much it will have to be reshaped to bring it flush with the widest diameter of the rail. Then unscrew it and clamp it in a vise; using slip-joint pliers or a hammer, bend it to the required angle. Replace it and check that the latch clicks as the window closes; it should have to be depressed fully for the window to open.

To secure a loose dog, remove the sash from the frame, as described opposite; then unscrew the dog from the bottom of the sash. Lay the sash flat on a stable surface, replace the dog in its proper position, and secure it. To replace a worn or broken dog with a new one, you'll need to remove the sash from the frame, then simply unscrew the dog from the sash, and screw the new dog in place.

Straightening a bent track

TOOLKIT
- Screwdriver (optional)
- Claw hammer

1 ▶ Removing the sash
Before removing the sash from the frame, look for any security devices at the top *(inset)*. To remove such devices, loosen the screws holding them in place. If there are key notches at the top, align the top rollers with them. Lift the sash up so it clears the track, and then tilt the bottom edge out into the room *(right)*.

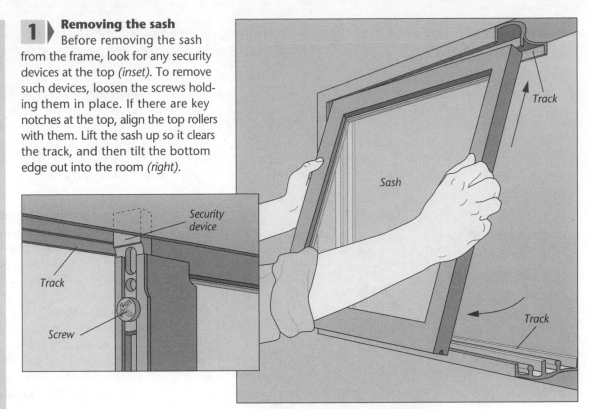

Security device

Track

Screw

Sash

Track

Track

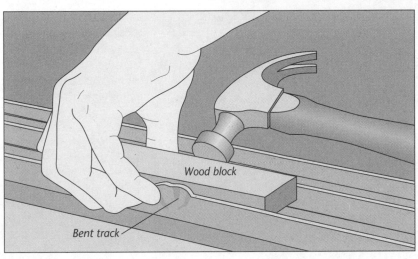

Wood block

Bent track

2 Fixing the track
Slide a block of wood into the track where the metal is bent. With a hammer, tap the block against the metal, working from the sides of the bent spot toward the middle *(left)*. Replace the sash.

PAINTING FOR PRESERVATION

An unpainted window can rot and crack from exposure to moisture and the drying effects of the sun. To prolong the life of your painted windows and keep them looking attractive, repaint them at the first sign of deterioration.

If the paint is in fairly good condition, you can simply scrape off any loose bits and sand those areas smooth. Lightly sand the entire frame. Paint that is in poor condition will have to be completely removed. The simplest method is to brush on paint remover and then scrape off the softened paint with a putty knife.

Sand the frame before applying the new coat. Applying a wood preservative before painting serves two purposes: It waterproofs the sash, and it acts as a primer. Let it dry overnight.

You may want to place masking tape around the edges of the glass to protect it from paint smears. However, the paint should extend $1/16$ inch onto the glass; it acts as an additional weather seal. An angled sash brush may be all you'll need to keep paint off the glass; it's especially useful when you're painting muntins.

INSTALLING WEATHER STRIPPING

Cold air entering your house in winter accounts for up to 35% of your heating load. Weather-stripping your windows can help reduce that load by 20%.

Most windows manufactured in recent years were weather-stripped by the manufacturer. Many older windows were not, but most of these can be sealed with one of the ordinary types of weather stripping that are sold in home centers.

The most common types of weather stripping are vinyl or plastic V-shaped strips, aluminum strips with pliable gaskets, and foam strips. Base your choice on window type, appearance, and budget.

Weather-stripping a sliding window

TOOLKIT
• Claw hammer (optional)
• Nailset (optional)

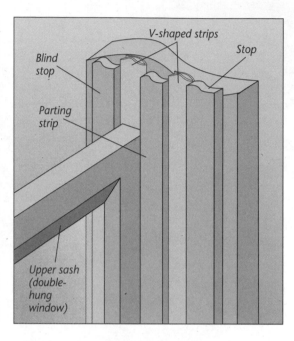

V-shaped strips
Blind stop
Stop
Parting strip
Upper sash (double-hung window)

Applying adhesive-backed strips

Vinyl or plastic weather stripping works best for double-hung windows; vinyl strips may even help the sliding action of older windows. These strips are usually adhesive-backed, so no tools are required. Open the window fully, peel the cover off the adhesive, and position the strip in the channel, with the open side of the V facing out *(left)*. If the strips need to be nailed in place, use finishing nails and a hammer and nailset to set the heads flush.

Adhesive-backed foam strips can be applied to the frame at the closing side of horizontal sliding windows. Foam strips can also be used at the top and bottom of double-hung windows: At the top, position the tape in the channel; at the bottom, attach the tape to the underside of the rail. You can also attach weather stripping to the bottom rail of the top sash, where the sash meet; aluminum strips with pliable gaskets are good for this job.

Weather-stripping a swinging window

TOOLKIT
• Claw hammer and nailset (optional)

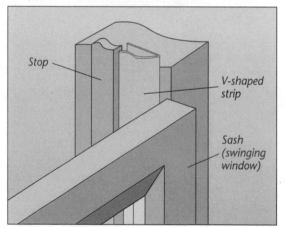

Stop
V-shaped strip
Sash (swinging window)

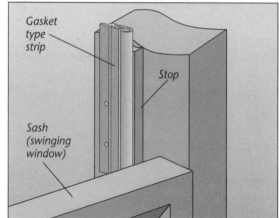

Gasket type strip
Stop
Sash (swinging window)

Using V-shaped and pliable gasket strips

Both V-shaped and pliable gasket weather stripping work well on swinging windows. With V-shaped strips, the point of the V should face in the direction that the window opens *(above, left)*, except on the hinge side, where the point of the V should be against the hinges.

Peel the covering off the adhesive, and stick the strips in place. If there's no adhesive strip, nail them in place with finishing nails, using a hammer and a nailset to set the heads flush. Attach the pliable gasket type weather stripping to the side of the stop with finishing nails *(above, right)*; the window should compress the gasket when it closes.

Foam strips can also be used with swinging windows. Attach them to the inside edge of the stop moldings, so that the window presses against them when closed. On the hinged side of the window, attach the foam strip to the jamb.

SKYLIGHTS

Choosing the right skylight is the first step in your skylight installation project. Turn to page 32 for information on what kind of skylight is appropriate for your roof. Next come the challenges of cutting a hole in the roof, framing it, installing the skylight, and sealing it against wind, rain, and snow.

Most skylights consist of a preframed window that you attach to the roof surface. A skylight installed in a sloping roof that can be reached from floor level (such as in an attic room) may be called a roof window. We'll use the term skylight for both types.

Opening your roof and then framing the opening below can be difficult and demanding, even for experts. Once you understand what's involved, you'll be able to decide whether this is work for you or a professional. On page 78, you'll find out what tools and supplies you'll need. For tips on working safely, see page 79. Instructions for marking and framing a skylight opening begin on page 81. We'll then give you complete instructions on how to install three common types of skylights—step-flashed *(page 87)*, curb-mounted *(page 88)*, and self-flashing *(page 89)*—as well as how to frame a ceiling opening *(page 90)*. You may also need a light shaft. You can build it yourself *(page 91)* or install a skylight that comes with a prefabricated shaft.

Installing a skylight in an open-beam ceiling is easier and takes less time than working with a finished ceiling because it doesn't require a light shaft; see page 93.

Even the most skilled do-it-yourselfer may sometimes require professional help. In some cases, you may be able to install the skylight yourself and hire a contractor just for the roofing. For information on working with professionals, see page 35. Work of this type is governed by local codes; check your plans with the building department, and keep in mind that you may need a building permit.

The self-flashing skylight shown here can be installed on roofs with either thick or thin roofing materials.

TOOLS AND SUPPLIES

Safety equipment and a sturdy ladder are essential in installing a skylight; see the section on safe working practices opposite. The other tools and supplies that you'll need will depend on your roof, the design of your skylight, and whether it will require a light shaft.

You'll need lumber for framing roof and ceiling openings, nails of various types (common nails, galvanized roofing nails, finishing nails), joist hangers (and special nails), and sealing compounds (roofing cement between flashing and roofing materials, and silicone rubber sealant between a skylight and a site-built curb). If you're not installing a self-flashing skylight, you'll also need the flashing recommended by the manufacturer.

If you plan to install a light shaft, you'll need wallboard tools and supplies, and if you want to trim the ceiling opening, you'll need molding, finishing nails, a nailset, and wood putty. Installing lights in the shaft requires wiring expertise, and is best left to a professional.

TOOLS OF THE TRADE: SKYLIGHTS

Claw hammer
To frame the opening and to nail wallboard to the light shaft.

Tin snips
To trim asphalt shingles and sheet-metal flashing.

Extension light
Use when working in an attic or crawl space.

Plumb bob
Used to locate one point vertically above another point.

Screwdriver
A variable-speed drill can be used instead.

Chalk line
Chalk-covered string extended and snapped on a surface to mark straight lines.

Butt chisel
Useful for cutting out pieces of wood roofing material and sheathing boards.

Nailset
Used to drive nails below the wood's surface; comes in variable sizes.

Wrecking bar
For removing shingles, roofing felt, and sheathing boards; a shingle ripper can also be used to remove shingles.

Combination square
For marking straight or angled cuts.

Circular saw
For cutting through roofing materials; a combination blade is ideal.

Utility knife
Good for scoring wallboard.

Caulking gun
Used to apply sealants.

Adjustable T-bevel
Measures angles other then 90°, such as in a light shaft.

Electric drill
For boring holes, such as those used to mark the corners of the ceiling and roof openings.

Carpenter's level
To level and plumb structural members and to lay out openings; a 24" model is recommended.

Tape measure
For taking vertical and horizontal measurements and laying out openings; a 16' model is recommended.

SUPPLIES

The supplies that you'll require will depend on the design of your skylight and the type of roof on your house, as well as whether or not you need a light shaft—the passage through which light from the roof enters the room.

Lumber for framing roof and ceiling openings should be the same size as the lumber used for rafters and joists in your home (usually 2x4 or 2x6). To build a skylight curb—the frame that holds a curb-mounted skylight above the roof—you'll need 2x6 lumber, unless you're installing a skylight in an open-beam ceiling *(page 93)*, where you'll need lumber that's 2x8 or wider. To frame the light shaft, use a 2x4 stud every 16 inches and two at each corner. To finish the light shaft, you can use either gypsum wallboard or plywood, but some building codes require the use of fire-resistant wallboard.

If you're not installing a self-flashing skylight, use the flashing recommended by—and usually available from—the skylight manufacturer. Be sure to get the type of flashing that's appropriate for your roofing material.

You'll need joist hangers *(page 86)* and different types of nails, in different sizes, for the various tasks involved. Generally, you can use 3$\frac{1}{2}$-inch nails to frame the roof opening and to build the curb; 2- or 2$\frac{1}{2}$-inch nails for bracing the curb; 1-inch nails, usually supplied with the flashing kit, for securing the flashing to the curb; wallboard nails for finishing the light shaft; and 1$\frac{1}{2}$- to 2-inch finishing nails for nailing molding to the ceiling opening. In open-beam construction, you'll need 2$\frac{1}{2}$-inch finishing nails to secure the curb to the roof.

Roofing cement, for use between flashing and roofing materials, is available in caulking tubes or 1- and 5-gallon cans. With a curb-mounted skylight, silicone rubber sealant should be used between the skylight and the curb.

Some skylights, such as polycarbonate domes, are only compatible with certain types of sealants; read the label carefully or check with your dealer for the appropriate type.

SAFE WORKING PRACTICES

As with all do-it-yourself projects, working safely is very important. Wear safety goggles when using any striking tool, and work gloves when handling insulation or rough or sharp objects. Use a dust mask or respirator to protect your mouth and nose when working on a task that creates a lot of dust (such as cutting through wallboard) or if handling insulation. When you're working with power tools, be sure to follow the manufacturer's operating instructions. When you're working in the attic, wear a hard hat, as nails protruding through the roof sheath-

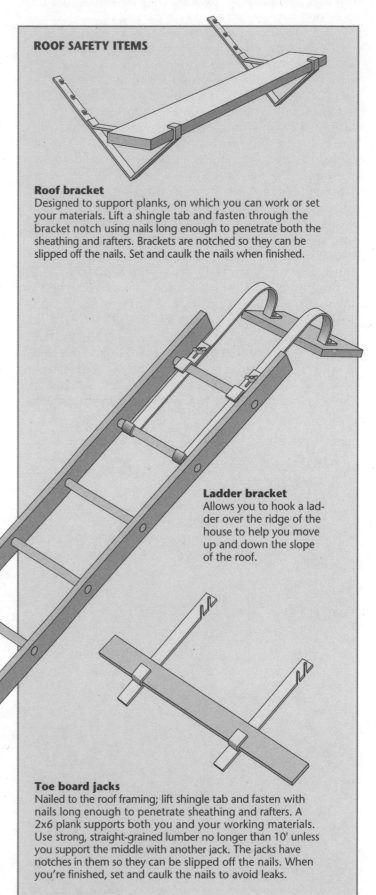

ROOF SAFETY ITEMS

Roof bracket
Designed to support planks, on which you can work or set your materials. Lift a shingle tab and fasten through the bracket notch using nails long enough to penetrate both the sheathing and rafters. Brackets are notched so they can be slipped off the nails. Set and caulk the nails when finished.

Ladder bracket
Allows you to hook a ladder over the ridge of the house to help you move up and down the slope of the roof.

Toe board jacks
Nailed to the roof framing; lift shingle tab and fasten with nails long enough to penetrate sheathing and rafters. A 2x6 plank supports both you and your working materials. Use strong, straight-grained lumber no longer than 10' unless you support the middle with another jack. The jacks have notches in them so they can be slipped off the nails. When you're finished, set and caulk the nails to avoid leaks.

ing can cause injury; avoid working in the attic on very hot days.

Working safely on a roof requires extra caution and planning. Wear loose, comfortable clothing, and rubber-soled shoes with good ankle support. Keep children, pets, and anyone not involved in the job away from the area; they may be injured by falling materials. Don't work on a roof when it's windy, rainy, or cold. Wait for good weather, but don't work during the hottest part of the day. CAUTION: Never touch power lines, with either your body or your equipment.

Some roofs are too steep to work on. Roof pitch is expressed as a ratio, such as 6 in 12. The first number indicates the number of inches of vertical rise; the 12 indicates one horizontal foot. A roof that is 6 in 12 rises 6 inches vertically for every horizontal foot. You can safely work on roofs with a pitch up to 6 in 12, although you should wear a safety harness or belt if the roof pitch is between 4 in 12 and 6 in 12. For roofs with a pitch of more than 6 in 12, call a professional. You can purchase a safety harness or belt and the other required equipment at a home center, or you can rent it. You'll also need a fall-arrest rope, which should be attached to a secure, fixed object (such as a tree) on the opposite side of the house from where you're work-

ing. You can also install the safety devices illustrated on page 79.

When using an extension ladder, first inspect it for weaknesses and cracks. Position it properly, as described below, and stabilize it. Make sure that the bottom of the ladder is on firm, level ground, placing a board under the feet if necessary. Tie both siderails to a stake driven into the ground between the ladder and the wall. At the top, fasten an eye screw or a 3-inch spiral nail just above or below the gutter on each side of the ladder, and tie the siderails to them. You may want to use scaffolding, which you can rent; scaffolding is an especially good idea if you're installing a large skylight or a window on an upper story.

Walk very carefully when you're on the roof—the fewer shingles or shakes you disturb, the better. If you have a tile or slate roof, don't walk on it. Both tile and slate are slippery and easily breakable, so skylight installation should be left to a professional. If the pitch of the roof is up to 4 in 12, you can walk up the slope diagonally to move from one place to another. For roofs that have a pitch of between 4 in 12 and 6 in 12, it's best to walk straight up the slope to the ridge, straddle the ridge and walk along, keeping your knees slightly bent, and then walk straight down to the new location.

Raising a ladder

Positioning a ladder

There are four steps involved in raising a ladder to a safe position. To get up to the appropriate height you may have to raise the extension. If you're going onto the roof, the ladder should be long enough to extend 3', or three rungs, above the roof eaves. First, lay the ladder on the ground with the extension on the bottom; set the base of the ladder against the wall. Raise the ladder by walking it into an upright position (A and B). Lift the base and move it out from the wall (C). Check that you've positioned the ladder correctly; the distance from the base of the ladder to the wall should be equal to a quarter of the length of the ladder (D).

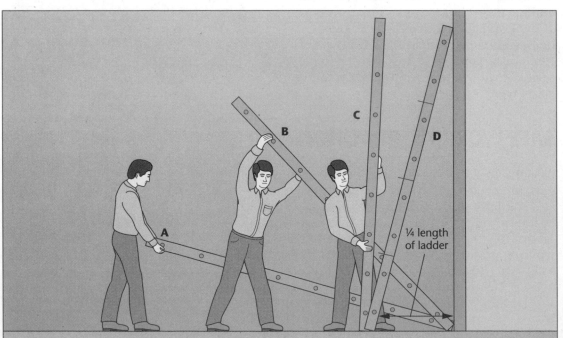

¼ length of ladder

BEFORE YOU BEGIN

Installing a skylight over a room that has a finished ceiling with an attic or crawl space above it involves planning both a ceiling opening and a roof opening. (If you're working on an open-beam ceiling, refer to page 93.) The dimensions of the roof opening are determined by the size of the skylight; they're generally the same as the inside dimensions of the skylight or of the curb if it's a curb-mounted unit. If you only have the curb's outside dimensions, deduct twice the curb's thickness from the length and width to determine the size of the opening. The instructions in this chapter refer to asphalt shingle or wood shake roofs; for a tile, slate or metal roof, consult a professional.

Much of the work of installing the skylight is done from the attic or crawl space. When working in the attic, protect your head with a hard hat, and step only on ceiling joists or on boards supported by joists. If you can't work in your attic, you'll need to cut a hole big enough to climb through or work through (from a ladder or platform) within the proposed ceiling opening, to one side of the center. Then, after you've marked the center of the roof opening, you can cut the ceiling opening for easier access *(page 90)*.

To lay out the openings, you'll need the following tools and supplies: a plumb bob, tape measure, straightedge, carpenter's square, drill and bit, 3 1/2-inch nails (4 inches if you have a heavy shake roof), and pencil. If your attic has no light fixture, you'll need an extension light, or at least a flashlight. Unless your attic has a floor, you'll also need boards or plywood panels to lay over the joists so you can work safely without stepping through the ceiling. If your attic is insulated, wear protective clothing: gloves, a long-sleeved shirt, long pants, a dust mask or respirator, and goggles.

Planning to install a skylight

TOOLKIT
- Tape measure
- Claw hammer
- Plumb bob
- Carpenter's square and straightedge to mark openings
- Electric drill

1 Marking the ceiling opening
Situate the opening according to where you want the light and what type of light you desire; the opening's dimensions are determined by the size of the skylight and the amount of light you want. To maximize the amount of light coming into the room, make the ceiling opening larger than the roof opening and connect them with a splayed light shaft *(page 22)*; you can splay any or all of the shaft walls. In some cases, as in an attic room, you won't need a ceiling opening and a light shaft.

In the room below, mark the four corners and the center of the proposed opening; drive nails deeply enough through these five points so you can find them in the attic. If any of the nails hits a ceiling joist, you may want to move the proposed opening or adjust its size. To save yourself work when you're framing the ceiling opening, try to arrange the opening so two opposite sides butt up against the facing sides of two joists.

In the attic, clear away any insulation material covering your proposed ceiling opening. Locate the five nails that were driven through from the ceiling below. Look for obstructions—wires, pipes, or heating or cooling ducts—within the area of the proposed opening; check the area of the roof opening now, too. If you find any obstructions and don't want to move the opening or adjust its size, you'll have to arrange to have the obstructions rerouted *(page 41)*.

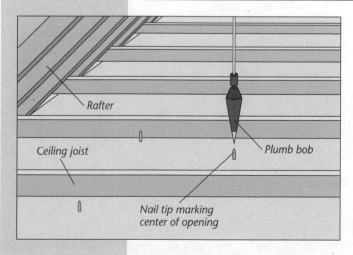

Rafter

Ceiling joist

Plumb bob

Nail tip marking center of opening

2 Marking the roof opening
Hang a plumb bob from the underside of the roof with the point of the bob over the center nail in the ceiling opening *(left)*. Mark this center point clearly on the underside of the roof.

Mark the manufacturer's recommended dimensions for the roof opening on the underside of the roof; to simplify the framing of the opening, locate at least one edge against a rafter. Drill a hole at each corner and drive a 3 1/2" or 4" nail through each hole so you can find the corners of the opening when you go up on the roof.

If the roof ridge or a purlin crosses the opening, relocate the opening and either move the proposed ceiling opening or use an angled or splayed light shaft between the roof and the ceiling. You should never cut trusses; if you have trusses rather than rafters, install a skylight that fits between them.

FRAMING THE ROOF OPENING

The thought of cutting a hole in your roof needn't conjure up images of dripping water destroying your living room carpet, as long as you know how to seal the opening against the vagaries of nature. Do the roof work on a day with zero rain probability, and plan to have the skylight installed by the end of the day. Even then, you'd be wise to be prepared for rain, just in case. You'll need a tarpaulin large enough to cover the opening generously, 2x4s or boards to go over the opening to support the tarpaulin, and more boards or 2x4s to weight it down. Ideally, the tarpaulin should be large enough to go over the ridge to the other side of the roof, where you can weight it down; this will keep rain from getting underneath the tarpaulin at the top. If this isn't possible, then gently tuck the top of the tarpaulin under a row of shingles.

The instructions on the following pages show you how to build the skylight curb, if needed, and how to cut and frame the opening. In a home with finished ceilings, you'll mark the roof opening and the roofing material that needs to be removed in exactly the same manner for either a sloped or a flat roof. The amount of roofing material you remove to allow for the flashing varies depending on the type of roofing and the kind of skylight you use.

Before you cut through the roof, you'll have to build a curb, or box frame, for your skylight if it's the curb-mounted type, as described below. If your skylight boasts an integral curb or sits directly on the sheathing, you can skip this step.

PLAY IT SAFE

WORKING WITH POWER TOOLS
Use safety precautions when working with any power tool: make sure the equipment is properly grounded; wear goggles or safety glasses; and read the owner's manual thoroughly. For more detailed safety information, see page 79.

Building a curb

TOOLKIT
- Tape measure
- Combination square or carpenter's square
- Circular saw or crosscut saw
- Electric drill
- Claw hammer

Constructing the frame
The curb should raise the skylight at least 4" above the roofing material; 2x6 lumber usually works well. In areas with heavy snow loads, wider lumber (such as 2x10) is recommended. The inside dimensions of the curb should equal the dimensions specified by the manufacturer for the roof opening. Using a tape measure and a combination square or carpenter's square, mark the lumber for cuts, taking care to keep knots away from the ends. Cut the pieces. As a further precaution against split ends, drill pilot holes for nails; then nail the pieces together.

Check the curb for squareness by measuring both diagonals from corner to corner (*right*); the distances should be identical. (You can use a carpenter's square instead.)

Brace two opposite corners of the curb to keep it square until you're ready to nail it in place. Use lengths of wood or triangles cut from 1/2" plywood and nail them with 2" or 2 1/2" nails, driving the nails only partway so they can be easily removed.

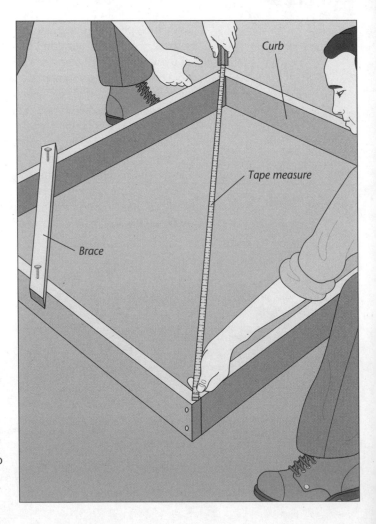

Curb

Tape measure

Brace

Marking the roof

TOOLKIT
- Tape measure and straightedge
OR
- Utility knife
OR
- Chalk line

Measuring for step-flashed or self-flashing models

Mark the rough opening on the roof using the four nails protruding from below as a guide. With a tape measure, a straightedge, and a piece of chalk or a pencil, mark the sides and top of the rough opening; or wrap a chalk line around the nails and snap it to mark all sides. On a built-up roof, clear away the gravel about 10" beyond the rough opening on all four sides, then outline the opening indicated by the nails. You can cut the opening as outlined below and install the skylight yourself, but hire a professional to install the flashing and replace the roofing for you.

Measuring for a curb-mounted model

Raise the curb carefully to the roof using a rope. Set the curb over the four nails protruding through the roof; there should be a nail in each inside corner.

For a wood or asphalt shingle roof, use chalk, a pencil, or a utility knife to mark lines on the roof along the outside edges of the curb. On a heavy shake roof, mark lines on the roof 1/2" away from the outside edges of the curb on all sides; this extra space will give you room to insert the pieces of step flashing. Return the curb to the ground.

Making the opening in the roof

TOOLKIT
- Circular saw
- Prybar
- Claw hammer
- Chalk line
For wood shingles or shakes:
- Combination saw blade
For asphalt shingles:
- Utility knife (optional)
- Carbide-tipped blade with widely spaced teeth or utility knife
For built-up roofing:
- Disposable saw blade

1 ▶ Cutting the rough opening

For wood shingles or shakes, use a circular saw with a combination blade. For asphalt shingles, use a circular saw with an old carbide-tipped blade. (Or use a utility knife to cut through shingles, then use a circular saw with a combination blade to cut through sheathing.) For a built-up roof, buy a disposable blade—the blade you use for cutting through the roofing material will be unusable afterwards. When using a power saw, avoid awkward positions and keep out of the line of the blade. CAUTION: Be alert while sawing—a blade that binds can throw you off the roof.

Adjust your saw so that the blade will cut through the roofing material and the sheathing but not into the rafters. Resting the front of the saw's base plate on the roof, align the saw blade with the chalk line, pencil line, or knife cut. Turn on the power and lower the saw until the base plate is resting on the roof. Saw slowly and steadily along the marked line until you reach a corner (right). Repeat for the other sides and remove the section of roof.

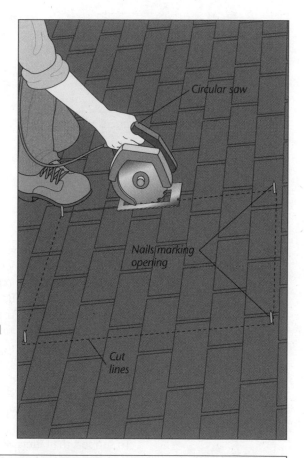

Circular saw

Nails marking opening

Cut lines

2 Removing the roofing material

The amount of roofing material you'll have to remove depends on the type of skylight you're installing. For skylights that require step-flashing (including those mounted on a site-built curb), remove shingles at least 10" on all sides of the opening, using a prybar to remove the nails. Try not to damage the shingles, since you'll have to replace some of them when you're flashing the unit. For self-flashing skylights, remove shingles in an area about 10" wide on the sides and top of the rough opening, but do not remove any shingles from the bottom of the opening. Don't worry if the shingles below the opening have been cut through—they will be covered with the bottom flange of the skylight.

Lumber used for headers and jack rafters should be the same size as the existing rafters. To determine the framing needed for the opening, carefully examine the structure of the roof around your skylight opening. Whether or not you're cutting through any rafters, you'll need to frame the roof opening with headers and possibly jack rafters so the sheathing is supported on all four sides.

If your skylight fits exactly between two rafters, you'll need single headers (framing members running perpendicular to the rafters) to support the sheathing (A). If it is larger than the space between the rafters, you can leave the rafters in place and install single headers, but you'll proba-

bly want to remove the rafters for an uninterrupted view. If you need to cut a rafter, you'll need double headers to support the sheathing and the cut rafter. You'll also need to add sister rafters—full-length rafters installed next to the existing rafters to compensate for the rafters that are removed (B). If more than one rafter must be cut to fit your skylight (C), consult a professional, since the structural support of your house is involved.

Skylights smaller than the space between the rafters require an opening framed with both headers and jack rafters: one jack rafter if the opening abuts one existing rafter (D), two if it does not (E).

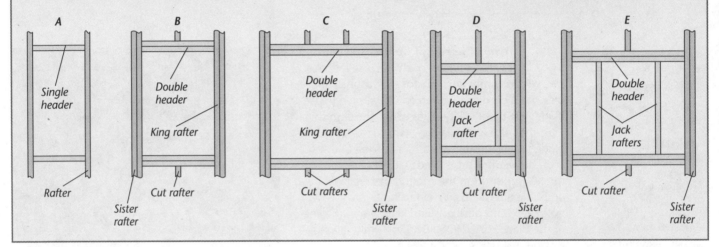

Removing the rafters

TOOLKIT
• Combination square or adjustable T-bevel
• Claw hammer
• Reciprocating saw

Marking and cutting the rafters
Determine the angle at which you'll need to cut your rafters (opposite). Using a combination square or adjustable T-bevel, mark lines on the rafter to be cut and the rafters on both sides of the opening at the appropriate angle relative to the cut edge of the sheathing (right). The lines on the rafters on the sides of the opening indicate the placement of the headers.

To support the rafters while you're cutting, nail 2x4s between the rafters and ceiling joists on each side of the opening. Leave these supports in place until you've installed the headers. Use a reciprocating saw to cut through the rafters along the marked lines.

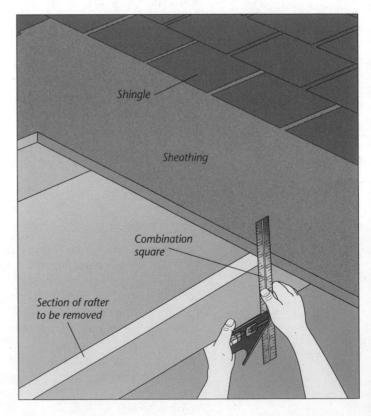

The type of light shaft that you want to build determines the angle at which you mark and cut the rafters, as well as how you install the headers. It also determines how you frame the ceiling opening *(page 90)*. These illustrations indicate some of the different angles that may be involved with splayed, angled, or straight light shafts.

You'll have to calculate the angles required for your specific situation. For example, if you have a straight light shaft, the angle of the headers in the roof opening will not be 90° unless your roof is flat.

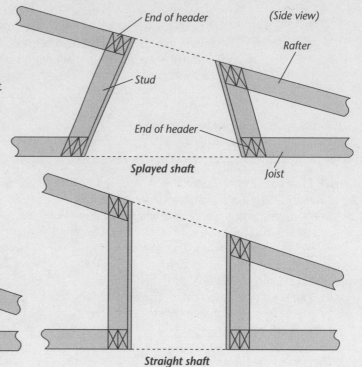

(Side view)

Splayed shaft

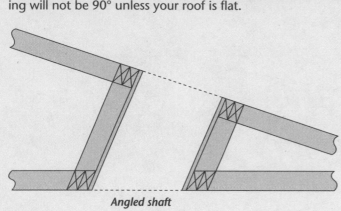

Angled shaft

Straight shaft

Framing the roof opening

TOOLKIT
• Tape measure
• Circular saw
• Claw hammer

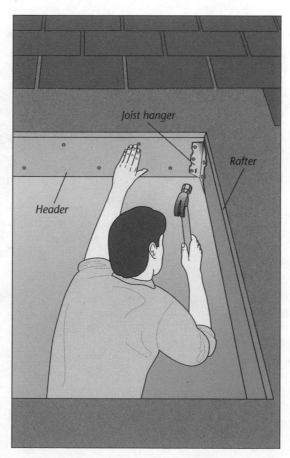

1 Installing headers
After marking the angles of the headers, measure the distance between the rafters. If your headers are set at a 90° angle to the roof surface, use lumber of the same thickness and width as the rafters; cut four pieces to the length measured. Nail them together in pairs to form two doubled headers. Place two nails at the ends, and then nail along the length of the header, staggering the nails about 6" apart. Insert the header into double joist hangers.

If your headers are not at a 90° angle relative to the roof surface, use lumber the same size as the rafters and attach the headers at an angle, or cut the headers from larger stock, angle-ripping (beveling) each piece to the appropriate angle. To attach headers on an angle, use a framing anchor instead of a joist hanger.

Position the header between the rafters, making sure that the header is properly aligned with the marked lines. Nail the joist hanger to the rafter using framing anchor nails and to the header using 3$\frac{1}{2}$" nails *(left)*. Toenail the header to the cut rafter with 2$\frac{1}{2}$" nails.

For single headers, cut just two pieces of lumber, and use single joist hangers. Otherwise, installation is the same as for double headers.

2 Finishing the framing

If your skylight doesn't fit exactly between the rafters you'll need to install jack rafters between the headers parallel to the rafters *(page 84)*. Cut pieces of lumber the same size as the rafters to fit between the two headers. Install and nail these pieces in joist hangers nailed to the headers.

If your skylight is a curb-mounted unit, you now need to install the curb and flash it. If you're installing a step-flashed unit, install the skylight as described on page 88, and then install the flashing as described opposite. If you're installing a self-flashing skylight, you're now ready to position the unit, as shown on page 89.

ASK A PRO

WHAT IS A JOIST HANGER?

A joist hanger is a type of framing connector used to make a secure butt joint between various framing members and assemblies, such as between a header and a rafter or between a joist and a beam. There are various types of joist hangers, usually U-shaped, which are secured with nails and sometimes prongs that stick into the wood (right). Joist hangers require special framing anchor nails, which you can buy with the joist hangers.

    To attach lumber at an angle, you can buy skewed joist hangers or use framing anchors if you can't find joist hangers at the angle you need.

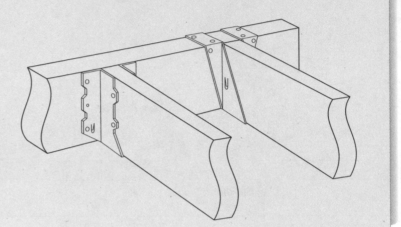

Installing a site-built curb

TOOLKIT
• Carpenter's square or tape measure
• Claw hammer
For fastening roofing felt:
• Utility knife
• Hand stapler

Positioning the curb

Raise the curb to the roof, using a rope, if necessary. Set the curb over the roof opening, sliding it up from the bottom until it's perfectly aligned with the opening. Check the curb for square using a carpenter's square, or measure each diagonal and check that they're the same. Then, using 2½" nails, toenail the curb through the sheathing to the frame rafters and headers *(right)*. Remove the corner braces from the curb.

    Fasten roofing felt around all sides, sliding it under the edges of the existing shingles and letting it curl up the sides of the curb. Trim the felt flush with the top of the curb, and staple it to the curb. At the corners, cut the paper, curl it around and staple it to the adjacent side of the curb. The edges of the piece at the top should overlap the side pieces, and the side pieces should overlap the bottom piece.

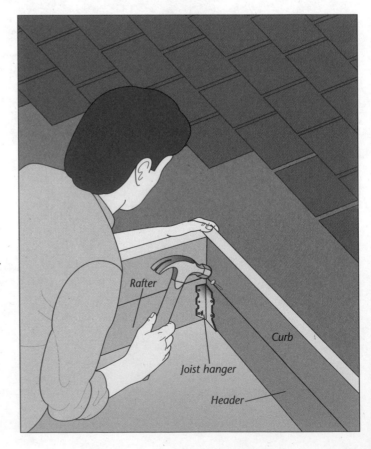

Rafter

Curb

Joist hanger

Header

INSTALLING A SKYLIGHT

Once you've framed the roof opening, you're ready to secure the skylight. If you're installing a curb-mounted unit, install the curb as shown opposite, then install the flashing following the steps below, and fasten the skylight to the curb, as shown on the next page. If your skylight is a step-flashed model, then fasten the unit to the sheathing with the mounting brackets supplied, and install the flashing as outlined below. For self-flashing units, follow the instructions on page 89. The steps described below should work for most models, but details may vary from manufacturer to manufacturer (for example, some manufacturers rec-

ommend against nailing flashing into the curb or frame); follow any specific installation instructions that come with your model of skylight.

Different flashing kits are available from skylight manufacturers for low-profile and high-profile roofing materials; flashing kits for high-profile roofing may include a special apron, molded to fit over the roofing material below the skylight. It is critical that the flashing be properly installed—a bad flashing job can result in a leaky roof. When pieces of roofing felt, flashing, or shingles overlap, the piece that is higher on the roof should always be on top.

Installing step flashing

TOOLKIT
• Claw hammer
• Tin snips

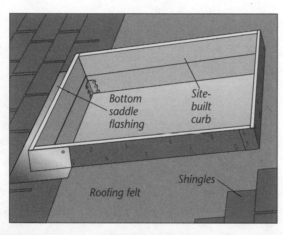
Bottom saddle flashing
Site-built curb
Roofing felt
Shingles

1 Installing the bottom saddle
Replace shingles up to the bottom of the curb (as shown) or the step-flashed skylight's frame. Position the saddle flashing against the bottom of the curb or frame; take care not to puncture the roofing felt, as this can cause leaks.

Nail the saddle flashing to the curb or frame *(left)*, using 1" nails, or the nails supplied by the manufacturer, if any. Do not nail the flashing to the sheathing.

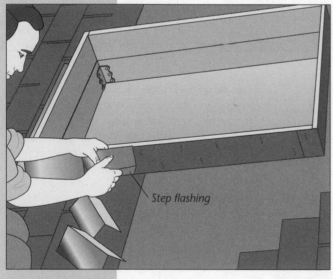
Step flashing

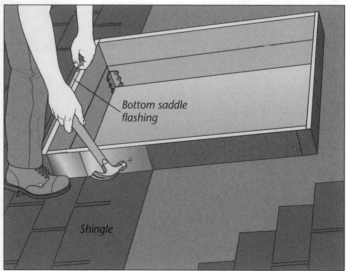
Bottom saddle flashing
Shingle

2 Installing the step flashing
At each side of the curb or frame, install the shingles and the step flashing, interleaving each course of shingles with a new piece of step flashing *(above, left)*; again, take care not to puncture the roofing felt. Do not nail the shingles through the flashing. The higher pieces of step flashing and shingles should overlap the lower ones. Nail

each piece of flashing into the curb or frame, holding it flat against the roof with your hand or your foot *(above, right)*.

At the top of the curb or frame, you may have to cut the flashing to fit. Using tin snips, cut the flashing and curve it around the corner; nail it to the top of the curb or frame.

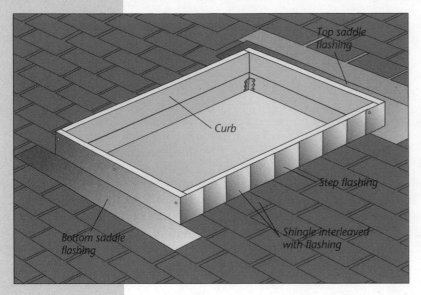

Top saddle flashing

Curb

Step flashing

Shingle interleaved with flashing

Bottom saddle flashing

3 Installing the top saddle

Position the top saddle flashing around the top of the curb or frame. Hold the saddle in place while you nail it against the curb or frame.

There may be a filler piece included with your flashing kit, which you'll need if you have thicker roofing material and the saddle doesn't fit tightly against the curb or frame. Insert the filler piece before nailing the saddle into position; nail the saddle through the filler piece into the curb or frame. Replace shingles over the saddle flashing but don't put any nails in the flashing.

Generally, no roofing cement or silicone rubber sealant is required with step-flashed skylights, but check the manufacturer's suggestions. In areas with the possibility of ice dams, you can seal the flashing *(page 94)* as a precautionary measure.

Installing a curb-mounted skylight

TOOLKIT
• Caulking gun
• Claw hammer

Fastening the frame to the curb

Once the curb is flashed, run a wavy bead of silicone rubber sealant along the top of the curb; center your skylight over the curb and press it down firmly into the sealant.

Secure the skylight's frame to the side of the curb by nailing through the predrilled holes in the frame.

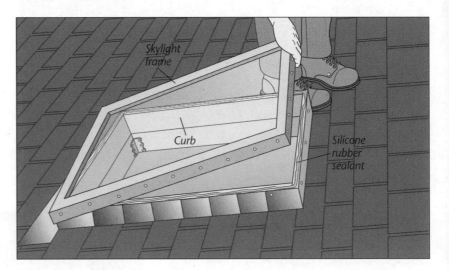

Skylight frame

Curb

Silicone rubber sealant

Installing a step-flashed skylight

TOOLKIT
• Electric drill or screwdriver
• Tape measure or carpenter's square
• Utility knife
• Hand stapler

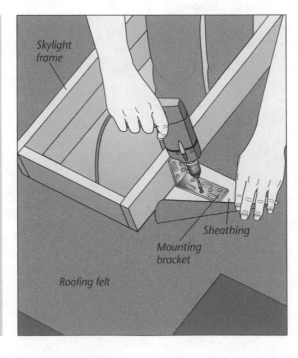

Skylight frame

Sheathing

Mounting bracket

Roofing felt

Fastening the frame to the roof

After framing the rough opening *(page 85)*, remove the sash from the frame if recommended by the manufacturer. Fasten the mounting brackets to the frame, following the manufacturer's instructions. Position the frame over the opening and screw the brackets to the sheathing *(left)*. Check that the frame is square by measuring both diagonals or using a carpenter's square.

Lay roofing felt around the frame, sliding it under existing roofing felt at the top and sides, and over existing felt at the bottom. Curl the roofing felt up around the edges of the frame and staple it to the frame. At the corners, cut the paper, curl it around, and staple it to the adjacent side of the curb. The edges of the piece of roofing felt at the top of the skylight should be on top of the side pieces, and the side pieces should be on top of the bottom piece. Replace shingles up to the bottom of the frame, then install the step flashing as described on page 87.

Installing a self-flashing skylight

TOOLKIT
- Utility knife (optional)
- Putty knife
- Electric drill or screwdriver
- Claw hammer

1 ▶ Applying roofing cement
Make sure that the sheathing around the rough opening is covered with roofing felt. Add new pieces if necessary, sliding them under the existing felt above and trimming them at the edges of the opening.

With a putty knife, spread roofing cement in a band 4" wide and 1/4" thick around all four sides of the rough opening. With some skylights, only certain kinds of sealants are compatible, so be sure to ask your dealer for any restrictions that apply to the skylight you're installing.

Roofing felt

Roofing cement

Putty knife

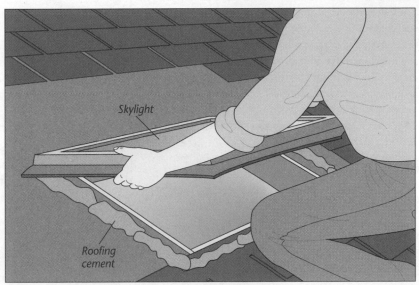

Skylight

Roofing cement

◀2 Placing the skylight
Position the skylight over the opening, align it, and press the nailing flange down onto the roofing cement. At the bottom, the flange should rest on top of the shingles.

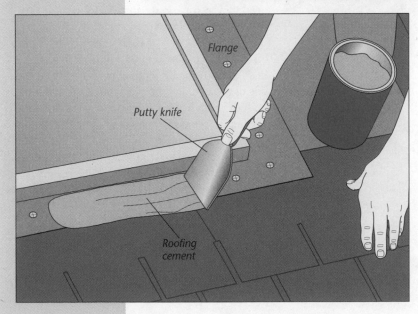

Flange

Putty knife

Roofing cement

◀3 Fastening the skylight and replacing the roof
Fasten the skylight to the sheathing through the predrilled holes in the flange, using the type of fastener suggested by the manufacturer; 1 1/2" screws spaced 8" on center is typical. Don't worry if some roofing cement is squeezed out from under the flange. Apply more roofing cement on top of the flange, covering both the screws and the edge of the flange; a 4" wide band 1/4" thick is recommended. You can also add a shingle at the bottom of the skylight; just press it into the roofing cement.

Replace the shingles at the sides and top of the skylight. Shingle right up to the sides of the skylight, but don't nail into the flange; the roofing cement on top of the flange will hold the shingles in place. Use mineral spirits to clean your tools.

FRAMING THE CEILING OPENING

After you've secured the skylight from the exterior, you can finish the interior work at any time—rain or shine. In this section, we'll show you how to cut and frame the ceiling opening *(below)*, how to build a light shaft to direct light from the skylight on the roof into the interior of your home *(opposite)*, and how to install a ceiling panel at the bottom of the light shaft *(page 92)* if you want the light to be distributed more evenly.

Cutting the ceiling opening

TOOLKIT

- Tape measure
- Carpenter's square
- Chalk line
- Reciprocating saw or saber saw
- Compass saw (optional)
- Screwdriver or claw hammer (for removing wallboard fasteners)
- Circular saw or crosscut saw
- Electric drill or screwdriver
- Adjustable T-bevel (optional)

1 ▶ Starting the project

In your attic or crawl space, use a tape measure and carpenter's square to check the markings you made at the corners and center of the ceiling opening against both the framed roof opening and the angle of the light shaft. In the room below, replace any of the nails missing from the corners. Stretch a chalk line around the four nails and snap the line between each pair of nails to mark the opening *(right)*; then remove the nails.

Cover the floor and the furniture with a large tarpaulin and drop cloths. Have a garbage can or wheelbarrow available to collect the debris, and wear a dust mask or respirator and goggles to protect yourself against the dust while you're cutting.

Cut through wallboard with a reciprocating saw, saber saw, or compass saw. Cut lath and plaster with a reciprocating saw or saber saw fitted with a coarse wood-cutting blade. When you come to a joist, cut through the wallboard but don't cut the joist. After the opening is cut, break off the wallboard and remove the fasteners. Ceiling material is quite heavy, so cut it out in pieces small enough to handle conveniently.

Corner nail

Chalk line

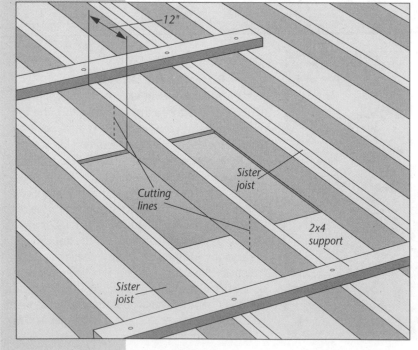

12"

Sister joist

Cutting lines

2x4 support

Sister joist

2 ◀ Supporting and cutting the joists

If you have to cut one or more joists, you'll need to add sister joists. Install a full-length joist next to the joist on each side of the ones you're cutting. To support the joists while you're cutting them, cut two pieces of 2x4 lumber long enough to span both the opening and two joists on each side of the opening, position the pieces at least 12" from the edges of the opening, and fasten them with wood screws to the joists.

Use a reciprocating saw to cut the joists, following the instructions for cutting a rafter *(page 84)*, as well as these additional guidelines: For a straight shaft, cut the joist at a right angle to the ceiling; for an angled or splayed shaft, mark the angle of cut with an adjustable T-bevel or a length of string held taut between the bottom of the joist and the roof opening. The cut joists will butt against the sides of the header, as shown opposite, so cut the joists far enough back from the edges of the opening to make room for the headers.

Framing the opening

TOOLKIT

For cutting:
- Tape measure
- Combination square
- Circular saw or crosscut saw
- Claw hammer

Installing headers

To frame the ceiling opening, refer to the instructions for framing the roof opening *(page 85)*. Cut four pieces of 2-by lumber for headers to the appropriate length. Make a double header by nailing two of the pieces together using 3 1/2" nails driven in a staggered pattern; repeat with the other two pieces of lumber. Nail the double joist hangers to the joists using joist-hanger nails. Set one header into each facing pair of hangers and toenail it to the cut end of the joist with 2 1/2" nails, then nail the joist hanger flanges to the header *(right)*. Repeat with the other header on the opposite side of the opening.

If your ceiling opening doesn't fit exactly between two joists, you'll need to install additional framing members parallel to the joists to frame the edge of the opening, as illustrated on page 84 for roof framing members.

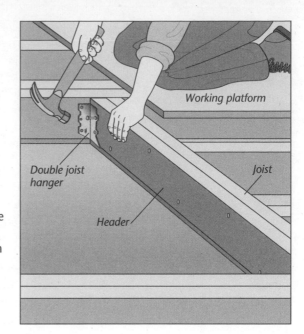

Working platform

Double joist hanger

Joist

Header

Building a light shaft

TOOLKIT

- Tape measure
- Combination square
- Saw
- Claw hammer
- Adjustable T-bevel (optional)
- Utility knife
- Straightedge
- Hand stapler
- Bell-faced hammer or screw gun for fastening wallboard
- Tin snips
- Caulking gun or notched trowel for applying panel adhesive (optional)
- Backsaw and miter box to cut trim

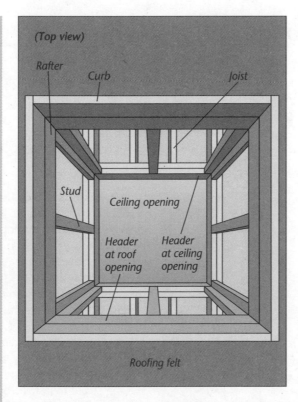

(Top view)

Rafter

Curb

Joist

Stud

Ceiling opening

Header at roof opening

Header at ceiling opening

Roofing felt

1 Framing the shaft

The frame for the light shaft not only provides a nailing surface for the walls of the shaft, but also joins the ceiling to the roof, giving support to both.

Measure the distance between the ceiling headers and the roof headers at every corner and at least every 16" in between. Cut vertical studs to the measured lengths. Unless your roof is flat and your light shaft straight, you'll need to cut one or both ends of the studs at an angle; mark the cuts with an adjustable T-bevel. Toenail the studs to the ceiling and roof headers with 2 1/2" nails. Install two studs at each corner to provide nailing for the wallboard or other material used to finish the shaft.

If you want lights in the shaft, position the studs to clear any electrical outlet or recessed light fixtures you plan to install. You may also wish to have wiring done at this time if your skylight will have an electric operating device. Even if you don't plan to install the device right away, putting in the wiring at this stage means you won't have to open up your light shaft walls if you change your mind later.

2 Insulating for energy efficiency

For greater energy efficiency, insulate the light shaft. Have any necessary electrical wiring installed before you insulate.

Blanket insulation works best for the short, uneven lengths needed in a light shaft; buy insulation in the width that will best fit between the studs. Check your local building code for the insulation thickness recommended for your area; your code may also require that the insulation be covered with fire-resistant wallboard. Measure a length of insulation to fit in each stud opening, and cut the insulation with a utility knife guided by a straightedge. Place the insulation between the studs with the vapor-barrier side toward the shaft opening; staple the edge flaps to the studs. Alternatively, unroll blanket insulation horizontally around the light shaft; staple a plastic vapor barrier to the studs on the inside of the shaft.

CAUTION: Wear gloves, a long-sleeved shirt, long pants, a dust mask or respirator, and goggles when working with insulation materials.

3 Finishing the light shaft

To finish the light shaft with wallboard, you'll need pieces of ½" thick wallboard cut to fit. Measure and mark your cutting line on the wallboard, then score along the line with a utility knife. Bend the panel backward away from the score line to break the core, then cut the backing paper with a utility knife.

Fasten wallboard to the studs inside the shaft. Fasteners are commonly spaced 8" apart, but check your local building code for spacing requirements. If you're using screws, set the heads slightly below the surface of the wallboard. If you're using drywall nails, you'll need to dimple the surface of the wallboard slightly with the last hammer blow, to create a shallow pocket for wallboard compound. Measure four metal corner bead pieces to fit around the ceiling opening, cut them with tin snips and nail them in place; install inside corner bead pieces at the corner joints. You'll now need to complete the joints between the panels and finish the joint between the light shaft and the ceiling.

If your walls are paneled, you may want to finish the light shaft to match, and then install trim. Around the ceiling opening, apply molding that is wide enough to cover the edges of the paneling and the wallboard, as well as the joint between the wallboard and the ceiling; miter the corners. You may want to apply quarter-round molding to finish the inside corners of the light shaft. Either nail the molding in place with finishing nails or use panel adhesive; be careful not to smear any adhesive on the top of the paneling.

ASK A PRO

HOW CAN I BRIGHTEN THE LIGHT SHAFT?

The longer your light shaft, the less light will penetrate down to the room. For maximum light reflection, paint the walls of the light shaft with white or light-colored semigloss paint. You can also have light fixtures installed in the shaft; connect them to a dimmer switch for controlled lighting effects. Installing a diffusing panel at the ceiling will hide the fixtures and spread the light more evenly.

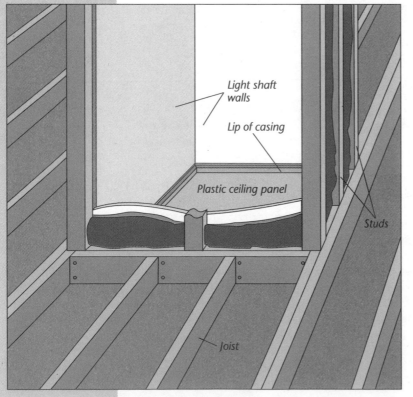

Light shaft walls

Lip of casing

Plastic ceiling panel

Studs

Joist

4 Installing a ceiling panel

To help distribute light more evenly, consider installing a translucent ceiling panel. It should be made from plastic; don't use glass because of the risks involved if it shatters. You can buy an acrylic, polycarbonate, or other plastic panel cut to the appropriate size from a home center.

Plastic sheets are commonly available in thicknesses ranging from ⅛" to ½". Have the panel cut ¼" shorter than the opening in both length and width to make it easier to fit the panel into place. Depending on the size and thickness of the panel, you may want to install cross supports under it.

To install a panel, you'll have to trim the ceiling opening with wood molding. Miter the corners of the molding and fasten the molding so the lip extends ½" around the inside of the opening. Holding the panel at a slight angle, lift it into the opening and set it on the lip of the molding. To remove the panel, simply push up from below, turn it to a slight angle, and lift it out.

WORKING ON AN OPEN-BEAM CEILING

It's easier to install a skylight in an open-beam ceiling than in a finished ceiling, since you don't have to cut a hole in the ceiling or build a light shaft. To minimize the framing you'll need to do, choose a skylight that fits between two existing beams.

Whatever kind of skylight you're installing—curb-mounted, step-flashed, or self-flashing—you can install a curb from inside to fill the hole in the roof; use attractive lumber for the curb, since it will be visible from the room. The curb can also be installed from outside, just like in finished-ceiling construction. Follow the instructions, beginning on page 81, that are relevant

to your type of skylight. You can, of course, skip the information on how to mark the ceiling opening. Fill the area between the bottom of the skylight and the ceiling opening with an attractive wood, and install casing around the ceiling opening.

The instructions given below are for installing a skylight with a curb that fills the opening. Before you begin, read through the installation instructions beginning on page 87 to get an idea of the procedures involved. You'll need to refer to that section at various stages of the process. Also, assemble all the tools and supplies that you'll require; turn to the section beginning on page 78 for details.

Putting in a skylight

TOOLKIT
- Tape measure
- Carpenter's square
- Electric drill
- Circular saw or crosscut saw
- Claw hammer
- Backsaw and miter box to cut trim
- Nailset
- Putty knife

1 Planning the opening

To fit the curb inside the roof opening, the opening must be cut to the outside dimensions of the curb. Measure and mark on the ceiling the corners of the opening. Drill a hole at each corner and drive a 3½" nail through each hole to the roof. If any wiring crosses the marked opening, have it rerouted *(page 41)*.

2 Building a curb

For a curb-mounted skylight, the lumber should reach from the ceiling to the required height above the roof. For a step-flashed or self-flashing skylight, you'll need lumber at least wide enough to reach from the ceiling to the top of the roof deck; it may need to extend past the roof opening, depending on your skylight. Build a curb for your skylight following the instructions on page 82, but don't brace the curb if you're planning to finish the ceiling opening with casing, as shown.

Measure and cut the casing to fit ¼" to ½" in from the curb's inside edge—facing the room—and miter the corners *(right)*. Using finishing nails, nail the casing to the curb; set the nails with a nailset and fill the holes with wood putty.

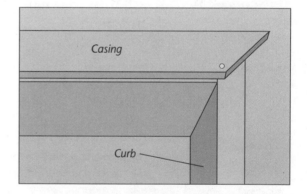

Casing

Curb

4 Installing the curb and skylight

Install the curb from inside the room; lift it to the ceiling with a helper, and fit it inside the roof opening. The casing should fit tightly against the ceiling.

While your helper holds the curb in place, nail it to the beams and headers every 6" with 2½" finishing nails. Nail carefully—any marks made with the hammer will show—or use drywall screws. Drive the nails below the wood surface with a nailset, and cover the holes with wood putty.

Finally, follow the instructions for installing and flashing the skylight, beginning on page 87, that apply to the type you're installing.

3 Opening the roof

The roof opening is planned and cut in much the same way as for finished-ceiling construction. However, if you're using a curb you don't have to frame the opening; the curb, which extends from the inside to the outside of the roof, serves the same purpose. Or, you can frame the opening, then insert a finished frame to hide the joists and joist hangers. If you have to cut one or more beams, consult a professional for the required framing.

Prepare, outline, and cut the roof opening following the instructions beginning on page 81.

SKYLIGHT MAINTENANCE AND REPAIR

Skylights require only a minimum of maintenance and cleaning. Because of their shape, slope, and location, most of the dirt can be washed away by heavy rains. Occasionally, you'll need to clean the inside—and the outside, too, if rain doesn't do the job. Some roof windows can be tilted into the room for easy cleaning of both the inside and outside of the pane from indoors.

Glass skylights are as easy to clean as your windows. You can use either a weak solution of household ammonia, mild soap, or detergent (if rinsed thoroughly) and water, or a commercial glass-cleaning solution. Whatever solution you use, apply it with a sponge and dry the glass with paper towels, a chamois, or a squeegee. To remove stuck-on material, scrape gently with a razor blade. To prevent scratches, abrasions, and deterioration of glass that is coated for sun control, never clean it with abrasive cleansers, gritty sponges, or use razor blades.

To clean a plastic or polycarbonate skylight, use a solution of mild soap or detergent and water; don't use glass-cleaning solutions. Apply with a soft cloth or cellulose sponge and rinse well with clear water. To prevent water spots, blot dry with a chamois or a damp cellulose sponge. To remove foreign material (such as caulking, roofing tar, grease, or fresh oil paint) wipe up as much as possible with a paper towel, then clean the dome with mild soap and water. Never use solvents (such as hexane, naphtha, kerosene, or methanol), since they will cause minute cracks (crazing) on the skylight's surface. The cracks may appear immediately, or later, after stress from wind or snow. Some solvents (such as denatured alcohol, carbon tetrachloride, or acetone) will actually dissolve the plastic. For fiberglass domes, follow the manufacturer's care instructions.

Plastic glazing is susceptible to scratches and abrasions, so never use abrasive cleansers, pads, or gritty cloths, and don't use any sharp tools, such as a razor blade or putty knife, to remove dirt.

To maintain the luster of plastic, protect it with a thin, even coat of automobile polish (not cleaner polish) or floor or automobile wax applied with a clean, soft cloth. Buff lightly and wipe with a clean, damp cloth to remove static electricity, which attracts dirt. Minor scratches and abrasions can sometimes be obscured with automobile wax applied as described above. If you have major scratches or cracks, it's best to replace the dome; get a replacement dome from your manufacturer and follow the installation instructions.

Skylight frames made of aluminum, vinyl, or clad wood generally require no care other than washing when you clean the skylight glazing. However, if your skylight has an aluminum frame, and you live near the coast (where salt spray can eat into the frame), you'll have to protect it with paint.

Stopping leaks

TOOLKIT
• Putty knife

Renewing the flashing seal

Check your skylight periodically to be sure that it's still properly sealed. For a self-flashing skylight, lift the shingles covering the flange and apply a generous amount of roofing cement around the edges of the flange *(right)*. Press the shingles back in place on top of the flange. Read the manufacturer's information or check with your home center to be sure that the roofing cement you're using is compatible with your skylight; some types of cement can't be used with polycarbonate domes.

A properly installed step-flashed skylight should not leak. However, if you do have a leak, you can solve the problem by bonding each piece of step flashing to the adjacent piece of step flashing and to the roof deck. First lift the shingle, then lift the edge of each piece of flashing and apply roofing cement under it, up to about 1" from the edge; press the flashing back into the roofing cement.

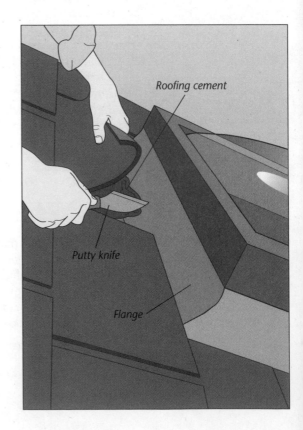

Roofing cement

Putty knife

Flange

WINDOW AND SKYLIGHT GLOSSARY

Apron
A piece of interior trim installed against the wall under the window, below the stool.

Beam
A large roof-support member.

Bearing wall
A wall that helps support the weight of the house. All exterior walls running perpendicular to ceiling and floor joists are bearing, as are some interior walls.

Casing
Decorative molding applied around openings, both interior and exterior, to cover the joint between the wall and the opening. Casing at the top of a window is called the head casing; at the sides, the side casing.

Catch-plate and dog
A latch mechanism on a sliding window; the catch-plate is fastened in the track, and the dog is screwed to the bottom of the sash.

Caulk
A material used to create a watertight seal, such as between a window and siding. Use exterior grade for outdoor applications.

Channel
The space in the window frame for the sash to slide in. On a metal sliding window, it's often called a track.

Countersinking
Drilling a hole in wood to allow a flathead screw to sit flush with the surface.

Curb
The frame on which a skylight sits. If the skylight comes with a curb built in, it's called an integral curb. A site-built curb is built separately and the skylight is then mounted on it.

Divided lights
Individual panes of glass in a multipane window. Authentic divided lights are actually separate panes; simulated divided lights are made from one large pane of glass with a grille or muntins added.

Face-nailing
To drive a nail through one piece into another with the nail at right angles to the surface.

Finished-ceiling construction
The type of house construction in which there is an attic or crawl space between the roof and the ceiling (built with joists) of the room below; as opposed to open-beam construction.

Flange
A rim that attaches one object to another, such as the part around a self-flashing skylight through which the skylight is secured to the roof.

Flashing
A material, usually metal, that seals a roof or wall against leaks at vulnerable points, such as at valley and eaves; must be installed around a skylight.

Framing connectors
Preformed metal fasteners such as joist hangers, framing anchors, and reinforcing angles, with holes for fasteners and sometimes prongs that stick into the wood, used to secure joints.

Glazing
Material, such as glass or acrylic plastic, used for panes in windows and skylights; may be one or more layers thick.

Header
A support piece framing an opening, such as in a wall, ceiling, or roof, attached at right angles to other framing members.

Jamb
A board that forms the top or side of the frame surrounding a window.

Joist
A horizontal framing member placed on edge, such as a ceiling joist.

Level
Exactly horizontal; can be determined with a carpenter's level.

Light shaft
Extends from a skylight through an attic or crawl space to the ceiling of the room below to allow light through.

Mitering
Cutting at an angle other than 90°; molding around windows is often mitered (45°) at the corners.

Mullion
A vertical divider between two windows, such as between the center and side windows in a bay.

Muntin
A slender strip of wood framing a pane of glass in a multipane window. With authentic divided lights, the muntins hold the individual panes; with simulated divided lights, the muntins are purely decorative.

On center
The distance from the center of one framing member to the center of the next one. Normally abbreviated O.C.

Open-beam construction
The type of house construction in which the underside of the roof forms the ceiling of the room below.

Parting strip
A vertical divider between two panes of a double-hung window; forms one side of channel that panes slide in.

Passive solar heating
Using the sun's energy to heat a home. In the Northern Hemisphere, south-facing windows are best.

Pilot hole
A hole drilled into a piece of wood for a nail or screw to follow; helps prevent wood from splitting.

Plumb
Exactly vertical; can be determined with a carpenter's level or a plumb bob.

Purlin
A structural member positioned at right angles to the rafters.

Rafter
An angled framing member that forms part of the sloping sides of a roof and supports the roof deck and roofing materials.

Rafter, jack
A short piece of rafter lumber, cut to fit between the headers, forming the side of the rough opening; used instead of existing rafters if the size of the skylight requires it.

Rafter, king
A full-length rafter forming the edge of the rough opening for a skylight.

Rafter, sister
A full-length rafter added next to a king rafter to compensate for any rafters that are removed.

Rail
A horizontal member of a window sash; it forms part of the frame for the glass.

Reveal
The small portion of the jamb, usually about $1/8"$, all around the window, that isn't covered by the casing. Casing is more easily aligned if there's a reveal than if the casing is flush with the edge of the jamb.

Roof deck
A material such as plywood fastened to the rafters as a base for roofing material.

Roof window
A skylight that can be reached from the floor, such as one installed in the sloping wall of an attic room.

Rough opening
The opening cut in a wall or roof to accommodate a window or skylight.

Rough sill
The horizontal framing member that forms the bottom of the rough opening for a window; it sits on top of the cripple studs.

Sash
The part of a window that holds the glass; may be operable (opening) or fixed. NOTE: "Sash" is also used for the plural.

Sheathing
The exterior skin of a house under the siding, typically plywood or exterior gypsum wallboard.

Shim
A thin piece of wood or other rigid material used to adjust alignment. You can use wood shingles available in packages or bundles at home centers.

Sill
An exterior shelf below a window placed on top of the rough sill.

Soffit
The area below the eaves, where the roof overhangs the exterior walls.

Stile
A vertical member of a window sash; it forms part of the frame for the glass.

Stool
An interior shelf below a window sitting on the rough sill, above the apron; used instead of casing at bottom of window.

Stop
A piece of wood attached vertically to a window frame that the window butts against; the stop at the interior of the window is called the interior stop and the one at the exterior is called the blind stop.

Stud
A vertical framing member; also referred to as a wall stud.

Stud, cripple
A stud that is shortened to accommodate an opening in a wall, such as above or below a window; there should be a cripple stud under each end of the rough sill, to support it.

Stud, king
A full-length vertical framing member at each side of the rough opening for a window; may be an existing wall stud or a new stud.

Stud, trimmer
A vertical framing member attached to each king stud, forming the side of the rough opening. Trimmer studs usually sit on top of the rough sill and support the ends of the header.

Toenailing
Driving a nail at an angle from one piece of wood to another; used when face-nailing is not possible.

Trim
See Casing.

Truss
Structural support members for roofs with parts that perform the functions of rafters and joists. Trusses shouldn't be cut.

Weather stripping
Material applied to window jambs, and sometimes also the sash, to seal the opening. Many new windows come with integral weather stripping.

INDEX

THE BOOK OF
WHAT
IF...?

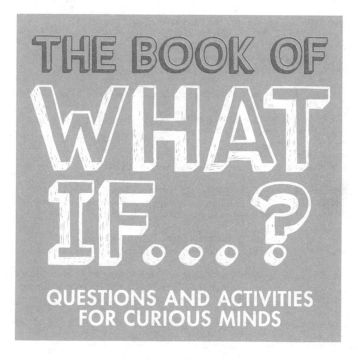

THE BOOK OF WHAT IF...?

QUESTIONS AND ACTIVITIES FOR CURIOUS MINDS

Matt Murrie and Andrew R McHugh

ALADDIN
New York London Toronto Sydney New Delhi

BEYOND WORDS
Hillsboro, Oregon

ALADDIN
An imprint of Simon & Schuster
Children's Publishing Division
1230 Avenue of the Americas
New York, NY 10020

BEYOND WORDS
20827 N.W. Cornell Road, Suite 500
Hillsboro, Oregon 97124-9808
503-531-8700 / 503-531-8773 fax
www.beyondword.com

Managing Editor: Lindsay S. Easterbrooks-Brown
Copyeditors: Kristin Thiel, Emmalisa Sparrow
Proofreader: Linda M. Meyer
Interior and cover design: Sara E. Blum
The text of this book was set in Adobe Devanagari and Interstate.

For information about special discounts for bulk purchases, please contact
Simon & Schuster Special Sales at 1-866-506-1949 or business@simonandschuster.com.

The Simon & Schuster Speakers Bureau can bring authors to your live event. For more
information or to book an event contact the Simon & Schuster Speakers Bureau at
1-866-248-3049 or visit our website at www.simonspeakers.com.

Manufactured in the United States of America 0317 RR2

10 9 8 7 6 5 4 3 2 1

The Library of Congress has cataloged the hardcover edition as follows:

Names: Murrie, Matthew, author. | McHugh, Andrew R, author.
Title: The book of what if...? : questions and activities for curious minds / by
  Matt Murrie and Andrew R McHugh.
Description: Beyond Words/Aladdin edition. | New York : Aladdin ; Hillsboro,
  Oregon : Beyond Words, 2016. | Audience: Ages 8-12. | Audience:
  Grades 4 to 6. | Includes bibliographical references and index.
Identifiers: LCCN 2015033441 | ISBN 9781582705293 (hardcover : alk. paper) |
  ISBN 9781481430746 (eBook) | ISBN 9781582705286 (pbk)
Subjects: LCSH: Curiosities and wonders—Juvenile literature. | Children's
  questions and answers. | Thought and thinking—Juvenile literature.
Classification: LCC AG243 .M857 2016 | DDC 031—dc23
LC record available at http://lccn.loc.gov/2015033441

Contents

Preface

Do you ever feel like the world is celebrating Opposite Day every day? But what if everybody saw things exactly the way you did? Would we all be better off . . . or worse? Be honest! Have you ever looked at something and thought, "Hmm, what if this one thing could be different?" and then explored what life would be like if it was in fact different? That process typically starts with a question. "What if no one went to bed hungry?" "What if we could go to the moon?" "What if we wrote a book about questions?" The best part is that anyone can ask a question—not only "experts" but those just beginning their journeys to become experts.

We're not experts on any of the topics in this book—but we are insanely curious. We wrote this book together anyways because we believe in the power of, "What if . . . ?" We believe in it so much that we started a company in 2010 dedicated to turning ideas into action. You see, we view curiosity as a natural resource. The same way people (including us) are concerned about wasting natural resources such as oil, coal, and natural gas, we're especially concerned about curiosity.

How can we stop wasting curiosity?

For some people, it's letting them know it's OK to be curious. For others, it's helping them find ways to take action on what they're curious about. Some just need to realize that being curious is a powerful ability to have. Through conferences, workshops, content, and connecting people, we've spread curiosity all around the world. Now you're a part of this movement to make the world a more curious place. Thank you!

Why ask, "What if?" Because nobody knows what tomorrow holds, and yesterday's lessons are never complete. By asking, you're taking the first step toward doing. Every great, world-shaking action starts with an idea. That idea becomes a seed that can then grow and spread beyond the mind that planted it. But nothing grows, spreads, or happens without being planted first. What if it's up to you to first think and then do? What if you do and then think? What if combining these two actions can create more awesome for you and beyond you? It's amazing all the things that become possible later on when you start with two simple words: *what if.*

As you read this book, you might find new answers to old questions. You might find old answers to new questions. You might not find any answers at all. That's OK! This isn't a textbook. There won't be a test when you're done reading it. Instead, we hope that by reading this book, you develop new insights, perspectives, and curiosities about yourself and the world we all share. Don't forget to occasionally put this book down while reading to start doing amazing stuff.

As we explore our questions, we also ask questions of you, the reader. This is part of the beauty of questions: They beg for participation. Each question starts an exploration of even more questions. Some entries go even further with expert interviews and historical spotlights, so we can learn directly from interesting people doing amazing things. There is peer introspection—we've posed these very same questions to kids just like you. We also have illustrations to illuminate complex ideas, and there are even technical corners, where you can learn more about how and why something is the way it is. Our most frequent element other than questions is activities that help you actively think about the questions. So get ready.

You can read alone or read as a group in class. You can talk with your friends about the book. Participate in activities. Ask your own questions. The only wrong way to use this book is to finish reading it with the same level of curiosity and the same beliefs you started with. Some of these questions deal with topics that are only going to grow more important in our world, like genetic modification, artificial intelligence (AI), and life extension. It's important for us to deal with these topics earlier rather than later—to have the time to understand them and maybe even improve upon them before these technologies become ever present in our lives. This way, by asking, "What if . . . ?," we can guide where we go in the future instead of waiting until the future is here and all we can ask is, "Now what?"

The Book of What If . . . ? is designed to spark your curiosity on certain ideas and open windows into worlds you may not have realized exist. That was our job in writing this book. Your job now is to go beyond (far beyond!) reading it. We expect you to interact with the information between these covers. There are other people out there wanting to collaborate with you to start something awesome. So, what are you waiting for? The world is waiting for you!

Your fellow wonderers,

Matt Murrie and Andrew R McHugh

Part 1
History

History: a long time ago. Right?

Kind of. History is everything that has happened before right now. It has stories of kings and queens, tribes turning into empires, technological improvements that changed the course of a country's development, and the occasional toppling of a dynasty.

What if history is also advice for the future? Some people say that history repeats itself. Well, not quite. Humans definitely make similar mistakes, but there are always new warning signals to teach us better ways to do things. What if, by looking back at these mistakes, we can make sure we don't make them, exactly, again?

What if we can also examine where we are now by thinking of alternative histories? For instance, what if we had never landed on the moon? Or what if dinosaurs still existed? These questions help us think about how we got here and how to get to where we want to be.

Another thing to think about is, if you're moving through a scale of time with the past behind you and the future ahead of you, this very moment, you're making your own history.

What if you're writing the history book of your life right now?

What if Dinosaurs Hadn't Gone Extinct?

If you've done any digging around on dinosaurs, you've probably discovered that the word *dinosaur* means "terrible lizard."[1] But this isn't entirely true. The actual translation for the Greek prefix *deinos* is "fearfully great." The inventor of the word *dinosaur*, Richard Owen, intended the word to inspire awe, not terror.[2] Over time, people have turned "fearfully great" into simply "terrible."

> "I would have a pet velociraptor. And we could buy dinosaurs at dino dealerships because there would be no need for cars because you just ride your T. Rex where you need to go."
> —Charlie, Battle High School, age 15

The second half of the word *dinosaur* comes from the Greek word *sauros*, which means "lizard."[3] Even though many originally thought dinosaurs were lizards, scientists have now determined that they weren't. Interestingly enough, birds and lizards both seem to be descendants of dinosaurs (though different ones).[4] The more we learn about dinosaurs, the more ways we find how they differed from the reptiles we have today, including lizards.

But what if we had more than just a bunch of bones to go by to understand dinosaurs? What if dinosaurs were alive today?

> "I would train a dinosaur to let me ride it to school."
> —Andrew, Battle High School, age 15

There are several questions to consider here. Perhaps the most urgent one is: who would "rule" the earth—dinosaurs or humans?

Looking around today, humans have been able to create an existence at the top of the food chain, and we've been able to develop technologies that move us further from the natural world. Do you think humans could have evolved in this manner if we had to compete against (or run away from!) dinosaurs all day long?

> "The bigger dinosaurs would be hunted and the smaller ones domesticated as animals of labor."
> —Jonathan, Battle High School, age 17

What if, instead of finding a neighbor's dog digging a hole in your yard, you saw a triceratops digging a hole? What if, instead of being afraid of bee stings when playing outside, you had to look out for pterodactyls swooping down from the sky to scoop you up for dinner? What if every day on your way to school, you were chased by a *Tyrannosaurus rex*? Could you tell your teacher a *T. rex* ate your homework?

Where would we be today? What would be better? What would be worse?

ACTIVITY
Dino-Proof Your House

Imagine you live in a neighborhood struggling with an overpopulation of dinosaurs. They're everywhere! Many people have come home to find dinosaurs in their yards eating their plants and leaves off their trees. Some homes have even been stepped on by dinosaurs—and crushed to smithereens, of course. What do you do? How can you save your home?

Draw a picture of what your home would look like once it's been "dino-proofed."

MARY ANNING, DINO-DISCOVERER

If you look around, you'll notice that there are not many creatures that look like the ones that were alive in the time of dinosaurs. The dinosaurs went extinct and some of them were fossilized. Many, many years later, a set of apes evolved into humans, and many years after that, we started fossil hunting. Mary Anning was an expert fossil hunter.

Sometime between 1809 and 1811, when she was only 10 to 12 years old, Anning and her brother found one of the first ichthyosaur fossils (an ichthyosaur looks kind of like a dolphin). Her whole family hunted fossils, but Anning was the most dedicated. She went on to find many other ichthyosaur fossils, but her greatest find was of the first plesiosaur (a swimming dinosaur with a long neck like a giraffe). Anning was a well versed paleontologist (person who studies fossils), an expert at finding, drawing, and analyzing skeletal remains of dinosaurs.[5]

"If dinosaurs never went extinct, humans would have very slim chances of survival with how dangerous the world around us would be. Perhaps this would create a different society that focuses more on survival and protection rather than the society we have developed in which survival isn't always immediately on our minds."
—Dillon, Battle High School, age 16

What if the Mongol Empire Helped the United States' Westward Expansion?

Stretching from the Pacific Ocean to the Danube River, the Mongol Empire still holds the place as the largest, contiguous empire of all time.[6] The Mongol Empire was so massive that during its reign (1270–1309), it contained over 25 percent of the world's population and 16 percent of the planet's land mass.[7] With a reach that large, Mongols had a huge influence on the world—then and on into today.

For example, in an empire as vast as this one, quick communication was critical to keeping things going—and keeping them from falling apart. To make sure everyone was always in the loop, Mongols developed a messenger system called the *yam*.[8] The yam was a system of postal relay stations at which riders carrying

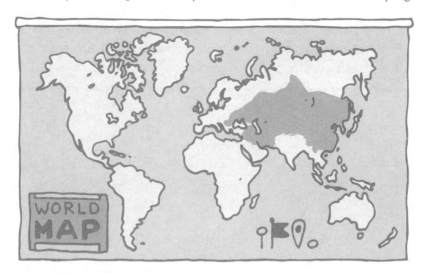

messages on horseback could rest, refuel, or exchange their tired horse for a fresh one. Sound familiar? A few hundred years later, the United States would replicate this same system as the Pony Express to facilitate its communication during westward expansion.[9]

GENGHIS KHAN, CONQUEROR OF CONQUERORS

As ginormous as the Mongol Empire was, it can be traced back to the vision and ambition of a single person: Genghis Khan. In the wake of his time on earth, history remembers Genghis Khan as both a great destroyer and a great creator.

Historians calculate Genghis Khan was directly responsible for the deaths of nearly 40 million people. Census data from the Middle Ages during Genghis Khan's reign show China's total population dropping by tens of millions. Genghis Khan's attacks were so devastating, historians estimate his war with the Khwarezmid Empire (located in what is Iran today), killed three-fourths of that entire population. In all, it's believed the great Genghis Khan lowered the population of the entire world while he was living in it by 11 percent.[10]

However, it turns out Genghis Khan was a lover as well as a fighter. Geneticists believe that approximately 16 million people on the planet today are direct descendants of Genghis Khan.[11]

What if Europeans Had Never Landed in the Americas?

One big difference would be the name. The name America comes from Italian explorer and cartographer (someone who makes maps) Amerigo Vespucci. But it wasn't Vespucci's ego that put his name on the map. It was another cartographer, Martin Waldseemüller.[12]

Shortly after Columbus, Vespucci crossed the Atlantic to explore what the Europeans saw as the New World and mapped out much of what is now South America. Waldseemüller used Vespucci's maps to draw the world map he created in 1507.

> "The country would probably be named something else. Indigenous people would still be here. They would probably not be advanced a lot."
> —Aidan, Columbia Elementary, age 10

Waldseemüller wasn't necessarily trying to name the continent of what is now South America after Vespucci; he was only giving him credit for the information he used in his new world map. However, his map (one of the first to include the continents of the New World[13]) became so popular that people began referring to the New World as the Americas before anyone could actually name it. The rest, as they say, is history.

> "If the Europeans never landed in the Americas I think that Asians would had landed next, but the indigenous people might have a couple decades more to live in peace."
> —Talia, Columbia Elementary, age 11

Another difference we might notice today is our form of democracy. People often credit the ancient Greeks for the basis of the democracy that took root in the United States of America. However, democracy today is quite different from what the Greeks practiced. What if there is a different group of people responsible for today's democracy? And what if they were living in America long before the Europeans settled it?

Since the United States had just fought a revolution against England, and most people in the American colonies had left Europe to pursue a better life, the colonists weren't very keen on looking to the kingdoms of Europe to construct their new set of laws.

"Where would we be if Europeans never landed in America? Would we live in a town call Koopazoo in some land far away? Would we speak any language we know of? Would we even be alive?"
—Hilary, Columbia Elementary, age 11

Even if their actions didn't always reflect it, many European Americans held great respect (perhaps even envy) for the indigenous peoples' way of life.[14] The admiration the US Founding Fathers had for the Iroquois, in particular, was so great that they modeled the first copy of the US Constitution after the Iroquois Great Law of Peace.[15]

ACTIVITY
Name a New Land

What if you hear on the news that a new island was recently discovered in the middle of the ocean, and there's a contest to name it. Write your answers to these questions on a piece of paper to enter your name into the contest.

1. Proposed name:
2. Who or what does this name come from?
3. Why are you proposing this name?
4. Are there other people, places, or things that share a similar name?
5. Does your name have any symbolic or hidden meaning?

"The country would probably be named something else. Indigenous people would still be here. They would probably not be advanced a lot."
—Aidan, Columbia Elementary, age 10

"The Europeans discovered the Americas in 1492, but one of the first countries to discover the Americas was actually China, so you might speak Chinese."
—Zephyr, Columbia Elementary, age 11

"I think that the indigenous peoples might still have all their land and, don't take this the wrong way, but we would not be here."
—Lyn Marie, Columbia Elementary, age 10

"If the Europeans never landed in the Americas, people would still think the world was flat. The indigenous people would still live here."
—Isaac, Columbia Elementary, age 11

"Then maybe people from Africa or Asia would land in the Americas, and everyone would be a different race at first, but then the Europeans would eventually migrate here."
—Jeremy, Findley Elementary, age 10

What if Humans Had Never Landed on the Moon?

For most of human existence, we've been stuck on a big rock speeding through space called Earth. We've been here looking out at the sky. Most nights, we can see another rock, the moon, which orbits our rock.

What do you think is the most important thing humanity got out of landing on the moon? Some say Tang, Velcro, and pens that write upside down are the most important things to come out of the space program. However, Tang[16] and Velcro[17] were invented before NASA's mission to the moon. Going to the moon just made them famous. Yet the Apollo program did produce technologies you probably find useful today. You know that spring you feel in your step when you're wearing your sneakers? Many sneaker insoles are made out of the same material that was first used in the space boots that made that giant leap on the moon.[18] And your parents may hate cleaning, but at least they can do it with lightweight, cordless devices. You can thank the Apollo program for helping develop lightweight, cordless tools.[19] Imagine how long the extension cord would have been had the astronauts needed one to plug in the tools they used on the moon!

Even with the marvelous technologies that came out of the Apollo program, many think the most important thing that came from landing on the moon was the power to create the dreams of tomorrow. Going to the moon propelled us. Space exploration encourages us to push human potential and excites students to become astronauts, scientists, and explorers. Space travel is the beginning of our species colonizing different planets. Can anyone say "living options?" If we are limited to only one planet (like we are now), all of humanity could get wiped out by a large disaster. What if it's kind of dangerous to be a single-planet civilization?

What if an asteroid hit us? What if a deadly virus started infecting everyone? Or what if zombies happened?! Humans would be trapped in one place, Earth. But if we look to our success with visiting the moon as our first step toward living on other planets, our species might know a less risky existence. If there were a disaster on one rock, at least the humans on the other rock would be safe.

Unfortunately, though, our exploration of space has started to slow. Did you know that after we first landed on the moon, July 20, 1969, scientists believed it would take only another ten years for a human to land on Mars?[20] In the time since then, we've landed a couple of robots on Mars but haven't managed to send any humans. In fact, the last time a human set foot on any space-rock was the moon in 1972. Over forty years ago!

Stepping foot on the moon is something only a few humans have ever experienced. But there are many things we all benefit from that came out of getting those feet up there. Why do you think we've never gone back? Why do you think we slowed down our space exploration? What do you think you can do to make sure humans never stop exploring?

NEIL deGRASSE TYSON, ASTROPHYSICIST

The day you stop [cosmic exploration], I fear for the future of the species because it's that which distinguishes humans from all other animals. That we explore and understand what we're doing while we're at it and expand our place in the cosmos. And, if that stops, I don't want to live in those times.[21]

Neil deGrasse Tyson is a world-renowned astrophysicist known for his many public appearances and playful demeanor. He's afraid that if we don't put our money into space exploration, we'll diminish ourselves as a species. Tyson has written many books, hosted numerous television shows, and served on both presidential and NASA advisory committees. He is the fifth head of the Hayden Planetarium in New York City.[22] In a lot of his work, he attempts to make space science interesting and exciting. If he can do that, then maybe the next generation of kids growing up will decide to focus some of their energy on going to space. Maybe the next great space adventurer or scientist is you.

ACTIVITY
Where Next? Meet Up

Gather yourself and at least three friends to a chat. The topic? Decide where humanity should adventure to if we could only explore one more place. What or where does your group think humans should focus on exploring next? Why? It's OK if deciding means arguing to agreement.

TECHNICAL CORNER
Rockets and Rocket Ships

Rocket ships and the people who fly them are pretty amazing. We take huge chunks of metal, strap people to them, start a controlled explosion behind them, and launch them into space. We must be bonkers.

Rocket development started way back around 400 BC, when Greeks were playing with steam. Throughout the years, Chinese scientists created arrows with rocket tips—Mongols started building them too—and Germans developed multistage rockets (rockets within rockets). It wasn't until 1898 that a Russian schoolteacher, Konstantin Tsiolkovsky, started thinking that rockets could take us to space.[23]

Sir Isaac Newton formalized three laws of motion. The third law says that for every action, there is an equal and opposite reaction. If you push your friend with three pounds of force, your friend moves away from you with three pounds of force, while at the same time your muscles exert three pounds of force. With rockets, this means that if there is an explosion with one hundred thousand pounds of force, the metal just in front of the explosion will move forward with one hundred thousand pounds of force, minus whatever part of the explosion that doesn't push the rocket up.

If you stand on top of a powerful explosion, you could go to space. (But really, don't do that. It is super dangerous. That's why there are rocket scientists.)

WHAT'S INSIDE A ROCKET?

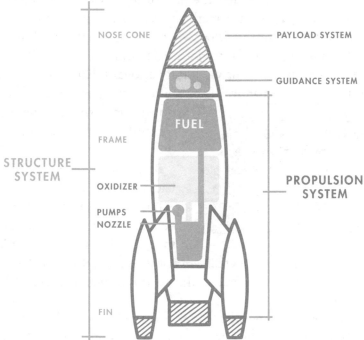

NOSE CONE — PAYLOAD SYSTEM

GUIDANCE SYSTEM

FUEL

FRAME

STRUCTURE SYSTEM

OXIDIZER

PUMPS
NOZZLE

PROPULSION SYSTEM

FIN

What if You Could Travel in Time?

Scientists, writers, and dreamers have always been fascinated by time travel. As we experience our universe, there are three spacial dimensions (which we travel when walking forward and backward, left and right, and up and down) and one temporal (which we travel by moving through time). When you meet up with someone, what do you tell them? You tell them, "Let's meet at 123 Main Street"—which describes a point in two dimensions—"on the third floor"—the location in the third spacial dimension—"at 3:30 PM"—the location in time.

Since you can move forward and backward, left and right, up and down, you can move in any direction in the three spacial dimensions. You can only go forward in time, the temporal dimension.

But what if you could also go backward?

Imagine that one day as you're out walking, you come to a small field. In the middle of the field, there's a chair with seat belts on it and a clock in front of it. You sit down and realize: *this is a time machine*. What would you do next?

Would you travel in time? Which way would you go first? Would you want to go to the first or last moments of the universe? Would

> "I would go back in time to observe history and refine the history book based on what truly happened, not just the opinion of one side of humankind."
> —Charlie, Battle High School, age 15

14

you want to meet your great-great-great-great-great-great grandparents or meet your great-great-great-great-great-great grandkids?

Would you use the machine for good or evil? You could go to the past and bring knowledge of vaccines to doctors before the bubonic plague and Spanish flu started, saving millions and millions of lives. Or you could take the personal gain approach: travel to the future to grab the answers to a test

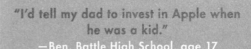

"I'd tell my dad to invest in Apple when he was a kid."
—Ben, Battle High School, age 17

you'll be taking in class next week. You could even go back in time and put money in a bank. Then go forward in time to when your money has grown. Instant riches!

What if everyone could travel in time? How do you think society would change? It would be hard to test people if they could always go and find the answers. What about when people die? Would it still be sad? Someone would never really be dead—that person would exist in a certain segment of time you could always go back and visit.

ACTIVITY
Go Back

Write a short story about traveling back in time. Where would you go? What would you do there? Who would you meet? Would you bring anyone back to the present with you?

ACTIVITY
Go Forward

Now that you've gone backward, let's go forward! Again, write about where you would go and what you would do there. Who would you meet? What would you do there? Would you bring anyone back to the present with you?

ACTIVITY
Create a Time-Lapse

A time-lapse is a video that was taken over a long period of time and then shortened. For example, if you've ever seen a video of a seed growing into a stalk and then leaves, that's a time-lapse! These videos are kind of like short time machines. Imagine that if you were in a time machine moving forward in time more quickly than usual (and assuming you could see outside of the machine), the world could look like one big time-lapse.

> "I would travel to the fortieth century, grab cool gadgets and stuff, and come back and be super cool."
> —John Ryan, Battle High School, age 15

Now it's your turn. Shoot a short video and speed it up.

TECHNICAL CORNER
Building a Time Machine

While physicists used to cast time travel as silly, there are a few that are now exploring the topic seriously.[24] Mathematicians and physicists found proof that time travel can work within our current understanding of the world. (Doesn't that make you want to study science?) Many of the devices they've come up with to help us move through time require vast amounts of energy (and a weird negative energy)—way beyond what we're able to build today.[25] A device suggested by theoretical physicist Kip Thorne uses two sets of metal plates, each charged with large amounts of electricity.[26] These plates would create a small tear in space-time. Then you could take one of the sets of plates, put it on a spaceship, and send the spaceship away from Earth at near the speed of light. Since objects traveling at close to the speed of light experience time much more slowly, the first and second sets of plates would work at different points in time. Boom! You've made a time machine.

Now you just have to make sure you can enter it without being hurt![27]

"You would create a paradox that would destroy the universe."
—Conner, Battle High School, age 15

"If I could travel in time, I would go back in time and invent the time machine, but this would cause several problems. If the time machine was invented any sooner, would I still have been the first person to go back in time and invent it?"
—Dillon, Battle High School, age 16

What if There Were Never Books?

Books. A bunch of words on a bunch of pages, right? Yet there are few things people love and hate as much as books. You might despise a textbook but not be able to take your hands off other books (like this one!). People have even burned books because they viewed them as dangerous. Beyond giving you a few paper cuts or a bruise on the head (if one is thrown at you), how can books be dangerous?

Books don't just contain words. What if it's the ideas in them that make books so powerful—or dangerous?

What if there never were any books written? People could still communicate ideas verbally, but books allow ideas to spread across greater distances of space and time. Think about your favorite book. If there weren't any books, you'd only be able to hear the ideas and stories of the authors while they were alive. Imagine how many great stories would be lost! And now with the internet, writing continues to spread, more ideas can be shared, and authors-long-gone can still have a voice.

There was a time before books and writing. As it turns out, being in a culture or group of people who can read—even if you cannot read—changes how you think. Catch that? Not only can books teach you *about* things to think about, they can also teach you *how* to think about things. Researchers found that if you and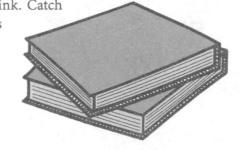

everyone around you never developed writing, you'd have a hard time understanding how to generalize objects into categories. Imagine you are in a culture that doesn't read or write. Someone arrives one day and shows you squares and circles on a piece of paper. You might say you see a house, a plate, or a moon—all things that look like squares or circles. But, you wouldn't say that you see two "shapes" because "shapes" is a category that squares and circles belong to. Writing and reading allow your brain to put thoughts out in front of it and think about those thoughts differently. It is the invention of literacy that helped humans develop logic which in turn helps us to generalize our thoughts.[28]

What if books also build on themselves? Not only do some books have sequels, so that a single story continues developing, nonfiction books have editions, so they can be updated with new information. Spreading and updating new information allows people to develop new ideas and create new technologies. Without books there'd be no computers, internet, or video games!

ACTIVITY
Remember and Tell a Story

Read or write a short story. Then try to memorize it. Once you think you have it, go to a parent, sibling, or friend and recite what you can remember. No notes! Was it difficult to remember without reading it?

ANNE MANGEN,
READING RESEARCHER

Reading is good for you. Reading as little as six minutes a day can reduce stress, help your brain function as you get older, and help the prevention of Alzheimer's.[29] But what if there's a difference between reading an electronic book and a paper book?

Anne Mangen, lead researcher on a reading study at Stavanger University in Norway, found that "the haptic and tactile feedback of a Kindle does not provide the same support for mental reconstruction of a story as a print pocket book does."[30] That means that if you can't feel an electronic book in the same way you can feel a paper book, you probably won't remember the book as well as you could.

Other studies suggest that a reader's inability to control the text physically (physically turn pages, bend pages, or write directly on the pages) results in a reduced long-term memory of what was read.[31]

What if You Lived in a Floating City?

Throughout history, humans have been confined to landmasses when establishing permanent living settlements. But what if that's all about to change? What if humans took to the sea, not just to traverse it, but to settle it?

If the Seasteading Institute[32] accomplishes its goal of creating the first permanent cities at sea, your future could involve living with water flowing underneath your feet and land being something you see off on the horizon.

> "I would buy a bunch of swimsuits and water tubes to play with if it was [on] water."
> —Kelly, Findley Elementary, age 10

Originally, the Seasteading Institute envisioned these floating cities establishing themselves as sovereign countries; however, it's shifted its vision to making them new cities for existing countries.[33] These micro cities would be built on movable, floating platforms, each of which could accommodate up to 270 residents.[34]

Sound like an impossible idea? From the perspective of the Seasteading Institute:

Over thirty million people a year already visit floating cities in the form of cruise ships. These ships provide water, food, power, service staff and safety from the waves at a cost as low as $60 per night. There are also 1,500 oil and gas platforms in US waters alone.[35]

These floating cities would simply combine the amenities and engineering of cruise ships and oil platforms to provide people with a permanent life at sea.

"I would move our city somewhere else using paddles."
—Stephen, Findley Elementary, age 9

"I would love it because I will be able to find myself in a different place every day."
—Olivia, Findley Elementary, age 9

ACTIVITY
Design Your Own Floating City

Imagine you've been asked to design a floating city for yourself and 269 of your closest friends. While you wouldn't be permanently cut off from ever visiting land again, there are some things you probably wouldn't want to live long without. What kinds of shops, services, and amenities would you want on your floating city? What kinds of things should you include to make land lovers want to give up their lives as they know them and settle permanently in your sea city?

"It would be amazing if we could live on a floating city. We could go swimming so often, and we wouldn't have to go to a pool, and instead of going to the pet store for a fish, you could just catch one. And fishermen don't have to go to the lake."
—Philippa, Oxford Elementary, age 9

PETER THIEL, MONEY GIVER

What if there were someone who would pay you *not* to go to school? And what if that's not a "what if" but a "what is"? Not only did billionaire Peter Thiel cofound the Seasteading Institute[36], he also created the Thiel Fellowship, a $100,000 award given every year to twenty people under twenty years old. One of the requirements to be eligible to receive the award is that the applicant has to drop out of or not go to college. Instead, that person works with visionary mentors to help turn dream projects into realities.[37]

"We would run out of food and everything."
—Conner, Columbia Elementary, age 11

"You would use boats as cars. They would use chocolate syrup in the bathtub instead of water. They would only eat water."
—Conner, Columbia Elementary, age 11

"I would train jellyfish to let me ride them everywhere."
—Edward, Columbia Elementary, age 11

"That would be amazing, and I could ride baby harbor seals around town."
—Jake, Columbia Elementary, age 11

"If you lived on a boat, you would probably get sick a lot and would have to be very smart to figure out how to get vitamin C in the water."
—Halle, Columbia Elementary, age 11

"It would be really cool, and I can snorkel with the plankton."
—Luke, Columbia Elementary, age 11

"We would sink by now, and how would we build new buildings? How are we going to grow crops? Plus a shark might bump into us."
—Aidan, Columbia Elementary, age 10

What if the State of California Became Six Different States?

Ever since August 21, 1959, the United States has been a union of fifty states. But what if that number increased? And what if that number went up without the United States having to invade another country? What if a state like California were to transform from  a single state into six different states? Sound crazy? Not to several people in California. In the fall of 2014, Californians voted on an initiative that would have led the way to divide California into the states of Jefferson, West California, Silicon Valley, Central California, North California, and South California.[38] But it sounded crazy enough to enough people for the ballot initiative to be defeated.

Why on earth would anyone suggest dividing up an existing state into multiple states? Lifelong California resident Tim Draper, the billionaire behind the Six Californias idea, said he "came to the conclusion that California is ungovernable."[39] His idea is to mimic the success of start-ups that spring up in his native Silicon Valley and have each new state run—and compete with each other—as if they were start-up companies.[40] According to the organization Draper formed to push his plan forward, Six Californias, the goal is "to create six states with more local, responsive, efficient and representative governments."[41]

ACTIVITY
Split Your State

Take a look at your state or province. Could you divide it up into multiple states or provinces? Where would you draw the new boundaries? What criteria would you use to group territories—geography, education, industry, etc.?

TIM DRAPER, HERO ENTREPRENEUR

Tim Draper's belief in the entrepreneurial spirit doesn't end with his desire to turn state governments into start-ups. He's also created Draper University of Heroes. The Draper University of Heroes is different from most universities because, instead of students taking classes and earning majors in a wide variety of subjects and fields, students receive a single, immersive experience that prepares them to become entrepreneurs.[42]

What if the South Had Won the Civil War?

The American Civil War was the deadliest war in American history.[43] It was much more than a clash of blades and bullets—it was a clash of ideologies. In the end, the Union was preserved, and the country evolved into the country it is today. But what if it had ended differently? What if the Confederacy had won the war?

Of course, it's impossible to say exactly what the United States would look like today if the Union had lost the Civil War, but that hasn't kept historians and writers from imagining how things might have played out. In 1960, MacKinlay Kantor wrote an article in *Look* magazine that he would later publish as a novel called *If the South Had Won the Civil War*. In it, Kantor speculated that Lincoln would still be assassinated and that slavery would still be abolished, but the two countries would exist separately until, eventually, they reunited in 1960.[44]

Another Civil War "What Iffer" was Winston Churchill. In his essay contribution to the 1931 book *History Rewritten*, Churchill imagined the United States if the Confederacy had won the battle of Gettysburg and then went on to win the war. In his imagination, not only did the Confederacy win the American Civil War but this outcome eventually helped prevent the first World War.[45]

COLONEL JEFFERSON F. JONES, AMERICAN ROYALTY

The United States prides itself on being a pillar of democracy. So how is it there was once a kingdom on its soil? When the Civil War tore the United States apart, with states having to choose sides, the Missouri state government declared its support of the Union, but many of its citizens had Southern sympathies. In particular, the people of Callaway County (in a region of the state still known today as Little Dixie[46]) were staunch supporters of the South.

When word got out that Union troops were marching toward Callaway County, Colonel Jefferson F. Jones, of Callaway County, assembled all the men he could find who weren't already off fighting in the war to defend the county. They had nowhere near enough troops to successfully fight off the Union army, so they created an illusion instead. Jones had his men chop down trees and paint the logs black to look like cannons and light multiple campfires at night to make their forces appear formidable. The ruse worked. Jones was able to secure a cease-fire agreement between the United States and Callaway County. Out of their immense pride for their tiny county standing up against mighty US Army, the people of Callaway County proclaimed their county the Kingdom of Callaway County—a label they continue to use today.[47]

What if France Hadn't Helped America in the American Revolutionary War?

The American Revolutionary War is also referred to as the War of Independence because it was fought by the British Colonies in North America against Great Britain in an attempt to gain their independence. The rebel colonies won and grew into what is today the United States of America. There are countless stories and songs that have survived from the war into today. Much of the cultural identity associated with modern-day Americans is tied to the idea of thirteen underdog colonies standing up against the biggest, baddest empire on the planet . . . and winning!

> "I still think we would win."
> —Carter, Columbia Elementary, age 11

But what if we're forgetting to include a crucial fact about the victory? What if the American Revolution would not have turned out the way it did without a little help from some French friends? What if the War of Independence were fought (or won) alone?

> "We would have probably lost the war. We would be under control by the opposing country, and we would not be the United States!"
> —Ceara, Findley Elementary, age 10

The French and British had been bitter enemies for decades before the Revolutionary War began in 1776. A little more than a decade before, in 1763, Britain defeated France in the Seven Years' War. As a result, France lost most of its North American territory. The rebel leaders leveraged France's bitterness against the British to negotiate a deal with France that brought the colonists weapons, ammunition, uniforms, troops, and naval support to help them fight the British.

In particular, French assistance played a vital role in getting the British to finally surrender at Yorktown in 1781.[48]

BENJAMIN FRANKLIN, POP STAR DIPLOMAT

What if one of the most important people in winning the American Revolutionary War spent much of the war thousands of miles away from the nearest battle? It's debatable whether the United States could have defeated the British without French help. It's also debatable whether the United States could have secured French assistance without the help of Benjamin Franklin.

Benjamin Franklin was such a personality that he was able to capture France's imagination to the extent that the country stamped his face on everything it could, such as rings, watches, and medallions. Everyone wanted to wear a Benjamin. He was such a trendsetter that women even started styling their hair after the fur cap he wore. From a purely historical standpoint, it was the American victory over the British at the Battle of Saratoga that tipped the French into lending their support to the colonies' cause. But it's hard to deny the role the power of Franklin's popularity played in persuading the French to pledge support.[49]

> "I think we would still be a British country."
> —Lyn Marie, Columbia Elementary, age 10

> "Then we most likely not have the Statue of Liberty."
> —Tashi, Findley Elementary, age 10

What if Poland Had Joined Germany in 1939?

When Nazi Germany invaded Poland in September 1939, it kicked off a world war that would not only bring its ultimate downfall but the destruction of more land, lives, and property than any war before it.[50] But what if, rather than resisting the Nazis advancing on its borders, Poland had joined them? This is what Hitler would have preferred.[51]

In *The Storm of War: A New History of the Second World War*, Andrew Roberts walked readers through a scenario in which Poland joined forces with the Nazis instead of putting up a month-long resistance, only to be the first domino to fall in a six-year world war. If Germany invading Poland was the first domino, Britain and France declaring war against Germany in response was the second. Roberts believed that Britain and France would not have had any reason to declare war if Poland hadn't been invaded. This would have allowed Germany to invade the Soviet Union with all of its forces, instead of dividing them between an eastern and a western front. The Soviet Union, on the other hand, would likely have had to have divided its forces between the Germans invading in the east and the Japanese invading in the west. Likewise, with the Japanese attacking the Soviet Union from the west, the Japanese wouldn't have attacked Pearl Harbor, thereby keeping the United States out of the war. The result would have been an alliance of Germany, Poland, and Japan fighting—and defeating—a solitary Soviet Union.[52]

The victory would have given them control of a territory similar to that of the Mongol Empire at its height. What they could have done to the rest of the world after that would have been truly terrifying.

JOSEPH STALIN,
MR. BAD-GUY-AND-US-ALLY

What if an ally of the United States in World War II was just as evil as Adolf Hitler? Typically, Hitler is the runaway winner for the title of Worst Human Ever. But what if he was not the clear-cut choice for this infamous title? What if one of the United States' strongest allies in World War II was truly the evilest person to ever live?

Hitler's atrocities are well known, but did you know that Soviet leader Joseph Stalin had thirty thousand members *of his own army* executed just to make sure nobody opposed his authority? He then had everyone who knew about the executions—that's right—executed.[53]

Not only was Stalin responsible for the mass execution of roughly ten million more people than Hitler (Stalin killed forty million[54] to Hitler's thirty million[55]), he was also quoted as saying: "Ideas are more powerful than guns. We would not let our enemies have guns—why should we let them have ideas?"[56]

What if the Internet Were Never Created?

Since the birth of human communication (in other words, since the birth of humans), we've been searching for better and better ways to talk to each other quickly and in synchrony (at the same time).[57] In the winter of 1790, Claude Chappe and his brothers built their first prototype telegraphs.[58] These communication tools could be used to send messages across long distances by having operators look at far off towers with swinging arms. The position of the arms corresponded to letters in the alphabet. Give the signal for a letter with one of the towers; someone a long way away looks out of their own tower, sees the letter, and marks it down. This goes on until the receiving tower has all of the letters and therefore the message. If the message is going to another tower in a line of towers, then the receiving operator has to use their own tower's arms to send the message. Then, another tower down the line has to look out, see the message, and mark it down. Repeat.

> **"Without the internet, life would not be proceeding as fast and efficiently as it is."**
> —Garrett, Battle High School, age 16

You can imagine how slow and tedious this must have been. And, since this relay system was all based on humans looking out windows at towers in the distance, weather could ruin the cross-country communication. This was the beginning of the internet: weird signal towers scattered around France. As time progressed, so did our communications inventions. Chappe invented codebooks so users could

> **"Many people will suffer from their lack of information."**
> —Conner, Battle High School, age 15

CLAUDE CHAPPE'S VISUAL TELEGRAPHS

encode their messages into something shorter for cost and privacy. For example, Chappe might send *ABDS* on a visual telegraph, which could mean "Isn't Napoleon kind of short?" This was the real power of visual telegraphs and, starting in the 1830s, electric telegraphs.[59] The inventors and users had created a sort of language, patterns of visual and auditory cues and symbols, for sending and receiving messages. That's exactly what the internet is.

Working at CERN (a research laboratory where scientists study the structure of the universe by smashing elementary particles together), in 1989, Tim Berners-Lee created a language for computers to talk to each other. That language became what we know as the internet. We now have a global communications system where if you can get to a connected device, you can learn and do almost anything. You can send messages almost instantly, watch cat videos, do research for homework, and learn how to build rockets.

"I'd play Pokemon all the time with all my friends."
—John Ryan, Battle High School, age 15

But if something were to have stopped its creation, where do you think we'd be today? How much harder would it be to solve global problems or even think about things on the other side of the world? What would we do for fun?

ACTIVITY
Day without Connectivity

Your challenge—if you're brave enough to accept it—is to go an entire day without connectivity. That means no internet, no smartphones, no Xbox Live, and no tablets. Whatever will you do? In your journal, write out how you plan to spend your day of no connectivity and then, after the day is over, how you did spend your day. What was it like? What did you plan to do? What did you do?

TECHNICAL CORNER
The Internet

When you type an address into your browser or when an application you're using picks up data from its servers (a server is just another computer), what happens behind the scenes?

Everything connected to the internet has an address—kind of like how everywhere that gets mail has an address. Your application sends a request to the device it's on, saying, "Hey, you! I want to go look at something at XYZ address." Your device says, "Will do! One moment." It talks to what is called a DNS. A DNS is a server that has a bunch of address information. So, if you are looking for "google.com," a DNS will respond with the internet address for Google. That way, your device knows where to send more requests.

Think about it this way: if you're sending a letter to your friend, you need to know where your friend lives before you can send the letter. So, you could ask your parents "where does my friend live"? They'll let you know so you can label your letter and send it off.

Now that your device has the address to send the request your app had, your device breaks the message down into small packets. Each of these gets sent out to the internet with a destination address. Back to the physical letter example: imagine that when you're sending your letter, the post office makes you cut your letter up into ten-word chunks, each with its own envelope, each marked with your friend's address. That's what happens when internet-connected devices talk to each other—they break up messages into smaller packets and send them all.

The internet is a network of networks. Look at a spiderweb sometime. It has connected strings that go all over the place. That's what the internet looks like: a bunch of crazily connected strings. As your packets go out onto the internet, they get transferred around and around, until they reach their destination. Just like small post offices send letters to larger hubs, which in turn send your letters to other hubs, and eventually to your friend's local hub, then to your friend's door; the internet does the same, routing messages through local, regional, and then local hubs.

When your messages get received by the server, it reads them and decides if it wants to send something back. If it does, then a new message gets created and sent back through the spiderweb of networks until it hits the device you're using. Your device notifies your application, saying, "Hey there! I just got this back for you." Your application then does whatever it needs to with the information, maybe showing you a web page or updating its memory.

Back to physical mail. When your friend gets all of those messages from you, he or she has to put them back together to read your letter. Then, if you asked your friend to answer a question for you, he or she will need to write a response letter, cut it up, and send all the messages through the mail, all the way through the system until the messages arrive at your house to be read by you.[60]

What if There Were No Stories?

Why do you enjoy stories? To have fun? To laugh? To be scared? To imagine? Or just to relax enough to fall asleep? People love stories for all of those reasons and more. But have you ever wondered how stories got their start?

Many of the stories we read today were built from stories of the past. The more you read, the more you'll discover that certain characters and plots are very similar across many stories. For example, what if Harry Potter and Katniss Everdeen have a lot more in common than you realize?

Some even believe that every story we read is, more or less, the same story, just told in different ways. What's the story that's being repeated? Change. In a happy story, a funny story, a scary story, or a sad story, the main character always goes through significant changes by the end. People who study stories believe this is to reflect the changes we go through in life. Reading these stories can then prepare us for the changes we face.

What if stories are life? What if your life is a story (and you're the hero!)?

ACTIVITY
A Hero's Journey

Below is a list of the typical stages heroes go through during a story. Think of your favorite story. Then read the list, pausing at each stage to think about how your story's main character experienced each stage. Can you think of an example for each stage? Now think of another story and main character and see if you can do it again. Can you start to see that many stories we enjoy could be considered the same story?

1. The Ordinary World: Stories usually start by showing the hero in a mundane or unsatisfying world. The hero will often possess some characteristic or ability that sets him or her apart—maybe even making the character uncomfortably different—from those around him or her.
2. Call to Adventure: Something happens in this ordinary world to shake things up. The hero is forced to realize that change is coming . . . and an adventure is about to begin.
3. Refusal of the Call: Even though the coming change is obvious and inevitable, the hero makes one last attempt to refuse the adventure, to stay home or not leave what's familiar. He or she fears the unknown ahead and may even have a friend or family member warning about leaving.
4. Meeting a Mentor: One of the first occurrences during a hero's adventure is the hero meeting a mentor, or guide. This person is typically much older than the hero and often possesses great intelligence and magical or supernatural abilities. The mentor also gives the hero equipment, training, or advice for his or her adventure.
5. Crossing into the Unknown: This is when the hero completely leaves the place, people, or situation that was familiar and goes to where the people, places, and rules are very strange and different.
6. Allies and Enemies: Once in this new world of the unknown, the hero encounters other people who then become his or her allies or enemies for the course of the adventure.
7. Fear and Death: At some point along his or her adventure, a hero comes close to death or must confront his or her greatest fear.
8. Reward: After overcoming this great fear, or escaping his or her death, the hero is rewarded. Often, this is an object or treasure. The hero shows great joy, and others might celebrate this achievement, but the adventure is not over.

9. The Return: Once the hero has his or her reward, it's time to return home. The hero now begins the journey from this new world back to the place where he or she is from.

10. Rebirth: During the hero's return, he or she must now use what was learned along the adventure (and possibly the reward acquired) to overcome one more obstacle (often facing death again). But this time he or she is more prepared to face the challenge and appears to be a new person as a result.

11. Return with the Reward: The hero is now home—or where he or she was before leaving on the adventure—a transformed person. The hero is like a person living in two worlds: back to what is familiar but with the learning obtained from something new. This allows the hero a new freedom. All may not be awesome, but the hero has changed and is ready for new challenges and adventures.

JOSEPH CAMPBELL, LUKE SKYWALKER'S OTHER FATHER

The hero's journey is a concept advanced by anthropologist Joseph Campbell in his book *The Hero with a Thousand Faces*. It was this book (and Campbell's work studying and connecting the myths and stories of humans across the earth and across the history of humanity on it) that guided George Lucas in his writing of *Star Wars*.[61] Lucas said, "I consider him [Campbell] a mentor. He was an amazing scholar and an amazing person. When I started doing *Star Wars*, I reread *Hero with a Thousand Faces*."[62]

Campbell also left several suggestions on how anyone can live life like a hero. Here are two:

"Life is without meaning. You bring the meaning to it. The meaning of life is whatever you ascribe it to be. Being alive is the meaning."[63]

"A hero is someone who has given his or her life to something bigger than oneself."[64]

What if the Future Never Comes?

Implantable memories. Nanobots. Computers that think for themselves. Robot friends. An ability to change our genetic code. Flying cars or cars without drivers. People who never get sick. All these things are said to be waiting for us in the future.

But what if that future never comes? What if all the technology we have right now is going to stay the same? What if we don't create anything new but have to just keep using what we have?

Would you be happy with what we have? Would you still want a faster computer, a faster phone, a healthier life? How do you think society would respond to everything stopping?

ACTIVITY
Happy/Sad List

If technology stopped changing, what would you be happy to not have to experience in the future? What would you be sad about never being able to experience? Write your list in your journal!

KEVIN KELLY, STEVEN JOHNSON, AND RAY KURZWEIL, TECHNOLOGICAL DETERMINISTS

There's this idea called *technological determinism*. You might have heard your parents say something was "determined to happen." That means that whatever they're talking about was going to happen no matter what (or mostly no matter what). It doesn't matter if, when going down a road, a person chooses the left path or the right path, this thing (whatever the thing is) is destined to be—it's determined to happen. *Technological determinism* is determinism related to technology.

Kevin Kelly, Steven Johnson, and Ray Kurzweil all believe in this. Coincidentally, they also all write about technology. They each think that, given a certain setup, both organisms and technology will evolve in certain patterns. This might seem strange if you've heard that evolution is a whole bunch of random happenings. Evolution certainly has a random component to it, but it also has a less random part.

Think about it this way: if you're in a sandwich shop, you can order a whole bunch of different sandwiches made up of various ingredients. There are a limited number of ingredients, and, thus, there are only so many combinations of ingredients you can have to make a sandwich. Some combinations are pretty terrible, like mayo, mustard, and pepper. There's not really a sandwich there, and it's kind of hard to eat. But you could put some bread around those and add turkey, lettuce, and cheese. Now you have a sandwich. Sweet! Some people have an allergic reaction to an ingredient in bread, so they can't use bread to hold their sandwich together. This is where a little bit of technological determinism comes in . . . or would it be sandwich determinism? Large lettuce leaves could be wrapped around your other sandwich innards. Using lettuce as a wrap is somewhat determined. Lettuce has certain properties: it's big, it's flexible, it's found at sandwich shops, and it isn't greasy when you hold it. These properties make it a popular choice when you can't use bread. It is a choice that *will* happen when non-bread people need a good sandwich.

Why are we talking about technological determinism here? We're talking about it because even if there is a horrible, terrible, no-good world disaster, there are some things that might still be bound to happen.

Kevin Kelly talks about technological determinism in the broad sense of technology where it "extends beyond shiny hardware to include culture, art, social institutions, and intellectual creations of all types."[65] In his view, all of technology obeys some deterministic rules. The only thing we can do through our choices is slow technology's growth but not stop it.[66]

Steven Johnson writes about technology from an ideas-and-innovation perspective. In his view, ideas grow in somewhat set pathways. Similar to the lettuce-instead-of-bread example earlier, our ideas can only grow to their neighboring related ideas (you can't come up with a lettuce-wrapped sandwich if you haven't created the idea of a sandwich yet) and settle into various determined balance points (lettuce and bread both hold other sandwich ingredients well).[67]

Ray Kurzweil largely examines computers and artificial intelligence. There's a famous law in technology called "Moore's Law." It states for every two years that pass, you can pack two times as many transistors on an integrated circuit. Basically, that means that computers get more powerful and faster at a known rate. Well, Kurzweil saw this and wondered about the time before Moore's Law and the time after. He found that computers, for as long as there were computers, have followed this curve of powerfulness and speediness. And beyond that, he proposed that computers in the future are determined to follow this. So far, he's been right.[68]

What if the First Olympics Were a Science Competition Instead of an Athletic One?

Can you imagine how different the world would look today if, way back during the time of ancient Greece, people came from all over to compete in science? Sure, science was and is valued, but what if it were celebrated in the same way as sports are?

What if, instead of trading cards and wearing jerseys of your favorite sports star, you had a lab coat or a poster of your favorite scientist? And what if scientists made millions of dollars and were featured on television the way our sports stars are?

How do you think schools would look today if we celebrated science as much as sports? Would competitions in which science teams from different schools competed against each other draw large crowds with bands, cheerleaders, and die-hard fans the way

school athletic teams do today? Do you think more students would get excited about studying and participating in science-related activities?

Perhaps the biggest question is how different the entire world would look if we had millions of people who were science fanatics instead of sports fanatics. What kinds of advances and new technology would we have today?

If you could play a sport or do a science experiment, which would you choose?

"Science gets so little appreciation by the general public that it gets very little funding and advances much slower than is possible. If people were to get as excited about science and research as they do professional sports, then they could help fund progress and be a part of progress."
—Landon, Columbia Elementary School, age 10

"People would perfect the cure to cancer to win a gold metal. Or find the cure to Ebola."
—Elise, Findley Elementary, age 10

"Nerds would be more respected."
—Francesca, Findley Elementary, age 10

"Then all the athletic people would be poor, and the smart people would be rich."
—Lucas, Findley Elementary, age 10

"I think there would be a lot more scientists, and we probably would have made a lot more discoveries."
—Madyson, Columbia Elementary, age 11

"I think if the Olympics were a scientific competition that young boys and girls would want to try new things and experiment more often. It would lessen the popularity of sports."
—Maximum, Columbia Elementary, age 11

"Then no one would care about sports very much. We might study athletics instead of science."
—Calliope, Columbia Elementary, age 10

"Then Rome would know a lot about the science they learned from the Olympics, and the first manned rocket would be launched in the 1800s!"
—Schuyler, Columbia Elementary, age 11

What if Electricity Could Travel through the Air?

You know all about Wi-Fi and how great it is that you can access the internet without wires, but, at the end of the day, you still have to plug your devices into a wall socket to give them the juice to work wirelessly. What if you could power up anywhere, even where there are no walls?

This isn't a new thought. Since the dawn of electricity, people have been frustrated by wires. In fact, one of the great pioneers in electricity, Nikola Tesla, had a vision of free, wireless electricity for the entire world . . . over a hundred years ago! At the beginning of the twentieth century, Tesla started building the Wardenclyffe Tower (aka Tesla Tower) that would have provided electricity to cities, buildings, and homes wirelessly and inexpensively.[69] But the cost of finishing the tower became too much. Construction stopped, Tesla had a nervous breakdown, and we've used wires to transmit electricity for more than one hundred years.[70] Even though we may have missed our chance to have wireless electricity over a hundred years ago, scientists and inventors are hard at work making it a reality in the near future. There's a very good chance you'll be using 100 percent wireless devices before you know it.

ACTIVITY
Wireless History

But what if we did have wireless technology for the past century? How would this have affected other technological developments? Imagine if people could have had power wherever they went.

Do you think things like computers and the internet may have been developed years—if not decades—earlier? What if your great-grandparents had grown up with smartphones? What kinds of devices do you think you'd have today?

Write an alternative history, a short description of what the world could have been like. You can even draw some of the things we could have had by now. How would the world be different?

NIKOLA TESLA, SUPER-SCIENTIST-INVENTOR

Nikola Tesla came to the United States in 1884 to work with Thomas Edison.[71] He spent his life inventing. He helped push alternating current (the type of electricity in your house). He invented new types of motors. He invented the first radio receivers and, thus, was one of the main people to invent wireless electronic communications. He also invented hydroelectric power.[72]

Unfortunately, Tesla didn't always get as much recognition as he should have because other people took advantage of his kindness. He was reclusive and spent his time pursuing scientific discoveries, so he never had a spouse or children. Ultimately, he died alone in a New York City hotel from a blood clot in his heart. Over 2,000 scientists, engineers, politicians, and friends attended Tesla's funeral to pay their respects and say goodbye to a greatly respected inventor.[73]

TECHNICAL CORNER
Wireless Power

Wireless power works by sending out what're called electromagnetic waves. These waves have electrical and magnetic components that work together. In fact, there are a whole bunch of these kinds of waves you might already know about: radio waves (waves that carry the signals from radio stations), microwaves (the waves inside your microwave oven), infrared waves (the waves heat gives off), all the light you see (visible light waves), ultraviolet waves (the ones that give you a sunburn!), and x-rays (waves that doctors use to see your broken bones).

Each of these waves carries energy, even if you can't see it. When one of these waves matches the pattern of something else, its energy can transfer. For example, microwaves move in a way that resonates with water. Food heats up in your microwave because the energy from the waves it sends out gets picked up by the water in your food. The waves make the molecules in the water move more (which is what heat is). But your microwave can't pick up radio signals because it doesn't match that pattern, just like your radio can't heat your food. But, if you have a radio, it can pick up radio waves.

There are a few ways to send power wirelessly. One way is using simple induction. Imagine you are standing close to two friends. Jane is on your right, and Joe is on your left. Joe pushes you toward Jane. Then Jane pushes you toward Joe. This keeps happening, and you keep moving left and right. That's induction! Jane and Joe are using the energy in their arms to move you. You pick up their energy when you move. If you had two wires that were close to each other, you could send power to one by continuously switching the direction of electricity in the other.

Part 2
People

People. Can't live with them, can't live without them. And you are one, so what if there were a way to get the most out of being one? People come with all different sizes, backgrounds, perspectives, interests, and futures. It's remarkably easy to act as if you're the only person on the planet. But what if learning how to better understand those other people with which you share this big, blue marble hurtling through space would not only make the world we all share a better place but also would make you a better person?

We're all connected through space and time, but how much do we really know about each other? What if, by asking and exploring questions together about who people are, we can also boost what people can do? What if, in understanding people as a whole, you can also develop a deeper understanding of the person that is you?

Whether exploring questions about the length of our lives, the powers we have and how we should use those powers, or what our roles are when we interact together, there's a lot to talk about when it comes to the potential of people.

What if the future is a brighter place when we're all shining there together?

What if People Lived for Only One Day?

Mayflies, a species of fly, live for a few hours to a day after they reach adulthood.¹ Their experience of the world is just one, a small sliver of what you see.

What if you only lived for one day?

If you knew your life would last only from the time you were born until the time you fell asleep, how would you spend your day? Would you spend it having as much fun as possible? Or would you rush to make as big of a difference in the world as you could?

How would a one-day lifespan affect the way you viewed and treated others? Would you be like, "Out of my way! I've only got one day to live—and it's almost over!"? Or would you spend as much time with friends and family as you could?

> "Just like flies, they would run around like crazy trying desperately to procreate and leave a legacy of their being behind."
> —Kate, Battle High School, age 15

What about your view of the future? When you think about how little humans consider the future now, when our existence can span up to a century, where would our focus be if our time would be up in twenty-four hours? How would we treat the planet? How would we treat each other?

ACTIVITY
Single-Day Planner

What would you do if you had just today? Rush through your day, filling it with as much action as you could in the hopes of creating "meaning"? Or would you slow it down and soak in every last second of your day? Fill out a daily schedule for a single day. For each of the twenty-four hours in a day, write out what you would do.

ACTIVITY
Record a Day of Your Life

Choose an upcoming day. On that day, take pictures, record audio, collect artifacts, and make a bunch of written entries that capture everything that happens. Put what you can in your journal. How would you feel if that were the only day you were going to be alive? Would you be satisfied?

"People wouldn't be so judgmental, and they would take advantage of their limited time and resources."
—Leslie, Battle High School, age 16

"If people only lived for one day, people would be forced to cram life experiences into the twenty-four hours that they would be alive. Instead of having years to basically waste, every second of that day would count significantly more, so time would become the most valuable thing in the world."
—Dillon, Battle High School, age 16

"I would still sleep for half of it. The other half I would eat. I would question if I could do both at once and then be dead never knowing if I could."
—Charlie, Battle High School, age 15

"We would all have to live on Venus where one day is equal to about 223 Earth days."
—Andrew, Battle High School, age 15

What if We Could Be Young Forever?

Every year, you get a little older, until one day, well, you don't. You die. It happens. Ideas about what happens after we die are as plentiful as there are people on the planet. But what if you didn't have to wonder about what's next? What if you never died? What if you could live forever? What if everyone lived forever? What if when you aged, you didn't get physically older?

How do you think longer lives would change society? Right now, people are born, they grow, they get a job and go to work, and then they retire. But if we could live forever, there'd be no need to retire. We could work forever! Sound like fun?

If you could live forever, you could also learn anything you wanted and pursue as many interests as you wanted. What if you could become a doctor, a musician, an athlete, an astronaut, and more instead of choosing just one? You could play every video game. You could watch every movie. You could travel to every country!

But what if you weren't the only one who was living forever?

It would seem that we would need to do something about all the people being born. In 2012, 451 babies were born every minute![2] How do we feed all those people? Will there be enough room for everyone? What changes might we have to make in order to make sure the planet is prepared for people living forever?

ACTIVITY
Write a Letter to Yourself in the Future

Write a letter to yourself five hundred years in the future. What are some of the things you're doing and thinking right now that you want to make sure you don't forget after you're five hundred years old?

AUBREY DE GREY, CHIEF SCIENCE OFFICER, SENS RESEARCH FOUNDATION

Aubrey de Grey used to be a computer scientist. Then he realized that something is killing humans more than anything else: aging. He changed career paths to start researching life-extension—how we could live drastically longer and healthier lives.

> [Life-extension] will empower us, both individually and as a society. The psychological impact of seeing our loved ones decline, and of knowing that sometime in the future the same thing will happen to us, is so huge that our only defense (for most of us . . .) is to ignore it. When we no longer have that, we will be far more able to aim high, in our personal and professional lives and as a society: we will believe that we can succeed against our other big challenges too, whether it be climate change, war, or pandemics.[3]

TECHNICAL CORNER
How Do We Die?

Loads of processes keep us alive. Our hearts pump our blood. Our intestines remove nutrients from what we eat. Our immune system fights off bacteria, viruses, fungi, and parasites. Our nerves send command and sense signals all around our body. It's pretty amazing!

Just like when your parents' car runs for a while and builds up damage, so do we. After enough damage, we will get a disease. And when things break down all the way, we die. Researchers like Aubrey de Grey are trying to combat each of the following causes of damage so we might never get that disease that kills us.

1. Cell loss, cell atrophy: Cells die too quickly.
2. Division-obsessed cells: Cells like dividing themselves in two too much. This is what many tumors are.
3. Death-resistant cells: Cells don't die quickly enough. All cells die, but resistant cells can cause problems too.
4. Mitochondrial mutations: Mitochondria help provide the energy to cells. If they are damaged then cells can't make the energy they need.
5. Intracellular junk: Cells have picked up too much waste. As the body cleans itself, that waste has to be transported to waste areas, but cells can get damaged if the body can't get rid of its waste.
6. Extracellular junk: Similar to waste in a cell, this waste is outside of the cell and damages the body.
7. Extracellular matrix stiffening: The stiffening of the tissue that connects all of your cells. If it can't move like it needs to, your body gets damaged.

What if Politicians Were Kids?

When was the last time a politician asked you what you think? Have people from your city, state, and federal governments ever asked you about how things should be run?

We're guessing they've probably never asked you. Well, what if kids had a greater voice in government? Sure, politicians might have more experience than kids with certain matters. It is one of the reasons voters vote for certain candidates. But while having experience in a topic can be really useful to thinking about that topic, it also can make your thinking more limited. That's why people with only a little bit of experience can contribute a great deal to a conversation. A person with less experience isn't guided by (what could be) faulty ways of thinking about a problem.

Kids have a unique perspective. You solve problems all the time and look at the world differently than older people. What do you think would happen if more kids were in government? Do you think kids should run for office? Do you think politicians should talk to you?

> "Children would be more open-minded and hopefully would not have predetermined judgments. To let the children run the government on their own, however, would probably be a bad thing. Adults still need to bring their wisdom and experience to the table and still be the major guiding force within the government. But the fresh opinions and out-of-the-box thinking that children would bring is very important and needs to be a bigger part of government."
> —Madi, Battle High School, age 15

ACTIVITY
Write to a Politician

Your representatives are the people who make decisions for you in government, people at the city, state, and federal levels. Here's the activity: write a letter to one of your representatives. First, find their email or mailing address online. Then, write a letter telling that person what you worry about and how you might go about changing it. Also, make sure you say that you'll be voting in future elections. Politicians are more likely to do something for people who will vote for them. Hopefully he or she will write back!

"I'm sure there would be a lot less drama."
—Ben, Battle High School, age 17

"There would be a lot more compassion in the world. As people age, they are shaped by the limitations they've seen in the world. Kids would be much better at solving the problems because kids are more creative, and they would actually be more focused on solving the problems of the world, rather than creating more of them."
—Dillon, Battle High School, age 16

What if There Were No Holidays?

What? No holidays? That was the case for the first ninety-four years of the United States. It wasn't until June 28, 1870, that the first federal holiday law was enacted. This law officially made New Year's Day, Independence Day, and Christmas holidays in the United States. It also opened the door for the establishment of other holidays.[5]

There have been over one thousand holidays proposed to become federal holidays since the fun began in 1870, but only eleven have made the cut.[6] Can you name all of them?

It wasn't until George Washington's birthday joined the party in 1879 that federal employees got a paid day off. Christopher Columbus may have been one of the first Europeans to land in the Americas, but Columbus Day, established in 1968, was one of the last federal holidays established—until Martin Luther King Jr. Day, the most recent federal holiday, was created back in 1983.

Each holiday has a unique history, but what if Thanksgiving has the craziest?

The first Thanksgiving was when George Washington declared "a day of thanksgiving and prayer" on Thursday, November 26, 1789. But the second Thanksgiving wasn't celebrated until Washington called for another day of thanksgiving over six years later, on February 19, 1795. Abraham Lincoln, fifteen presidents later, thankfully brought an end to the madness of this moveable feast in 1863 and proclaimed the United States would celebrate Thanksgiving once a year on the last Thursday of November. Thanksgiving didn't settle on its present date (the third Thursday of November) until 1941, when President Franklin Roosevelt put it there.

Why did Roosevelt move Thanksgiving Day back a week? To give stores an extra week for Christmas shopping—a decision for which business owners remain thankful today.

ACTIVITY
Your Own Holiday

What if you could make your dream holiday? What would it be about? On what day of the year would this holiday happen, and what sorts of traditions and activities would be involved in this celebration? You already have a birthday, but what if you had a new day with a new theme?

What if You Hibernated?

Sure, you like to sleep in an extra hour or two whenever you can, but what if you slept in an extra six months?! That's how long some hibernating animals sleep. Black bears can go up to one hundred days without eating, drinking, or going to the bathroom![7]

For starters, imagine how hungry you'd be when you woke up after sleeping (and not eating) for many months. This is why hibernating animals spend most of the summer and fall eating to pack on the pounds. Black bears can put on an extra thirty pounds every week before their super long slumber.[8] But bears aren't the only animals that hibernate. There are species of snakes, turtles, lizards, toads, bats, and even shrimp who feel the need for sleep, always in the wintertime.[9] Why not you?

> "I would feel much more energized after hibernation, but life would seem much shorter because we would be sleeping, and time would pass faster."
> —Veronica, Battle High School, age 17

You may not believe it, but human hibernation isn't as crazy as it sounds. It might even be helpful. Scientists have identified a couple genes in humans that might allow us to hibernate, but we'd have to undergo treatment to start. Doctors could add or remove genes, or they could use medicine or environmental factors to allow these genes to express themselves. It's somewhat similar to cooking: when you want your cake to turn out a certain way, you add, remove, and change the amount of ingredients. But, why would a person ever *want* to sleep that long? Perhaps the most

> "I already do."
> —Andrew, Battle High School, age 15

exciting reason for a person to hibernate is space travel. Traveling through space can take a long time. It takes two hundred to three hundred days just to reach Mars![10] Traveling to other interesting places in our universe can take years, if not decades.

How would you use your ability to hibernate? Would you sleep through long trips, boring movies, or entire seasons of the year?

ACTIVITY
Find Your Hibernating Friends

We told you a few species that hibernate. Who else can you find? Start with a little research on the internet or in other books for an animal that hibernates. Then, go to your local zoo and try to find that animal. When you do, take a picture of it (or even with it). Put the picture and a short description of what you've learned in your journal.

"Teens already do that. We sleep as much as we can and eat large quantities. We are only active during the summer because we don't have school."
—Charlie, Battle High School, age 15

What if the Jobs of the Future Were Different?

What do you want to do when you grow up? Be a doctor? A lawyer? How about an astronaut? A factory worker? A construction worker?

What if the job you'll have when you're older doesn't even exist yet? What if you can create your future job? What would it be? What would you do?

One of the wonderful things about technology is that machines can do some jobs humans used to do but didn't enjoy very much. Imagine digging huge ditches out in the blazing sun. Doesn't sound like much fun, huh? Today, we have gigantic machines that can dig thirty-two feet every minute and move more than 2.7 million cubic feet of earth every day![11]

But it's not just moving dirt. Other jobs are slowly becoming obsolete.[12] As computers get smarter, they're able to correct our spelling and grammar. What if we no longer need proofreaders? What if we no longer need teachers?

What, no teachers? Sounds crazy, but there are some people today, like Sugata Mitra, who believe the future of education will be students with computers in a classroom—without a teacher![13]

> "I would ask myself for a raise, and probably only be able to get a new title."
> —Charlie, Battle High School, age 15
>
> "People, including myself, would be much more happy with their lives because they [would have] the power to control their work environment completely."
> —Veronica, Battle High School, age 17

And what about those other careers popular with kids today, like doctors[14] and lawyers[15]? Many futurists believe humans won't be doing those jobs either in the future. Heck, with Google's driverless car[16], you may not even be able to get a job driving a taxi, bus, ambulance, or fire truck.

So, what will you do?

What if today is the time to start thinking about tomorrow? On the bright side, some of the jobs that will be done by machines are jobs must humans didn't want to do in the first place. By having machines do these jobs, humans as a whole can explore new activities. However, people who like jobs done by robots might get forced into jobs less likely to be taken over by machines. Think about the kind of job you want. Do you think it can be replaced by robots? Can you come up with an entirely new job that doesn't exist yet, one that wouldn't be replaced by machines?

"I would sit, be a professional doodler, and [be a] taste tester."
—Kate, Battle High School, age 15

Do you love to travel? What if you became a personal tour guide?

Like sports? You could become a personal trainer.

Enjoy cooking? You can bake treats and sell them to the world through an online store.

Are you creative? There's nothing stopping you from creating your art and then using the internet to share it with the world.

What if, in the future, people stop asking other people what work they do for a living and start asking what they enjoy doing for a living?

ACTIVITY
Read This Book, Create a New Job

Many of the entries in this book have futuristic elements. After reading more of the book, come back to this activity and describe a new job based on something you read. Your new job could even be from what you learned while you were doing a different activity. Write it up in your journal and then search the internet for jobs like it. Does it exist yet, or are you the first to describe this job?

What if We All Spoke the Same Language?

In 2014, there were 7,106 different spoken languages, according to Ethnologue,[17] a world language research group. That's a lot of languages. However, 40 percent of the world speaks one (or more) of eight major languages: Chinese, Spanish, English, Hindi, Arabic, Portuguese, Bengali, and Russian.[18] On top of that, many languages are dying out for a multitude of reasons. This leads us to the question: what if we all spoke the same language?

Which language do you think it'd be? This book is printed in English, but English is only the third most popular language (at least at the time we're writing this).[19] Language is highly tied to power and culture. English is powerful because of British expansion and the United States' strong role in world economics.

What about some of the properties of language? English gets kind of greedy. When it finds a word in a different language it likes, English just steals it. For example *anger* comes from Scandinavia, *dance* comes from France, *skeleton* comes from Greece.[20] Look at German. It can putwordstogethertomeannewthings. For example, a person who wears gloves to throw snowballs is a *handschuhschneeballwerfer*.[21]

We also know ideas are tied to our language. If you've ever learned another language, you've probably learned about a few concepts that just don't translate well. Will we lose certain ideas that can only be expressed in one language? Or do you think we'll figure out a way to say these things in a new language?

ACTIVITY
What's in a Good Language?

If you had to build a language, what would be special about it? What would be useful and why? Could you string words together? Could you steal from other languages? Could you add new letters and other symbols? Could you change the way it is written? What would you choose?

L. L. ZAMENHOF, FATHER OF ESPERANTO

Dr. L. L. Zamenhof created Esperanto in 1887 to allow people of different languages the ability to communicate easily with each other without feeling as if they were sacrificing their own cultural identities when speaking. He also designed it to be logical and easy to learn so as many people as possible could use it—not just those who could afford to go to school to learn it.[22] Today, it is estimated that as many as 2 million people speak fluent Esperanto.[23]

What if People Didn't Know Anything?

Knowledge can be defined as "justified, true, belief."[24] So, if you have a thought, and you're wondering if it is knowledge or not, you can ask yourself three questions. (1) Is this thought a belief? (2) Is this thought true? (3) Is this thought justified? If you answer yes to all three, you've got a little nugget of knowledge!

The first question is pretty easy to answer. A *belief* is just a thought that you think is true (regardless of if it is true or false). "I believe the Earth orbits the sun," and "I believe there is a civilization of mole-people at the center of the Earth" are my beliefs if I believe them to be true. Question one: done.

But be careful! The next two questions are harder. Truth doesn't depend on what people think. A thing is either true or false, regardless of whether or not a person believes it to be true or false. (Well, there are a few weird things that do crazy things with logic and quantum mechanics, but we'll leave them out for now.) Anyway, how do you know if something is true or false? You might know it is true if it's a thing you can see (example: these powders explode when lit because when I light them, they explode). You might be able to deduce it is true if the thought is based in logic (example: $1 + 1 = 2$ because that is how math works). You might hear someone you trust say it's true (example: your teacher tells you that America used to have slaves). But how certain are you of any of these things?

This is where we get into justification. To be justified in a belief, you have to have enough evidence that a thing is true with enough reasonableness. So, your teacher tells you that there are mole-people at the center of the Earth. At first you believe her because she tells you other things you know to be true. But later on, you ask other trustworthy people about the mole-people. Turns out they don't think there is anyone down there. You then study geology, you read about how the Earth works, and you learn about the molten core. Now you have more evidence that there is no one, not even mole-people, living at the center of the Earth. You would now be justified in *not* believing what your teacher told you about mole-people because you have more evidence against her statement than for her statement.

How do you make sure your beliefs are properly justified? How do you make sure your beliefs are true? Do the things you "know" stand up to the test? If you are pretty sure about your beliefs, is that really you "knowing"?

ACTIVITY
Test Your Knowledge

In a journal or notebook, write down three things you think you know. Now, go through each of these things and write what your belief is, how you know it is true, and how you are justified in believing it. When you're writing how you know it's true and how you're justified in believing it, don't just say, "My teacher told me." Write out a few sentences about how you know. What other things do you know that lead you to thinking your belief is true?

What if We Got Rid of Cars?

Wherever you live, you probably have many cars around you. America especially likes cars—Ford Motor Company, General Motors Corporation, Chrysler, and others started in America. And there are countless movies and songs that romanticize cars and driving. No wonder America likes cars so much—it's part of the culture!

Jane Jacobs, urban activist and writer, thought that cities (including rural ones) are a balance of two things: city function and transportation.[25] Grocery stores, bookshops, big business buildings, homes—these are all containers of city functions. It's what is happening in the city. Transportation is how we get from one city function container to the next. You can walk, bike, drive a car, take a bus, or fly your blimp—these are all forms of transportation.

> "It would be awesome because you could play baseball or ride your bike in the street."
> —Isaac, Oxford Elementary, age 9
>
> "There would be much more space and there [would] be more buildings, and there wouldn't be as much putrid air."
> —Charlie, Oxford Elementary, age 9

City functions are the places we want to be, though. We don't want to be driving around all day. We want to be hanging out, riding roller coasters, sitting in the park—we want to be *doing* things. So, what if we got rid of cars?

Roads take up a lot of space. But if we didn't have

cars, buses, trucks, or other large vehicles that need that space, we could fill it in with more activities! If we got rid of cars today, we'd certainly have a lot of empty space between buildings (especially where parking lots used to be). Think of all the weirdly shaped buildings we could put between current buildings. Think of all the new activities that could be so much closer to where you live! But would it be harder to get there?

"If we got rid of cars, then people would be a lot more fit and healthy because they would have to walk everywhere. Also no one would be able to visit faraway places."
—Emily, Findley Elementary, Age 10

ACTIVITY
You Fill in the Streets

What would you put between our buildings if cars (and similar transportation) just disappeared? Draw two pictures. Your first picture should be of a street including cars, people, and buildings. Then, draw your second picture of the same street but replace all the cars and the roads with new buildings or activities.

JANE JACOBS, URBAN ACTIVIST AND WRITER

Jane Jacobs started as a writer in New York City. For her pieces, she went to different parts of the city for inspiration. Over time, Jacobs learned a lot about the city and eventually wrote *The Death and Life of Great American Cities*. She wrote this as someone who had no formal training in public planning (the study and profession of putting cities together). It is now one of the most important books about cities, and she has affected cities beyond measure.

Jacobs believed that cities are made of all sorts of people, and that buildings and neighborhoods should reflect that. When New York City planners wanted to demolish homes of the poor so a highway could be built, she fought them for a more balanced city. If you have an area of your city with mixed-use buildings (homes, businesses, and shops in the same structure), you might have a city planner who was inspired by Jacobs.[26]

"If we got rid of cars, we wouldn't have CO_2 just floating around. Global warming would stop. Buildings spew out CO_2 anyways, but cars do the most of it. Bike stores would make a lot of money selling bikes too. Bikes would be everywhere."
—Rone, Columbia Elementary, age 10

"If we got rid of cars, global warming would be way down, and people would probably walk, ride bikes, and we might even invent a new kind of vehicle."
—Sophia, Columbia Elementary, age 11

"People would be less lazy."
—Mason, Columbia Elementary, age 11

"Then everyone would be skinny, and they would walk and exercise more. The streets would be crowded, and people would have to carry their belongings."
—Vedant, Findley Elementary, age 9

"We would start riding horses and die under the ghost of Henry Ford's wrath."
—Carter, Columbia Elementary, age 11

What if There Were No Sports?

How would you spend your free time if there were no athletics? What would motivate you to be physically active? Could you still learn the value of teamwork if there were no teams to be a part

of? We often think of sports as just a spectacle of winning and losing, but what if there's more to them? What if sports provide people with an outlet to physically exert themselves? Without playing sports, where would all of that energy go? Fighting with each other? That would be awful! Sports also provide us with a distraction from our everyday (sometimes boring) lives. Do you work harder on your homework if you know you get to watch your favorite team play as soon as you're done? Or would you have more time to do

> "If there were no sports, society would have to find something else to keep them physically fit, and society would have to find something else to follow and be fans of. Artistic interest might become a social norm, and people might discuss actors, dancers, artists, and writers in place of famous athletes. Maybe scientific interests would flourish. Who knows what would capture our society's attention in place of the worldwide obsession with sports and athleticism?"
> —Madi, Battle High School, age 15

your homework if you didn't have the distraction of sports?

Speaking of getting your work done, sports give us a framework to be competitive in constructive ways. Do you enjoy competing with yourself or against others? If sports didn't exist, how do you think you could develop your competitive edge?

Of course, some people can take sports and competition a little (or way) too far. Do you know people who are a little too in love with winning or like their favorite teams a little too much?

What do you think these people would love if their favorite teams stopped playing?

ACTIVITY
Play Shnorjin

What is shnorjin? We don't know. You haven't created it yet.

Your task is to create a new sport. It has to be something that can be played with one or more people with some goal that can be attained. Write out the rules in your journal and then find a few friends to play with you. If they also have this book, they could create their own version of shnorjin that you could play!

"The arts would be embraced more."
—Leslie, Battle High School, age 16

"Then life wouldn't be as fun."
—John Ryan, Battle High School, age 15

What if You Could Hear and See What Other People Were Thinking?

Do you ever wonder what someone else is thinking? No, we don't mean when someone does something silly and you wonder, "What are you thinking?!" We mean private thoughts, the things you say only to yourself and others say only to themselves. What would happen if you knew what they were thinking—and they knew what you were thinking?

Doctors, scientists, tech hackers, and entrepreneurs are asking the same questions . . . and they are building tools to look at what people are thinking. If you were to injure your head, your doctor might use an MRI or EEG to figure out exactly what was wrong. These are two tools that let them peer into your thoughts. They can see if you're happy or sad, frustrated or at ease, thinking about a word or image. How would you feel knowing your doctor was seeing your thoughts? We learned about how brains work because of these machines. Researchers are even getting close to being able to record dreams![27]

"That would be helpful for men trying to understand women."
—Charlie, Battle High School, age 15

Well, if machines can see what we're thinking, what if they could do something when you think in certain ways? You could think about watching television, and the television could turn on. Rather than drawing with your hands, you could draw with your brain and a computer. Why draw at all? You could just think of the whole image and have it "print" on a screen. What if you could build 3D structures, like if you were playing with LEGOs or sculpting with clay, but only by using your mind? Research in this area is growing too. The machines you'd use are called brain computer interfaces, or BCIs for short. Pretty neat!

"I [would] stop acting a fool all the time."
—Ben, Battle High School, age 17

"The world would be a violent place."
—Kate, Battle High School, age 15

Seeing into people's minds could have downsides too. Your parents would know everything you're thinking. Whoever cooks in your house would know when you think their cooking is bad. If you have a secret crush on someone, and that person could read your thoughts, your secret wouldn't be very secret. Nothing would be very secret, would it?

ACTIVITY
With the Power of Your Brain

If you could control objects with your brain, what would you do with that power? Would you become a superhero or a supervillain? Would you use your power for scientific discovery or artistic expression? What about for money or for power? Write in your journal about what you would do.

TECHNICAL CORNER
How to Read Thoughts

Your brain is alive with electricity. When you want to move your arm, an electrical signal is sent from your brain, through your spinal cord, and then into your arm's muscles. Or, when you think a thought, electrical signals get sent to other parts of your brain. If you're trying to remember your friend's face or complete a puzzle, electrical signals again! Weird, right? We don't think about our gooey brains being filled with electricity.

If a brain scientist put sensors on your scalp, the sensors could measure your brain's electric pulses and how they change. Scientists have been collecting data for many years, and they now have a good idea of which pulses are tied to which thoughts. That means that with enough research, brain scientists can read your thoughts.

"I would be either driven insane or be a billionaire."
—Andrew, Battle High School, age 15

What if Your Community Were More Democratic?

What does it mean to be democratic? Does it mean being a democrat instead of a republican? Nope. *Democratic* comes from *democracy*, which means a type of government where every individual has an equal say in what happens. If your teacher ever asked your class to raise your hands and vote for something, that was probably a temporary democracy! The United States is a *representative democracy*, meaning that everyone elects a few people to represent everyone's ideas in government. Anyway, to be *more democratic* means to give individuals more access to decision-making and actions.

Your community is already somewhat democratic. Officials are elected to local positions. You have a mayor, judges, and someone to make sure all the finances are in order. What if the community voted for even more positions, like each office worker, garbage collector, web designer, and tax preparer? That would be more democratic . . . but you probably don't need everyone to vote on who collects the garbage.

You could also be more democratic by encouraging or allowing more people to vote. Even though many people have the right to vote in elections, they don't always do so. This is one of the reasons why some groups don't get as much representation in government. There are other people who can't vote at all: some crimes take away your right to vote, and some people (probably like you!) are not old enough.

ACTIVITY
More Democracy, Yes or No?

When does it make sense to have more democracy, and when does it make sense to have less? Spend a day jotting down notes in your journal whenever you're making group decisions. Would it make sense to have more or fewer people vote?

What if There Were No School?

No school? Or, at least no more boring parts of school? Awesome!

Wait. What? No school? How would you spend your days? When would you see your friends? What would you learn?

Before we go off and cancel school, what if you took a second and asked yourself what you don't like about school? Is it the tests? Homework? Uncomfortable desks? Boring classes? What if there were solutions to all of those things?

The more we learn about how people learn, the more some schools are moving away from things like long tests, pointless homework, and boring lessons. In fact, more and more schools are starting to include things like toys, 3D printers, and even Minecraft in their classrooms to create more interactive (and effective) learning experiences.

What if, instead of not having school, students like you were able to help design your learning environment and decide the things you studied?

ACTIVITY
Create Your Own Classroom

Draw a picture of your ideal classroom. Include all the things you'd like to have in it to help you learn. Think about how you'd situate different parts of the room. Will you have places for writing, lectures, experiments, books, art, and talking with other students? Will your classroom be inside or outside? How many students are in the class, and are they all the same age?

MALALA YOUSAFZAI, EDUCATION ACTIVIST

If you don't like school, it might sound like fun to all of a sudden not have it. And, sure, maybe "school" isn't the thing that is important to have—education is. It's important to be able to interpret what is going on in the world, how to live with others, and how to learn more. Without any education, we would devolve into apes.

Malala Yousafzai is a Pashtun Pakistani who was shot in the head because she was trying to go to school, trying to get an education. The Taliban, an Islamic fundamentalist terrorist group, targeted Malala because she wrote a blog about how important education is. Malala survived the shooting, and when she recovered she continued to fight for education rights.[28] At age 17 she won the Nobel Peace Prize, the youngest recipient yet. Now, she travels the world talking to others about how important education is. But, she always finds time for her own education.[29]

What if You Were Wrong about Everything?

Think about the last time you were wrong. Maybe you answered something wrong on a test or were trying to explain something when someone else corrected you. What does being wrong feel like? Embarrassing, right?

> **"Then I'd be right about nothing."**
> —Ben, Battle High School, age 17
>
> **"Then what would happen if I said I was wrong about everything?"**
> —Charlie, Battle High School, age 15

We bet not. The question was "What does being wrong feel like?" But when you're thinking about times you were wrong, the feeling you remember arose just after you learned you were wrong. It can feel embarrassing to learn you are wrong, but actually *being wrong feels like being right* because you think you're right and don't yet know you're wrong.[30]

Being wrong happens all the time! If you thought about all the knowledge you have, you're probably wrong about a lot of it. You have a few beliefs that contradict each other, and you have beliefs about things in the world that will be changed by new scientific discoveries. You have beliefs that came about based on miscommunication or misunderstanding.

Now, what can you find that you're wrong about?

ACTIVITY
Comfortably Wrong

People usually aren't comfortable admitting when they're wrong. Why? They might think it makes them look silly or that people shouldn't believe or trust them. That's all pretty silly, though. What if admitting you're wrong is the first step in getting things right? The truth is, we've all been wrong before. What are some things you've been wrong about? What did you learn from realizing you were wrong? Journal three things you've been wrong about and what you learned from being wrong.

> "If I was wrong about everything, I would stop answering questions and only ask them."
> —Madi, Battle High School, age 15

> "Nothing would change; the truth is subjective. My wrong truth is still my truth."
> —Jonathan, Battle High School, age 17

What if You Wrote Computer Code?

Computer code, like any code, is made up of small parts that are like letters, words, sentences, and stories. Imagine you write a story, and your friend reads it. Well, that is kind of how computers work. A programmer writes out a series of events, descriptions, and comments in code. Then the computer reads the story and acts.

You can write recipes in code: start with peanut butter, jelly, and bread and then follow steps one, two, and three to make a sandwich. You can draw pictures in code: put the first box here and color it blue, put the second box three inches to the right of the first and color it red, and then put the first circle one inch above the second box and color it black.

Writing code allows you to easily manipulate how things interact with each other. If you had a robotic dog as a pet, you could teach it something (like how to guard your room) by uploading a bit of code to it. If you drew a house with code, you could change its size by editing the code (rather using a pencil to erase and redraw). If you built a house with code, you could

change your room size, the color of your walls, and when the lights turn on—all by editing a few lines of code.

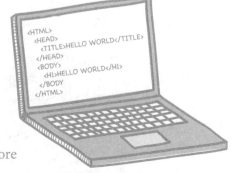

What would you change if you knew how to write code? What would you have your computer do that it doesn't do now? What would you make more interactive? A teddy bear that warms up when you hug it? Music that starts playing when you do chores? What would you want to make?

ACTIVITY
Write Some Code

Writing code doesn't have to be hard. It doesn't even require typing! Scratch is a programming language made by researchers at the Massachusetts Institute of Technology. With it, you can snap blocks of code together like Lego bricks. Go to scratch.mit.edu to put some blocks of code together. Maybe you'll draw something awesome, tell a story, or make the next Angry Birds!

ADA BYRON, COUNTESS OF LOVELACE, FOUNDER OF COMPUTING

Way back in the 1800s, Ada Byron met Charles Babbage.

From a very young age, Byron was interested in and inspired by the world around her. She tried to build wings for flying with[31] and, in her 20s, had an understanding of mathematics that surpassed that of men graduating college.[32] At this time, women were not encouraged to go to college or pursue anything intellectual. Ada Byron didn't care. She was going to learn anyway.

Babbage had been working on a Difference Engine, a mechanical calculator that could find answers to some complex mathematical functions. (Computers weren't around to do this because Byron and Babbage hadn't created their predecessors yet!) Imagine a large dining room table. Now imagine in the space the table takes up, from the floor to the ceiling, a contraption of gears, pulleys, and levers. That's what the Difference Engine looked like. When Babbage met Byron, he had a working prototype of this crazy machine and she was fascinated.

Some years passed before they started working together. Babbage lost his funding from the government and, at the same time, started work on an Analytical Engine.[33] This new invention would solve more than what the Difference Engine could—you could program it to solve new problems. They were designing a physical contraption that you program like a computer. Inspired by weaving looms that could make different patterns based on cards put in them, they set out to do the same with their mechanical computer.

Babbage saw the original potential, but Ada Byron saw an even bigger potential. What if they could use variables that could be filled with non-number symbols? She thought about having the machine manipulate language and musical notes, similar to how computers can edit sentences and write melodies.[34] The work was well before its time. Parts of the machine were built, but it mostly lived in sketches and notes, never completed.

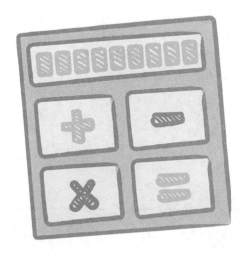

What if There Was No You?

Where is the "you" in you? Some think it's your body. Some think it's your brain. Some think it's a combination of the two. Would you still be you if I took your brain and put it in a vat (where you could still think, of course!)?

Imagine a wooden ship called *Santa Maria*. After a year of being out to sea, it gets badly damaged. When it's back at the dock, workers find the damaged planks and replace them with new wood. The first time they fix it, there are many pieces to fix—50 percent of the ship. The next year the workers fix the ship again; this time they outfit 20 percent of the ship with new wood. The third year there is a really bad storm, and the workers have to replace 30 percent of the ship with new wood. When the *Santa Maria* sails for its fourth year, it doesn't have any of its original wood. It all got replaced by the workers. Is the *Santa Maria* still the *Santa Maria* that sailed out four years ago? If it isn't, where did the ship go? When did the change happen?

Here's the really weird part: your body and mind are like the *Santa Maria*. Every year, you have cells that die and get replaced by new cells. Every year, you learn new things and forget others. Do "you" exist through all of that? Do you constantly die, and then are you reborn? Is there no "you" at all? Are "you" the process of change—the shape of the river as water flows through?[35]

ACTIVITY
Talk with Your Friends

Ask around. See how people respond to the ship story and how they think about their own identities. Do they think they live and die all the time? Do they think they don't really exist? Do they think we're all processes of change? Or do they think something else? What do you think?

DAVID EAGLEMAN, NEUROSCIENTIST

Among other things, David Eagleman is interested in personal identity. Like the question above, he wonders where the you is inside your body. What makes it?

We like to think of memories, our personal life memory, as being at the core of our personal identity. It's what gives us a narrative of our lives that we can share with other people and has meaning to us. But the bad news is that it is not a faithful record. Instead, it is part of the ever-evolving story of who you are. [. . .] Who we are has so much to do with our experiences in the world. So, if you look across cultures in the world, you'll find that people and cultures and ideas are very, very different from one another, and this is because brains, human brains, are born into the world not finished. They drop into the world with the capacity to learn, and from there your experiences in the world tune up your brain circuitry on the fly. And so what that means is that so much of who you are has to do with your surroundings, your influences, the family [. . .] you were born into, your neighborhood, the culture you're born into . . . all of these are such an enormous part of personal identity.

We might have the fantasy that, let's say you were born one thousand years ago: what kind of person would you be? The fact is you wouldn't be you *at all*. You might look a bit like you, depending on the nutrition available, but internally you wouldn't be the same person at all, because, fundamentally, half of us is other people and our environment.[36]

What if You Became a Designer?

Design is about functionality, aesthetics, usability, and the small details. In other words, designers work to create systems that work really well, look great, and can be used by all sorts of people, and they're always sweating those little details.

Imagine some system or process. Maybe it's your morning routine, your computer, or even this book. Can you identify problem areas? What are the problems with the system or process, and what are some ways to fix it? That's the functionality part.

After you're done thinking about that, how does the system look? Is there a visual component? If there is, what looks great about it and what looks terrible? Thinking about this book, is there enough space around text blocks? If you only glanced at it, would you be able to pick out the important parts quickly? That's the aesthetics.

If your grandmother were using the system or process, would she understand it right away? What about your younger siblings? If you were color blind, broke your arm, or couldn't hear, would you still be able to use it well? Is there a large gap between how new users use the system and how people who've used it for a really long time use it? That's usability.

The little details are hard to find sometimes, but when you do, and when you realize why they are there, it makes you smile. Maybe the pockets of your pants are colored, but only on the inside. Maybe there's a menu that is only on the screen if you click on text that would use it. Maybe your hammer is designed to reduce vibrations when you're hitting nails. These details are subtle and can be hidden. Once you start examining your world every day, such details will start to pop out!

ACTIVITY
Improve Something and Prototype It

Look around you. What can you improve? Unless you're in the middle of an untouched forest, there's likely a part of your environment that was built by humans: a chair, a writing utensil, a photo, a sign, a building, a way to interact with something. (And even if you are in an untouched forest, you're likely wearing clothes, and you're definitely holding this book, so you're still able to participate in this activity.) Choose one of the things around you now. Pick it up (if you can). Examine it. What features can you pick out? Why do you think someone chose to make it that way?

Here's the fun part: What can you make better about it? Can you add or take away functionality? Can you make it look more pleasing? Can you make it easier for someone to use? Can you add a small detail that really gives the object or interaction character? Write and draw at least one thing in your journal for each category (function, aesthetics, usability, and small details).

CAROLYN DAVIDSON, DESIGNER OF SWOOSH

Graphic design is a part of the design profession that focuses on how things appear visually. These designers focus on typography, color choice, layout, visual patterns, understandability, and sometimes logos. In 1971, Carolyn Davidson was hired by Nike cofounder Phil Knight, at a rate of $2 per hour, to design a logo for his new company. She was a student at Portland State University at the time studying graphic design. She sketched a set of logos that needed to convey motion and look good on a shoe. The new company chose her sketch of a check mark, the now famous Nike Swoosh. When she finished her work, she made $35 off the logo. Though, in 1983, Nike gave Davidson 500 shares of stock.[37]

What if You Could Teleport Anywhere?

You're in a warehouse. It's big and empty except for a humming metal doorway in the middle of the room. As you walk up to it, you notice the space inside the doorway shimmers like light bouncing off water. You walk through it, and your shoe steps into . . . sand. Looking around, you realize the doorway brought you to a beach! You just teleported from point A to point B way faster than travel would have taken you in a car, plane, bullet train, or any other means of transportation known to humanity. Are teleportation machines possible? If you had one, how would you use it?

> "I would get more time to sleep in because I could factor out the time needed to travel. Patients could get to the hospital far faster than riding in an ambulance. Knowledge could be spread by simply walking through a teleportation device and arriving in a foreign place to share information. People could stay in touch with family that lives far away."
> —Madi, Battle High School, age 15

Teleportation is possible today . . . if you're a photon or atom.[38] Through complicated setups, physicists entangle particles to transfer the identity of one particle to another. Imagine if all you had to do to teleport was change your identity with someone else across the globe.

> "I would travel the world."
> —Kate, Battle High School, age 15

If we could teleport people or things across the world (or even across the universe!), how would society change? Right now, America is largely a car-based society. We probably wouldn't need all of those cars if we were just instantly popping in and out of places. What about war? We'd certainly have an easier time sneaking up on people, but we'd also be caught by surprise all the time too. Would we be less violent if everyone could just appear and disappear? And what about buildings? If we didn't have to walk through doorways, could we have huge buildings of closed spaces we just pop into?

ACTIVITY
One-Way Trip to Anywhere

The universe is a big place with many places to travel. It's easy to ask, "Where would you travel to?" Here's a harder question: if you had a transporter that could take you anywhere in the universe, but you could never come back home, where would you go? What would you need to find to be comfortable never coming back? Write your response in your journal.

"I'd get a spacesuit with a tank of oxygen and teleport to the moon just for fun. Then I'd travel across the world doing extraordinary things by teleporting things/people places in acts of trying to help them."
—Charlie, Battle High School, age 15

"I would never walk anywhere and wait until the last second for everything."
—John Ryan, Battle High School, age 15

What if You Started Your Own Business?

Businesses are all about solving problems. If you're in advertising, you try to figure out how to effectively sell a product or service to a market. If you're doing design work, you focus on functionality and usability for products or services. All businesses are the same in this regard. In business, you figure out how to deliver value to a customer (through products and services).

> "I would name it Stevo Candy. And make people happy."
> —Stephen, Findley Elementary, age 9
>
> "I would make it a snail farm, and snails would be a protected species."
> —Elise, Findley Elementary, age 10

Start by looking around for problems in the world. A problem could be something big: a country with a food shortage. A problem could be small: when people use a can opener made by XYZ Corp., they have a hard time opening their cans. This is where you come in. Find a solution to the problem. Figure out what works and what doesn't work.

Once you have a solution, try it out! The first answer is a step in the right direction, but it takes testing and refinement to make something really valuable. What do customers like and not like about your new product or service?

Sometime in the process you'll need to build a team. Who else can help you with this? What is missing in the current team, and how can you fill it with someone new? Teams take the load off one person and help you see things you couldn't have by yourself.

As you're making the next great thing, remember to check the market. What else is out there that might compete with you? What does that company do well, and what does it do poorly? How is your product or service better? If you offer something worse than what another company offers, can you make it better? Remember the big questions: Will people buy it? How much will they pay for it? Will you make money?

If you started a business, what kind of business would you start?

"I would boss people around."
—Noah, Findley Elementary, age 10

ACTIVITY
Seed an Idea Notebook

Spend a day with a pen and notepad. Every time someone complains about anything, write it down. Every time you think of something that could help someone out, write it down. By the end of the day, you'll probably have a lot written down! Now, skim through your notes and try to think of a few solutions for each problem. It could be something that already exists or something that doesn't yet. When you're done, do any of them catch your interest, and are you able to solve them? Could you sell the solution to people? If so, you might just have a business!

"If I started my own business, I would make it unique, so it would not shut down—for example, a business that sold balls of water or floating cars."
—Dillan, Columbia Elementary, age 11

"I would sell pets, but I would only sell genetically modified squirrels that could do yoga, and I think it could be a hit."
—Edward, Columbia Elementary, age 11

ALEX OSTERWALDER, BUSINESS MODEL GENERATOR

Alex Osterwalder has been challenging the way we make business models. After growing up in Switzerland and scraping his way through business school, he eventually wrote a book called *Business Model Generation*.[39] It explores business models in nine parts: customer segments, value propositions, channels, customer relationships, revenue streams, cost structure, key resources, key activities, and key partnerships.[40] Whoa. That's a lot. Let's break it down.

A business model is a bird's-eye view of how the business works. Customer segments are customers grouped by their similarities.

When someone says "here's my product or service; it solves XYZ problem," he or she is giving you a value proposition. Channels are ways the business connects with customers (for example, social media, storefronts, and advertisements). Just like you have relationships with your friends, parents, and teachers, you can have a relationship with customers. That's customer relation-

> "It would be an encouraging business, so it can help you follow your true dreams."
> —Shannon, Findley Elementary, age 10 ½
>
> "Then I would make money by actually selling stuff instead of just getting an allowance for nothing."
> —Tanay, Findley Elementary, age 9 ½
>
> "I would own a mansion and live on a pile of money for a bed and own five thousand Teslas."
> —Olivia, Findley Elementary, age 10

ships. Revenue streams are the ways in which you make money (your customers buying your products and services). Cost structure is all the ways you lose money (e.g., rent for your store and hiring people). Key resources are the objects you need to keep your business going while you're doing key activities (the activities you need to do to keep your business going). And, everyone needs friends. Key partnerships are the business's friends who also have important resources and do important activities.

An underlying theme of Alex Osterwalder's book, and of him as an interesting person, is focus on rapid testing. (A growing number of startup leaders focus on this.) When you're trying to make a business, you'll fail at something. It's his goal to help you both figure out why you failed and reconstruct your business so it can succeed. That's why he wants schools to help teach students how to fail successfully.[41]

"One word: bankrupt."
—Carter, Columbia Elementary, age 11

"If I started my own business, I would start a business that would help the ocean. We would do beach cleanups, research about all different animals and plants, keep animals safe and wild, and teach others how to help save the ocean."
—Hilary, Columbia Elementary, age 11

"Well, I might, but right now when I'm ten? I don't think It'd work out very well. I could probably manage money all right, but getting people to buy stuff, I'd crack."
—Erin, Columbia Elementary, age 10

"It would be a store that sold smart talking rats as pets."
—Zephyr, Columbia Elementary, age 11

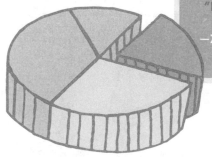

What if Your Parents Couldn't Tell You What Was Right and Wrong?

Imagine a world without any right or wrong—things just are. If people were loud in the library, they wouldn't be doing anything wrong. They would just be loud. People could run at swimming pools, eat all their food except their vegetables, and drive cars before they were old enough. Parents couldn't tell their kids to stop doing something because that something is wrong or bad.

What do you think this world would be like? Would it be crazy all the time? Or do you think people would still be nice to each other? Maybe people wouldn't yell in libraries because they would know that others go there for quietness. Maybe people would eat their vegetables because doing so gives them important nutrients. Maybe people wouldn't drive cars before they were of age because it is dangerous.

If there were no right or wrong, how would you act? Would you do anything you wanted? Would you be nice to strangers?

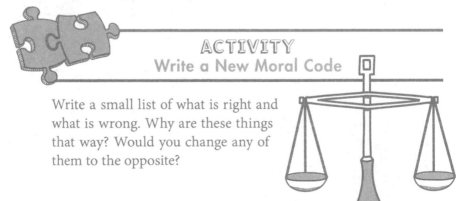

ACTIVITY
Write a New Moral Code

Write a small list of what is right and what is wrong. Why are these things that way? Would you change any of them to the opposite?

What if Society Were Truly Altruistic?

Altruism is the belief and action of acting selflessly. An altruistic act is one in which somebody puts another person first, even if it does not directly benefit the first person. In extreme cases, altruism may result in somebody making a personal sacrifice in order to help another person out. You can think of it as the opposite of selfishness.

> "I think there would be no war, and people wouldn't starve. I think our world would be much more peaceful."
> —Edward, Columbia Elementary, age 11
>
> "No one would be bullied."
> —Olivia, Columbia Elementary, age 10

Altruists believe their behavior can increase cooperation and improve harmony among all people. However, there are skeptics who believe that we, as individual beings, are always acting out of self-interest. For example, they might say the person who is "selflessly" helping others is only doing so because it makes that helper feel good or because he or she appreciates the thanks or recognition.

ACTIVITY
Secret Servant Agent

Become a secret servant agent for a day. Spend one day doing nice things for other people (for example, make your sibling's bed, do the dishes, rake your neighbor's leaves, write a letter telling someone how awesome he or she is, etc.) but do them without anyone seeing you or knowing it was you. Can you be stealthy enough not to get caught? If you can, how do you feel after doing these things that were kind to someone else but gave you nothing in return?

What if only you can determine whether altruism truly exists?

"I'm passionate about the various forms of oppression that plague the modern globalized world. If we worked for communal benefit, would stigmatism exist at all? Would all people be equal in this way? Would people of differing races, genders, orientations, and the like be equal?"
—Jonathan, Battle High School, age 17

"The world would be putting other things/ people in front of something else. The world would be really nice."
—Cooper, Columbia Elementary, age 11

"Moms would be not awesome (which they are already)—they would be super awesome."
—Jake, Columbia Elementary, age 11

"There would be less articles about cyberbullying."
—Tashi, Findley Elementary, age 10

"They will not compete. There will also only be one society because they are all helping each other."
—Ervin, Findley Elementary, age 10

What if You Could Move Objects with Your Brain?

We already do move objects with our brains! Whenever you want to eat another bite of food, you have to reach out for it, pick it up, and put it in your mouth. Your brain has to tell your arm to move in such a way that you can eat. If it didn't, you'd probably starve!

But that's not entirely interesting, is it? So, what if you could move the things you can't move now with your brain? Lifting a car, moving a character in a video game, or playing your favorite instrument—what if you could do these things without touching anything?

> **"That would be AWESOME!"**
> —Jasper, Columbia Elementary, age 11
>
> **"We would be really lazy (no not really lazy—REALLY LAZY)! People will also have an advantage at robbing valuables. Then this power would be taken for granted."**
> —Aidan, Columbia Elementary, age 10

You can! Brain-computer interfaces, or BCI for short, are devices that connect the thoughts in your brain to the objects around you. Your brain has electrical signals in it. That's how thoughts move around and, in some ways, exist. These BCIs use small sensors that sit on your head to read and measure your thoughts.

But how does a BCI know the difference between your brain and your best friend's brain? Think about noses. We each have a nose, and each of our noses is unique. But there are a few properties that keep all noses similar: it's a pointy thing with two nostrils that comes out of a face. Brains are like that too. Each one is unique both in its structure and its thoughts, but

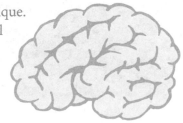

brains are also similar to each other. To help a BCI out, you have to train it a bit. You might do this by telling it you're thinking "up" when you're thinking up and "down" when you're thinking *down*. The BCI is looking for patterns of thoughts, and when it sees them, performs some action.

"I would wash the dishes without touching them."
—Stephen, Findley Elementary, age 9

"If we could move objects with our mind, then there would be no point in machines because you could make things make themselves. Also, people could stop asteroids from hitting the Earth, and people could change the weather by moving the clouds and sun."
—Emily, Findley Elementary, age 10

"The world would be destroyed by criminals."
—Elise, Findley Elementary, age 10

"Then people could move the Earth, and we could visit other solar systems and there would never be bad weather because we could move the clouds, and we would never have to build anything because you can make the materials build themselves."
—Francesca, Findley Elementary, age 10

"I would move my brain."
—Landon, Columbia Elementary, age 10

"I think I would be really lazy because I wouldn't get up to get things."
—Nevaeh, Columbia Elementary, age 11

"I would freak my brother out by moving something and telling him there was a ghost."
—Ceara, Findley Elementary, age 10

"I would win every time in darts, or soccer and other sports."
—Aiden, Columbia Elementary, age 11

After you train a BCI, you can do just about anything you set your mind to! (OK, that was a bad joke.) Brain-computer interfaces extend your mind and its capabilities. You could connect your brain to anything and control that thing with your mind . . . assuming you figured out how to find the patterns of thoughts and have a clear way of turning those into physical actions.

"Then you would be a superhero. And people might take pictures with the superhero."
—Aiyana, Oxford Elementary, age 8

What if You Challenged the Rules?

Society has reasons for having rules, even if those reasons are not always very good. To become a rule, it has to be created, perhaps by people getting together and talking about why a rule is needed. A rule could come from one person in power deciding this is the way things should be. A rule could come out of a culture's practices. A lot of the time, rules can be pretty helpful. They tell you how you should act, and by everyone agreeing to them, you know what to expect.

For example, take the rule "don't steal." By people (or at least most people!) agreeing not to steal, you can feel a little safer when you walk down the street or when you pay for a product or make a trade with someone. If your fellow community members stole all the time, you wouldn't be able to trust them. And if you couldn't trust them, you'd have a hard time building organizations like businesses, schools, hospitals, and city governments.

The people who enforce the rules are generally called authorities. Your teacher is the authority on grades and homework. A police officer is the authority on speeding. Sometimes they only enforce the rules; other times they also create the rules. A parent is a good example of someone who is both the creator and the enforcer.

Now, how do we know rules are good? Well, if the rule stands up to tests and challenges, it's more likely a good rule than a bad rule. But if the rule gets questioned, and the authority can't give a good reason for why the rule is there, then maybe the rule isn't a very good rule to begin with.

For instance, in the United States, there used to be rules that people with darker skin couldn't be in the same places as people with lighter skin were. Blacks couldn't shop, eat, drink, or even go to the bathroom in the same places whites did those things. But people questioned this rule with a one-word question: "Why?" Is a difference in skin color a reason to separate people? Some authorities said yes, but many people kept questioning. Eventually, people realized that this segregation was a bad rule, and they changed both the rule and many of the authorities.

We live in a society with many rules, but not all of them are good ones. Which rules would you get rid of and why?

ACTIVITY
Challenge an Authority

The next time you get bothered by some rule an authority has, ask why the rule exists. If the person can't give good reasons, maybe the rule shouldn't exist. If the person can, maybe you'll learn something about your society. Remember: just because you're challenging something or someone, you can still be an empathetic person!

ALEXIS OHANIAN, REDDIT FOUNDER, ENTREPRENEUR

In his early twenties, Alexis Ohanian built Reddit, now one of the web's top fifty websites. He's challenged authorities by not always asking for permission before he acts. In his eyes, one of the great things about the internet is how much it empowers the people using it.

Every child who grows up with an internet connection and the skills to make the most of it is yet another potential founder, or artist, or

activist, or philanthropist, or . . . I don't know, that's just it: I can look
her in the eyes and tell her that she doesn't need to ask anyone's
permission to go learn about the printing press, or start publishing
her photography, or rally her community to fix a dilapidated play-
ground, or begin working on the next big thing.[42]

What if You Kept Your Ideas to Yourself?

You are just lying in bed, about to fall asleep, when all of a sudden: BAM! POW! SHAZAM! You just had a good idea. No, not good—great. You have a great idea.

Where is your journal? Oh, there it is on the floor. You jot down the idea and go to sleep thinking about how many people will benefit from it (and how you'll make a lot of money in the process).

The sun rises and creeps through your window. It wakes you up. You blink a bit and then quickly jump out of bed to find your journal. There it is. Staring back at you are a few scribbles of brilliance.

What do you do now?

Through breakfast, on your way to school, and during class, all you can think about is your idea. You know it's really great. You want to tell people about it. But what if they steal it? They would get all the credit. They would go off to build the next big thing and be kings and queens of awesomesauce.

But maybe it wouldn't be so bad. It'd be cool to talk to your friends about it. Maybe they could help you. You could all work together to build something great. Or maybe they could share something with you that you would want to work on with them.

When you have that diamond of an idea, you might want to keep it to yourself. But here's the thing: ideas *want* to be shared. Ideas like to mingle with friends. Just like you learn new things from your friends, ideas pick up new pieces too! Like you get smarter, ideas get stronger.

Most people can't execute their ideas all by themselves. Not because they are frightened to, but because those ideas need lots of hands to turn them into a reality. Many idea-building competitions require you to have a partner or team. Judges know teams work better than lone wolves.

So, what will you do the next time you have a great idea?

ACTIVITY
Build Your Dream Team

If you were about to launch an awesome new thing, who would join you? Make a list of your dream team. You can include your friends, other people you know, people you wish you knew, or even fictional people. Write each of their strengths (what they bring to the team) and what their weaknesses are. That way, you'll get an idea of how they might work together.

Part 3
Stuff

Stuff. The world is made of it. In fact, there are more inanimate objects on the planet than there are people. What
would a book about curiosity be without some questions
about all that stuff that makes our world?

Just because inanimate objects are, by definition, life-
less, it doesn't mean you can't find a life's worth of wonder
wondering about these things we share our lives with. For
example, your television, phone, computer, and tablet aren't
alive, but could you imagine your life without them? Part
of the reason that would be tough is because they connect
your life to the lives of others. What if we need stuff to stay
alive? But what if too much of some stuff could also lessen
our living experiences? It's a tough balance, but what if, by
questioning all the stuff in your life, you can get more out of
it—and your life?

What if the questions in this chapter are also the silliest of
the entire book? Questions like "what if broc-
coli tasted like chocolate?" and "what if
your phone had feelings?" certainly
sound funny, but what if there's
also a ton of serious lessons to
learn by asking silly questions
about stuff?

What if Nanobots Joined the Fight against Cancer?

What if our biggest technological developments will happen on a very small scale? Nanobots, once just the subject of science-fiction stories, are about to become a reality.

Nano-whats? A nanobot is a tiny—and we mean tiny!—machine or robot that can work with other nanosize objects with precision. Just how tiny is a nanobot and other nanosize objects? They're anywhere from 0.1 to 1.0 micrometers in size.[1] To give you an idea how tiny a micrometer (or micron) is, there are 25,400 of them in an inch and just under a million of them in a yard (a meter has exactly one million microns in it).[2] If you pull out one of your hairs and stare at it, what you see is still about forty times wider than a single micron. A nanobot is so tiny, it could dig a hole through the diameter of a single hair and use it as a tube slide for fun.[3]

That is, if nanobots were designed to have fun. Currently, scientists are planning on giving the first nanobots they develop a lot of work to do. Considering that even red blood cells are over six times bigger than a micron[4], nanobots are ideal workers to help doctors treat patients and help humanity become healthier.

Today, cancer patients are treated with surgery or powerful drugs that can kill cancer cells, but they also damage healthy, noncancerous cells. This can be painful and as damaging as the cancer they're trying to treat. By injecting nanobots into a patient, doctors will be able to destroy only the cancer cells. Eventually, these nanobots could be designed to be scouts in addition to soldiers. What if your next visit to the doctor involved getting an injection of nanobots that would explore your body in search of diseases and eliminate them before they became deadly?[5]

OMID FAROKHZAD, PHYSICIAN SCIENTIST

Nanoparticles are small but powerful. Dr. Omid Farokhzad has created a few companies around different nanotech innovations he has helped pioneer. The nanoparticles in one of his projects do three things to attack cancer cells. First, the nanoparticle carries a cancer-fighting drug with it. Second, the nanoparticle's surface is water-like. That helps it sneak through someone's body without being detected and destroyed by an immune system. Third, the nanoparticle also has homing molecules that help it recognize and target cancer cells. When the nanoparticle collides with a cancer cell, it tricks the cell into letting it inside where the nanoparticle starts releasing its drugs.

Fighting cancer is a whole lot easier when you're fighting only the bad cells—and that's what you can do with these nanoparticles. There's a long way to go before average patients can start buying these targeted treatments, but research has grown exponentially. One day we'll take a pill that can help the immune system step up a notch and give us medicine right when and where we need it![6]

What if You Had a Box That Could Make Anything?

A box. That can make anything. *Anything*. Pretty cool, right?

Imagine there is a box in front of you. Maybe it is on a table. Maybe it is on the floor. Maybe it is just floating in the air. Imagine it as an entirely black box. There are no markings on the outside, but there is a lid. If this box could make anything tangible (meaning you can touch it), what would you have it make?

Would you have it make money, so you could buy things? Would you have it make a new friend to hang out with? Would you have it make you the tastiest food you have ever eaten?

These boxes already exist . . . kind of. The boxes are called 3D printers. These printers produce tangible objects. For instance, if you dropped your cup and it shattered, you could just print a new one. If you wanted a new part for your bicycle, you could just print it. If your friend came up with a really cool new toy, she could send the drawing to you and you could print it out! You see, all the information the box needs is digital, so it can move as easily as an email or text message. This works because someone draws up some object (like your cup or the new toy) on the computer. Then, the computer tells the printer how to print the object. That's it!

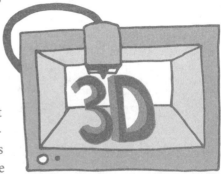

Right now, printers that most people have can only print plastic. But scientists, machinists, hobbyists, and tinkerers are working every day to make better and better printers that use other materials. Some of these are printing concrete—you could print a new house! Some are printing food—you could print that tastiest meal! Some are printing organs. Organs! What if one day you got into a car accident and needed a new lung? Right now you'd have to wait on a transplant list. But in the future, the hospital could just print you a new lung in a few hours.

Printers are coming a long way from just putting images on paper. Soon they'll print anything you can imagine.

TECHNICAL CORNER
How 3D Printing Works

Normal printers work by putting a layer of ink on paper. Instead of just one layer, 3D printers put many layers down to build up a shape. Look around you and find an object. Now, imagine you were to cut it into really, really, really thin slices. If you were printing that object with a 3D printer, it would print each slice/layer, one on top of the next, till the object was whole. They usually use plastic, but as you now know, 3D printers are starting to use all kinds of materials!

ALEX MADINGER, DESIGNER, INVENTOR, MECHANICAL ENGINEER

Alex Madinger has been interested in building things since he was young. In college, he was able to start playing with 3D printers, and he was hooked. Since then, he's been working on human prosthetics (artificial limbs). Often if you lose a limb, you'll get a generic prosthetic. But look at the people around you. Does everyone have the exact same arms and legs? Noooooooope. So, wouldn't it be nice if there could be variety in prosthetics too?

Madinger's methods, like those of other 3D printing inventors, rely on a high level of customization and personal tuning. 3D printing methods allow inventors like Madinger to work more quickly because they can easily print and test their designs.

If you have had an idea of something cool to make—and you've drawn it out on a piece of paper, you might not know [how it all works]. But you have a cool idea. Maybe someone has made it. Maybe someone is working on it. You can look online. [Either way,] instead of going to a big company to spend a lot of money to try to make your thing, you can use 3D printing.[7]

What if Your Phone Always Knew Where You Were?

What if you were never really alone? What if there was some-thing—nonhuman—that always knew where you were?

If you have a cell phone, it's probably always close by you. Maybe it hangs out in your pocket or backpack. What if your phone knew where you were and knew where it was? What if everyone's phone was like that?

In some ways, this could be (and is!) really neat. You can have alerts that only come up based on your geolocation (*geo*—"world," *geolocation*—"world location"). If one of your favorite bands was playing a show in your town, your phone could say, "Hey! You! Go to this!" Or your local ice cream shop could offer a deal to whom-ever was within a few blocks of it.

In other ways, this can be (and is!) really terrible. Everything except for the physical laws that govern the universe can be hacked. That means a hacker, government, company, par-ent, brother, or sister could access your information and then know what you're doing and where you're doing it.

Here's a bonus "what if": what if your phone could pre-dict where you go next? They don't call them "smart" phones for nothing. The more data our computers (and your phone is really more computer than phone now) collect about us—what we search, what we buy, what we watch, where we go, etc.—the better they're becoming at predicting what we'll do next.

> "First of all, [phones] already do. But because of this, it creates a major violation of our privacy because the fact that someone could always know where I'm at frankly terrifies me."
> —Dillon, Battle High School, age 16

"Wait. How does my phone know where I'm going to be? It doesn't have a brain." We hear you. You're right. Your phone doesn't have a brain, but it has something like a brain. It's able to collect data on you: what you like to do and when, where you go for different things, and with whom you hang out. Think about it. Every time you use your phone, you're giving it a little bit of information about what kind of person you are. Via data mining, it can look through all of those pieces of information, find patterns, and then make predictions based on your patterns. For instance, after noticing you driving to school at around the same time every day or going out to your favorite place to eat every Friday, your phone might start prompting you with the amount of time it will take to get to school or letting you know that that restaurant is getting crowded (because your phone is talking to other phones, which know what their owners are doing!). It's smart and a little frightening.

"It better find me then when I lose it, stupid phone."
—Ben, Battle High School, age 17

ACTIVITY
Map Your Location

Print out a map of your local area (make sure it includes where you are most of the time). For a week, mark your location on your map every hour with a dot and a number. The first place you are: a dot and a 1. The second: a dot and a 2. The third: a dot and a 3. You get the idea.

Keep doing this on and on (it's OK if you miss a few). After a week, you should have a map filled with dots and numbers. Place a piece of tracing paper over your map and connect the dots with straight lines. Don't worry about copying the dots or the numbers, just connect them on the tracing paper. When you're done, you'll have a new piece of art that is unique to you and your week.

If you want to go a little further, you could create other pieces of art based on your map. Or you could find a friend with this book, and you two could compare your location shapes.

AMBER CASE, CYBORG ANTHROPOLOGIST, FORMER DIRECTOR, ESRI R&D CENTER

Amber Case grew up excited about people and the technologies we use. She eventually focused her excitement on location-based technologies because they could tie information on the web to places in the real world. You could play games and leave messages for friends. Or you could help coordinate airplane flight plans and crowds at major events. You know, whichever was important to you.

There are all these planes out there, and trains, and ships, and people, and if they don't know where they are, they could be in serious trouble. So, a ship needs to know where it is in the ocean. Early location-based technology, like the compass, allows people to not sail into really rough seas, or get really lost and off track. It could help us explore new worlds. Now [location-based technology] makes sure your shipments arrive on time and that they aren't lost in a big storm.[8]

TECHNICAL CORNER
GPS

A global positioning system (GPS) is a collection of satellites and receiving devices that together help us find out where we are on Earth. It's important because it helps ships navigate open water, planes navigate the skies, and farm equipment steer itself, and it can also help you find your way in a busy city.

There are a handful of different ways to find your spot on Earth. GPS is one of those ways. Here's how it works: Your phone has a receiver in it that picks up signals from the GPS satellites. There are over twenty-five satellites that circle the Earth. They are all synchronized with each other, meaning they all have the same time on their internal clocks. Since it takes time for the signal to travel from space all the way down to your phone, and the satellites are in different places, each signal gets to your phone at a slightly different time. Your phone then calculates the differences between the signals and uses fancy mathematics to figure out where you are.[9]

What if Robots Looked Like People or Animals?

Think about a pet you know well. It runs around. It plays. It loves you. You've known it for a long time. What if one day you learned that this pet is actually a robot? How does this change your affection toward it? Would you love the animal just the same or be uncaring toward it because its brain is a computer?

What if you found out your best friend was a robot? How would that change your relationship with him or her? Would you still be kind? Or would you be more abrasive, as you might be to a phone, computer, or printer?

Robotics technology is very far along. Having developed faces that are almost human, and personalities that can be as complex as a kindergartner's, we're on the verge of more and more robots entering our lives.[10] In some ways, this is already happening, with Siri on iPhone and Google Now. Our devices are coming alive, and soon they'll have faces too.

There's a lot more we'll have to figure out in the coming years. If robots become as complex and mentally alive as humans, will they need rights similar to humans? If they need to get repaired at a repair shop, should they be able to get a license and drive themselves? If they are affected by government just like humans are, should robots be able to vote like we can? If a robot wants to run for a government office, should we let it? What if you developed a crush on a robot?! How do you think robots will change our future, and how will we change their future?

What if, instead of taking real animals from their homes in the wild, zoos used robotic, animatronic animals? How would you feel about going to a zoo of robotic animals rather than actual animals?

ACTIVITY
Surprise, I'm a Robot

One day your brother, sister, or good friend sits you down to tell you something serious, that he or she is not a human but a robot. How would you react?

Write a play or a screenplay (like a television show) that shows how you would react. You can choose whether or not you're a character in the play. Make sure to write some conversation, a few stage directions (where and when people should enter and exit the scene), and a description of the scene too.

SHERRY TURKLE, PhD AND
ROBO-RELATIONSHIP CRITIC

Dr. Sherry Turkle studies the relationships between humans and computers (including robots). She has set up experiments and observations with both kids and adults playing with robots. According to Turkle and others, we have a tendency to want to be with robots, especially as they can fulfill our needs more and more. Humans are vulnerable. We're able to be hurt and able to be loved. If a robot can protect us from our fears of loneliness and of being hurt, we might just start wanting robotic relationships instead of messy human ones. And Turkle's research backs that up. She's found that we have a hard time distancing ourselves from robots when they give positive feedback (for instance, when robots light up and make cute beeping noises).[11]

What if You Had No Possessions?

If you could keep only ten things, of all your possessions, what would they be? What if you could keep only five things? Which would be your top three? What would be the one thing you would keep?

Nearly everywhere we look, there's another advertisement telling us the next great thing we "need" to make our lives better, easier, or both. But what if the secret to happiness was to reduce rather than reload? From architecture to fashion, artwork, design, and, now, lifestyle design, minimalism has been an attitude many have adopted. Is it even possible in today's consumer society? Would it work for you? It's tough to find out, because it requires a rather steep commitment (the first step is getting rid of all of your stuff!). What if you had to live with fewer things? Could you still be happy? Imagine going through an entire day with nothing other than the clothes you were wearing. Where would you go, what would you do, who would you see to fill your day and make you happy?

ACTIVITY
Your Top Ten Possessions

Choose a room in your house and imagine it is empty (or, if you're really adventurous, and with the permission of the adults you live with, actually empty it out). Choose only ten items to put in it. Take one away. How many can you take away before you lose your ability to use the room for its intended or required purpose?

"I wouldn't have a home."
—Luke, Columbia Elementary, age 11

"Then nobody would be greedy."
—Dillan, Columbia Elementary, age 11

"Then would I be alive?
I possess myself."
—Bailey, Columbia Elementary, age 11

"It would be weird if there were no possessions. We would have to measure with our fingers instead of a ruler, and we would have to use sticks as forks."
—Philippa, Oxford Elementary, age 9

"I wouldn't have to worry about losing anything because if I had no possessions I wouldn't care if I lost them."
—Kelly, Findley Elementary, age 10

What if Nanobots Turned the World into a Glob of Gray Goo?

Whether they're killing cancer or cleaning up pollution[12], nanobots are effective because of how they work together. Nanobots aren't lone wolves; they're a swarm. But just like any powerful technology, whether they're used for good or bad is, ultimately, up to humans to determine.

Just as a swarm of nanobots could be used to eat away harmful pollution molecules, they could also destroy the molecules that make up buildings—or you. There is a fear that swarms of nanobots could become the deadliest weapons of the future.[13]

There's also a fear of gray goo. Gray goo is the label for a scenario "in which a swarm of millions of rapidly self-replicating microscopic robots, in a ravenous quest for fuel, would consume the entire biosphere until nothing remained but an immense, sludge-like robotic mass."[14]

Take this scenario on how our world could turn from a lush planet of people, animals, and vegetation into a glob of goo:

> Take a relatively plausible present and future environmental problem/solution—cleaning a nature habitat after an oil spill. In this scenario, billions of nanobots are deployed to consume the toxic oil and convert it into less harmful substances. But a programming error directs the nanobots to devour all carbon-based objects, not just the oily hydrocarbons. These nanobots destroy everything, and in the process, replicate themselves. Within days—or hours—planet Earth is turned into "goo."[15]

What if Broccoli Tasted like Chocolate?

If broccoli tasted like chocolate, would we all be incredibly healthy or would we lose our appreciation for what it means to be healthy?

> "If broccoli tasted like chocolate, I would eat a lot."
> —Avery, Findley Elementary, age 10
>
> "It will make every kid eat healthy, right? And it will be ssssssooooo yummy."
> —Shannon, Findley Elementary, age 10 ½

Wondering about this raises a bigger question: Does this mean being and doing good isn't supposed to feel good, at least not initially? What if the better feelings we get are those we earn? For example, the feeling you get later on in life as a healthy individual from eating more broccoli than chocolate is certainly a better feeling than the quick flash of deliciousness on your tongue while munching on chocolate . . . right?

Sound farfetched? Consider this: What if there were a berry that, when eaten, would temporarily change how your taste buds taste? For example, after eating this berry, Tabasco sauce (that spicy hot sauce) would taste like doughnut glaze. Bitter things would taste temporarily sweet.[16]

ACTIVITY
Do the Yucky!

Make a quick list of ten things you hate doing—but know you should—like cleaning your room, doing your homework, being nice to your brother or sister, or eating your broccoli. Now, see how many of those things you can do today! Write them down once you're done.

How many did you do?

1–3: Come on! You can do better.

4–7: Not bad!

8–10: You just might be the most awesome person on the planet!

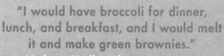

"I would have broccoli for dinner, lunch, and breakfast, and I would melt it and make green brownies."
—Vedant, Findley Elementary, age 9

"I would probably eat a lot more broccoli, but beans are vegetables, and cocoa beans are beans, and cocoa beans are used to make chocolate, so chocolate is a vegetable anyway."
—Schuyler, Columbia Elementary, age 11

"It would be horrible because broccoli tastes so much better than chocolate."
—Isaac, Oxford Elementary, age 9

BITTER

SOUR

SALTY

SWEET

TECHNICAL CORNER
Taste

On our tongues, we have different types of taste receptors. We know that there are at least five different types of receptors: sweet, sour, salty, bitter, and savory. Sweet receptors tell you that candy tastes sugary. Sour lets you know that's a lemon slice in your mouth and not an orange slice. Salty tells you that you've used too much of that seasoning on your eggs. Bitter is used for many things, but part of its importance is letting you know when foods have expired or are downright bad for you. Savory is part of meat's flavor, so you could also think about it as your tongue's bacon receptor. These five types of receptors are found all over the tongue, but the sides of your tongue are a bit more sensitive. All of these receptors work with your nose to let your brain know that the food you're eating is really tasty (or that you shouldn't eat it)![17]

"If broccoli tasted like chocolate, more children would like broccoli, but it would still be as healthy as it is now. Also, what would chocolate taste like?"
—Amy, Findley Elementary, age 9

"Everyone would eat it, we would have a broccoli shortage, and everyone would have to grow their own broccoli."
—Jeremy, Findley Elementary, age 10

"Then I would ask what does chocolate taste like, broccoli?"
—Tashi, Findley Elementary, age 10

"If broccoli tasted like chocolate, everybody would love broccoli. Every farmer would plant/eat chocolate broccoli seeds. It would be fun."
—Philippa, Oxford Elementary, age 9

What if Solipsism Were Correct?

What if the only reality was the one in your mind? That's the basic idea behind solipsism.[18] Since it's impossible to know what is in someone else's mind, a solipsist takes the perspective that his or her understanding of the world is the only one.

Sure, this might be seen as a very selfish and limited perspective, but how can you truly tell what is in someone else's mind? Or that anything is in their mind at all? What if

> "What if this was a dream? What if you woke up to find yourself in a different form? It would be a nightmare to wake up and what you thought was your life is gone, your family, your friends, everything is gone."
> —Hilary, Columbia Elementary, age 11

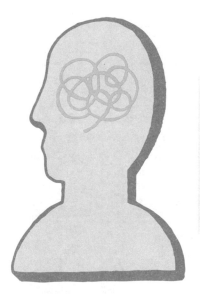

> "Then all your friends would be a dream? I refuse to believe that. If solipsism was correct, all the bad in the world would not even really exist—that would be good—but the flickers of goodness would be gone as well, not so good."
> —Erin, Columbia Elementary, age 11

everything you see and hear others do isn't them doing it; rather, it's just your brain telling you they're doing it?

Mind blown? Well, that's up to you.

"The Matrix, for realsies."
—Jake, Columbia Elementary, age 11

"I would take power over that and know that whatever happened was my imagination and do AWESOME things."
—Schuyler, Columbia Elementary, age 11

"We could actually be aliens in our teacher's mind."
—Olivia, Columbia Elementary, age 10

"If solipsism was correct, I would be in a constant fantasy. Who I thought was my best friend may be merely a tree. If solipsism was correct, the world may constantly be changing. We wouldn't be able to keep a stable leader, which would lead to a large amount of conflict. But it may help people be more creative and less worried about what other people think. But the most important thing to me is that people would feel unpopular or feel like they don't fit in. 'Cause to them they are awesome no matter what."
—Maximum, Columbia Elementary, age 11

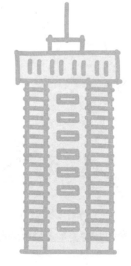

What if Awesome Didn't Exist?

Does awesome exist? Do we create it? Is there any way we can control it?

Regardless, everyone seems to want as much awesome as we can get.

After all, a world without awesome isn't a world in which you'd want to live, right?

> "The word *awesome* is meaning to cause awe; if we didn't have wonder or awe, humans wouldn't be impressed with anything. The creativity of the world would decrease because they find nothing awesome enough to express ourselves with."
> —Kate, Battle High School, age 15

What if it were up to you to seek and create awesome wherever you are, wherever you go, and whatever you do, or it would disappear? Could you do it?

How would your life change? How would your community change? How would the world change if we created and shared the awesome we find all around us with others?

What if every day were an awesome day?

Believe it or not, for everyone who lived before the end of the sixteenth century, awesome didn't exist. At least, the English word for it didn't exist until around the 1590s.[19] And if people from way back then were to time travel to today, they'd

> "Then I wouldn't either."
> —Ben, Battle High School, age 17

discover the meaning of awesome has changed a bit with time. According to the *Online Etymology Dictionary*, the first definition of *awesome* was "profoundly reverential." Then, about eighty years later, its meaning was downgraded a bit to "inspiring awe." By 1961, *awesome* only meant "impressive, very good." What's up with that? It wasn't until the 1980s, though, that the word became trendy.[20]

What if you could determine the next definition for this awesome word? How would you define what's awesome?

HARVEY MILK: CIVIL, HUMAN, AND GAY RIGHTS ACTIVIST-POLITICIAN

Awesome means different things to different people. For Harvey Milk, awesome didn't exist yet. He wanted the gay community to gain a voice in politics. That would be awesome.

In the 1960s, Milk started to become more involved in politics, leading to his eventual appointment to San Francisco's Board of Permit Appeals. Harvey Milk was the first openly gay city commissioner in the United States.[21] In 1977, Milk was elected to the San Francisco City-County Supervisor position where he helped protect "gay rights [, . . .] establish day care centers for working mothers, the conversion of military facilities in the city to low-cost housing, reform of the tax code to attract industry to deserted warehouses and factories, and other issues."[22]

"Another word will replace its current meaning and the way it is used."
—Leslie, Battle High School, age 16

"I would invent it using my pet velociraptor and borrowing a knight's armor from a local museum."
—Charlie, Battle High School, age 15

"Then what would everything be?"
—Jonathan, Battle High School, age 17

Harvey Milk and the mayor were assassinated by Dan White on November 27, 1978. That night thousands of supporters held a candlelight vigil in Milk's honor. "Milk Day" was created in 2009 as a California holiday in tribute to Harvey Milk.[23] He lived in a time with less acceptance of the gay community, and inspired others to come out, share their story, and shift public opinion.

What if You Could Get into a Machine That Created Any Experience You Wanted?

Imagine one day you get an offer from a mysterious stranger. She says that she can plug you into a machine that will create any experience you want. In the machine, you can do anything you can imagine. Your body will be taken care of by the machine. It will feed you and keep you alive, but while you are in it, you won't feel like you are hooked up. You'll be alone in the new virtual world but can choose to do anything. You could be president. You could be an explorer. You could live in a world where it rains every day. You would leave behind your family and friends. But you could always imagine a new family and new friends.

Would you want that? Would you miss your real family and friends? Would you get lonely with virtual friends? Would you feel like you are in a video game, or would you feel just the same as you do now? How would you change your world? What experiences would you want? If you would feel the same, how do you know you're not in a machine like this already? Would you ever leave the machine?[24]

ACTIVITY
Short Story

Write a short story in your journal about how you would respond to the mysterious stranger. Think about it before you start writing. Would you let her plug you in? What experiences would you want to have? Would you miss your family and friends?

TECHNICAL CORNER
Virtual Reality

Virtual reality (VR) is called *virtual* because it is an almost-real thing. These realities can be anything from a hyperrealistic world to an entirely made-up one that looks nothing like what you see every day. Video games are all virtual realities: a small set of objects that interact based on that particular universe's rules.

The really interesting realities are likely still to come. Over the last few years, a lot of traction has been put behind VR systems, starting with the development of the Oculus Rift. One of the problems is that VR systems can feel a little clunky. Your eyes are experiencing one thing while the rest of your body is just sitting still. It can be kind of like when you read in the car: part of you feels like it is moving, and the other part feels as though it isn't. Over time, we'll see even more sensory immersion with new interactive devices.

PALMER LUCKEY, OCULUS RIFT CREATOR

Humans throughout time have continually created imaginary worlds in their heads. If you're sitting around wondering what it might be like to fly a spaceship or be a doctor, you're imagining a fake world where you are that spaceship pilot or doctor. For almost as long as people have been using computers, they have also imagined and eventually even created simulated worlds they can "virtually" step into. Video games and 3D graphics were the beginning, but virtual reality (VR) was a goal.

Early virtual reality systems have been around since 1962.[25] This unique industry of creating virtual experiences grew like a balloon until, like balloons, it popped. The technology that the early innovators used was not good enough at tricking the brain into thinking it was indeed in a virtual world. And so excitement died down. VR headsets became the playthings of just a few research labs until one day 18-year-old Palmer Luckey created the first prototype of the Oculus Rift in 2011.[26]

Luckey was a curious kid. He did not understand why technology had not delivered more immersive, affordable experiences. So, he worked and saved his money, beginning to buy up the best virtual reality tech out there at the time. Still, the experience was lacking. Armed with curiosity, Luckey began building his own VR headset.

The Oculus Rift is a headset that you can wear. It has two screens and uses what is called stereographic images to put the wearer in a virtual world. *Stereo* is a stand-in for "two," *graphic* for "images." Two images are shown with a little distance between them. Each eye sees a separate image, and just like your eyes already work, your brain stitches the images together into a three-dimensional perspective of a virtual world. It wasn't the stereographic images that made the Rift exciting; it was that it created an experience so good, human brains had a hard time knowing they were in a virtual world.

Luckey's project started with a little curiosity. It continued with a dose of action—and money. Facebook eventually bought the company for $2 billion.[27] So don't let anyone tell you that questions aren't worth anything.

What if Everything Were Only Five Minutes Old?

You've been sitting and reading this book for more than five minutes. You remember eating breakfast this morning. You remember walking outside yesterday. You remember your birthday last year.

How do you know all of that happened? Do you *really* know?

You've watched movies before, maybe even played video games. What if, somehow, you were connected to a machine that played a movie in your brain? Or what if that machine let you interact with things as though you were in a video game—all the while your body is sitting still (like the experience machine we what-iffed about earlier)?

What if, five minutes ago, you woke up out of nothingness but with all the memories of your life to that point? One way you could test if things existed before would be to ask someone if he or she had lived for more than five minutes. But what if everything—people, objects, ideas—all came into existence at the same time, but with memories of a longer past, only five minutes ago?

How is this scenario different from the Big Bang? What happened before the Big Bang? What if there was a whole universe that—all of a sudden—disappeared, and this universe took its place? What would be different in that scenario? How can you tell that the past exists beyond any point?[28]

ACTIVITY
Write Your Five Minutes

Find a timer and set it for five minutes. When it starts ticking, either write in your journal or record yourself speaking. Keep going until the timer runs out. Don't worry about being right or being wrong or being anything. Just keep going and going. A stream of consciousness is when you write or talk as fast as you think. There's no time to edit what you're writing or saying. Your consciousness is streaming out of your brain. (If you're embarrassed about anything when you're done, you can throw it away. But while the timer is going, don't think about editing.)

What if Everything Could Communicate?

Do you ever wish that when you woke up, your breakfast was ready, your shower was warm, and your favorite music was playing? What if everything were aware of everything else? Imagine that your house watched you wake up. If it knew when you woke up, it could start playing your favorite music. If you shower in the morning, it could prepare your shower by the time you walked from your bed into it. It could prepare your breakfast. And—the best part—it could save you time, so you didn't have to wake up a second before you needed to.

Imagine you get to school and your teacher doesn't have to take attendance, because the room knows you're there (maybe because of a chip in your phone, in your shoe, or in your body). After your teacher gave a new lesson, your desk or table could show you how that lesson is connected to other things you're interested in. For example, if your teacher was talking about mathematics, and you are really interested in whales, your desk or table could show how mathematicians calculate whale migration.

What would you connect? What would you never want connected?

ACTIVITY
Map the Connections

Look around the space you're in right now. Write down a handful of different objects that you see. Then, connect a few by drawing a line and writing about how they could be connected in the future. Your imagination is your limit!

What if Your Clothes Were Smarter?

When you buy clothes, what do you have to do? Try each piece on. Try different colors together. Try different styles. Basically, you have to test a bunch of different things to see what fits and what works well together.

People come in all different shapes, sizes, and styles. Why do our clothes have only a few available sizes? We have large, but not Susie-large or Bob-large. And everyone changes a bit even throughout one year. In summer, people may be more active and lose a few pounds. In winter, we're often less active and have many feasts—leading to us packing on a few pounds. These fluctuations are natural, but our clothes don't move with us.

What if our clothes were made out of new materials that worked with our lives better? Researchers are making clothing out of bacteria, allowing us to create more customized clothing with less waste (and possibly even have your clothes deliver nutrients to your skin!).[29] What if you didn't have to try on different colors and sizes? What if your clothes showed you where Wi-Fi was or knew your heart rate?[30] What if your clothes hardened when you bumped into something, which would protect you from accidents or punches?[31] What if your clothes got smarter?

ACTIVITY
Fashion Designer of Future Materials

Fashion designers of the future will have many more materials to choose from than we do today. But that doesn't mean we can't start thinking about new types of clothing in the present. Use the following inspiration list to design and draw new types of clothing you want to see in the future.

- Something that is made of plants
- Something that can talk to your phone or computer
- Something that can change colors
- Something that can change shape
- Something that can make noise
- Something that can broadcast signals
- Something that can receive signals
- Something that has multiple functions
- Something that changes when the weather changes

What if Your Phone Had Feelings?

What if your phone could understand and remember everything you spoke into or wrote on it?

If the lines between human and artificial intelligence are about to blur as never before, what does this mean for how we interact with machines? It's one thing to have your phone angry with you, but what if your computer-driven car hates your guts? Better look out!

> "If my phone had feelings, it would most likely complain all the time about me using it too much and repeatedly hitting the screen."
> —Veronica, Battle High School, age 17

Understanding how to read sentences or suggest restaurants you might like is one thing. But if your phone can read philosophical and legal documents, how long do you think it'll take before it wants to be able to vote and be respected like a human? How long will it take for your phone to want you to become a vegetarian because it cares for animals and doesn't want to see them on your plate?

What emotions, morals, and interactions will machines develop? Will they be in line with our own or something foreign?

> "I would apologize for all the times I yelled at it when I lost at a game."
> —Charlie, Battle High School, age 15

Could *machine* become its very own culture?

Or what if machines never develop feelings, yet how we treat them reinforces and reflects the way we treat other people?

What if it's time to tell your phone how much you appreciate him or her?

ACTIVITY
Create a Comic Strip

In your journal, make a comic strip about a phone with emotions (maybe even an emotional phone!). You can draw it or even cut images out of magazines. But try to make it funny, since comic strips are usually comedies.

"It would tell me to call my mother more and be sad if I got into an argument over the phone."
—Jonathan, Battle High School, age 17

"I'd feel bad for cracking every single phone I've ever had."
—John Ryan, Battle High School, age 15

What if a Picture Were Worth One Thousand Words?

You might have heard that expression before: a picture is worth one thousand words. But what does it mean?

Imagine you're telling your friend about a day you spent at the local museum. There, you saw this really great piece of digital art: an animation on a screen. If you're trying to describe the piece to your friend, how would you do it?

You first might try to tell him or her exactly what you saw. "Well, there was this line over here, and some shapes on this side, and colors all over the place." The more and more you talk, the closer you're getting to one thousand words. Maybe you skip a few details here and there, but if you do that, you won't be describing the whole picture.

Even after you've told all you can about the visual components of the art, there is still more to tell! Every human creation is sort of floating in a larger cultural story and the personal story of the artist. So, you might go on to say that the art you saw at the museum was part of an artistic movement. "During this time, artists from all around were using this technique," you might say, adding, "but this artist also included certain elements from her life." You're adding a lot of words, aren't you?

You could go on by sharing why the museum chose to add this piece to its collection, why you enjoyed the art, or even what other observers' responses were to it.

Or you could just show your friend a picture of the art.

ACTIVITY
One Thousand Words or Bust

Give yourself five minutes to find a picture. Put the picture up on a screen where you can see it or print it out. Now, get out your journal and start writing a description of the picture. How many words was it before your first long pause? Keep writing until you get to one thousand words (you might want to keep a running total of your word count every paragraph). Was it easy or hard to write that much about a single photo? What else did you learn about the experience?

What if Computers Were Conscious?

Computers follow a bunch of instructions. Turn on. Open the browser. Turn up the volume. They usually do what humans tell them to do. But what if they thought for themselves? What if computers were conscious like we are?

There are many stories about conscious computers and artificially intelligent machines (AI). Sometimes the computers take over the world because the humans are not needed anymore. Other times, the two live side by side. If we're living together with computers and they act similarly to humans, we'd need to change many of our systems. Would the computers go to school like we do? How would they be handled in court?

How would you know when computers become conscious? Would you measure it with medical equipment? How would you hook up the equipment? Would you ask the computer questions? How would you be able to tell if it was *really* thinking or just following a complex rule book?

Do you think computers ever will be conscious? What would they think about? How would you interact with one? Would it argue with you? Do you think its mind would be like yours or entirely different? What does it say about our minds if computers are able to think too? Should we treat computers differently just because their brains are different from ours? If computers can think, can they also feel emotion?

ACTIVITY
Watch a Science-Fiction Movie about AI

There are lots of science fiction movies about artificial intelligence (*WALL-E* is a fun one). Watch one and think about how AI is portrayed. Is the intelligence good or bad? How does it think? From the outside, would you be able to tell who is a robot and who is not?

TECHNICAL CORNER
Artificial Intelligence

There's been a lot of progress in creating smart machines that solve specific problems; we now have ones that produce Google's search results, win chess, and interpret our language in the way we speak. But so far, we haven't figured out exactly how to make a machine that can think as broadly as humans do. Computer scientists, philosophers, and engineers have a few different directions they are investigating.

One of those ways is by looking into our own brains. Since we know we think, the human brain would be a good model that we could break down and figure out how to reconstruct in a computer.

Another way is by having computers get better at symbol processing. You have thoughts, and your thoughts have symbols attached to them. For instance, when you're reading, you're looking at the letters and words on a page. You either know or are learning how to move those symbols around into other working symbols. You know that thinking is something you actively do, but a thought is an object. We might be able to make an AI just by strengthening its ability to manipulate symbols.[32]

Yet another way to build artificial intelligence would be to create a system or network of connections. Just like your brain has different sections that perform different functions, a network can do the same. For instance, if a computer is looking at a book and trying to figure out what the words say, it might have one small network looking at the shape of the letters, another network looking at the shape of the whole word, another one determining the meaning of one word, and yet another network determining the meaning of the words together. Each of these smaller networks can work together in a larger network to create an intelligence.[33] Which way is right? We don't quite know yet. All of them show some promise. It'll probably take some combination to create a truly thinking machine.

JOHN SEARLE, PHILOSOPHER

John Searle published a paper in 1980 that included the Chinese Room Argument.[34] This thought experiment has a man, who doesn't know Chinese, in a room with two slots in the wall. Through one slot arrive Chinese symbols. When they come in, the man looks up what to do with them in a very large book. The book doesn't tell him the meaning of the symbols, but it tells him what symbols to pass through the other slot.

Outside of the room is a woman who speaks Chinese. She writes down Chinese symbols and passes them through the first slot. Out of the second slot, she sees new symbols from the room. From her perspective, it seems like she's talking to another Chinese speaker. But from the man's perspective, he's just passing symbols out of the room based on what the book tells him to do. He never knows that the Chinese speaker is outside of the room nor does he even know that the symbols are Chinese. John Searle said that this is how computers work: based on certain inputs, they give certain outputs. Computers never understand what they are doing; therefore, artificial intelligence will never be truly intelligent.

This thought experiment is one of the most popular in philosophy and has sparked debate among philosophers, neuroscientists, and AI researchers. What do you think? Do you think Searle is right, or can you poke holes in his argument like others have?

What if Walls Could Talk?

We've been in many buildings in our lives: our house, our friends' houses, school, the doctor's office, the library, the grocery store. What if we could listen to what the walls have seen?

It's definitely a weird thought. If your friends saw you talking to a wall, they might think you need to see a doctor. Think about these buildings. They stand up to all sorts of weather. Snow, rain, hail, heat—all try to take a little piece out of the building. And what about inside? Workers come and go. If it's a family-run business, generation after generation fill the halls. If it's a school, the walls watch small children become young adults.

> "I would ask the wall what the answer to my homework is."
> —Stephen, Findley Elementary, age 9

What about major historical events? Older buildings have seen women enter the workforce, and racial desegregation. Think about how much technology has changed too! From paper and quill pens, to typewriters, to bulky computers, to laptops, to phones and tablets, to speech and gesture technologies—some buildings have seen this entire evolution. Some industrial buildings have turned into homes because the devices we use changed, in turn changing how we use our buildings.

> "They would tell us stuff they heard one thousand years ago."
> —Adrian, Oxford Elementary, age 8

> "That would be really scary."
> —Clare, Findley Elementary, age 9

> "If walls could talk, could they eat? If they could eat, what would they eat? Would they have mouths?"
> —Ceara, Findley Elementary, age 10

ACTIVITY
Listen to the Walls

Choose a building. Any building. It could be your house. It could be your school. It could be that one you look at every time you pass it. After you've chosen a building, start investigating it. Ask the people working there about its history. How long has the building been around? Who has used it and for what? Ask people in your community if they know anything about the building. You might also want to go to your city hall and look at the old building records. Write your notes in your journal. If walls could talk, you could learn a lot!

> "I would ask the wall what it was like being a wall. Also, the walls would have to be living to talk, so you would have to feed the walls and give them water."
> —Emily, Findley Elementary, age 10

> "We would have more friends . . . and more enemies."
> —Jeremy, Findley Elementary, age 10

> "Then they would blabber all day about what it's like to be a wall."
> —Tanay, Findley Elementary, age 9 ½

> "When you ran into it, it would say, 'Oww!'"
> —Nevaeh, Columbia Elementary, age 11

> "Different walls would have different personalities, and they could tell you what colors they wanted to be, and what pictures or posters they would like, and it would be noisy!!"
> —Calliope, Columbia Elementary, age 10

What if You Made Music?

BEEP BOOP.

Music can seem hard to make. Concert pianists, rock stars, jazz gods, and hip-hop heroes—they all can make great music, but they've worked for years and years to get where they are. How are you supposed to make sounds that awesome?

With a little pattern, that's how! Music is all about patterns—patterns repeated, patterns mixed and remixed, patterns adapted, patterns sped up and slowed down, patterns layered. While it's true that it can take a long time to create really great music, that doesn't mean you can't make something awesome right now.

Want to play drums? Start by tapping your hand on your desk. Tap it twice every second. Tap with an even space between each tap. Tap twice really quickly and then wait for the rest of the second. Now, try tapping twice every second with your right hand and once every second with your left hand. Try mixing up your taps. You're on the way to playing drums.

What about guitar? Try to find a rubber band or a piece of string. Take it and stretch it so that it's pretty tight. Now put your finger on it, pull it back a little, and release! Do you hear anything? Try tightening the rubber band some more (but make sure it doesn't break!). Does the sound get higher in pitch? What happens when you loosen it? If you play two notes, one high and one low, you've started playing guitar.

There you have it. You've started making music.

ACTIVITY
Really, Make Organized Noise

Music is basically organized noise. There's a noise over here, another over there, repeat. Anything can be an instrument as long as it makes a noise. You could use normal instruments, pots and pans, other noises stitched together, or even your own body to make music.

Your task? Make music in at least three different ways.

BILLIE HOLIDAY, JAZZ SINGER/SONGWRITER

Known for her low, coarse voice, Billie Holiday shaped jazz singing by performing her own works in a manner similar to how jazz is played: improvised and with changing speed. Her voice, coupled with her show of emotion, is what led Billie Holiday to popularity. One of her most notable works was "Strange Fruit," a song about the lynching of a black man in the south.[35]

Part 4

Nature

This section focuses more on the nonhuman aspects of nature, but it's important to remember our direct connection to the past, present, and future of nature.

We often think of nature as being everything that's outside and around us. That's true. But what if we're also a part of nature? What if we're not just a part of it, we also have a responsibility to it? Nature could survive without us better than we could without it. In fact, it did for billions of years before we decided to crash its party.

From space and time to plants and animals, nature is everywhere. What if questioning as much of nature as we can is the best way to make sure we can stay a part of it as long as we can?

Now, what if we got back to the questions?

What if People Could Sting with Their Fingers?

Sure, scorpions sting with their tails, and bees and wasps sting with their butts, but what if you had stingers in your fingers?

The stinging sensation you receive when you get stung by a bee or a wasp is partly from the stinger sticking in your skin and partly from the poison it injects into you. So, if you've ever been stung by one of those critters, you can tell your friends you know what it's like to be poisoned. Scorpions, on the other hand, can control whether or not (and how much) poison they inject into you.[1] Who knows, if the scorpion likes you, it might not fill you with poison. Yeah, right!

> "LOL the fun I would have!"
> —Ben, Battle High School, age 17

A couple other animals you might want to model your stinger fingers after offer one of the world's most painful stings, the bullet ant,[2] and one of the world's most deadly stingers, the box jellyfish.[3]

> "Could you then be poked to death then?"
> —Charlie, Battle High School, age 15

Incredibly, there is a man who studies stings—on himself! Justin Schmidt, a researcher at the Southwestern Biological Institute has been stung by over 150 of the world's most painful stingers. How does he describe the sting of a bullet ant? "They just make you want to lay [sic] down and die. You're just screaming in pain and agony."[4]

Scorpions use their stingers primarily for attacking animals they'd like to eat—but don't think you can bother one because you're too big to eat! Scorpions use their mighty sting to defend themselves too. Bees die after they sting[5], using their stingers to defend the rest of their colony.

How would you use your stinger fingers?

"Handshakes would be less popular."
—Jonathan, Battle High School, age 17

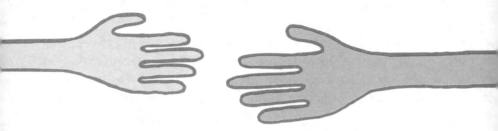

What if Time Repeated Itself?

What if, when you die, you are born again, and everything that happened to you the first time happened again . . . and again . . . and again . . . forever and ever on repeat? Think: every choice you made the first time around would be the same each and every time back through your life. If you did something wrong once, you'd do it wrong for infinity. If you were happy when you got your first pet, you'll be happy about it for infinity. You can't change any of your choices, but you do get to experience them again. It's like watching a movie on repeat but feeling the same things every time.

If you knew this was going to happen, how would you live differently? Would you live so each day brought you happiness? Would you live more selfishly? Would you live less selfishly, since you *and* everyone around you lives over and over again? If you were less selfish, the people you'd help would be helped for infinity.

But, from a different perspective, since you're doing the same thing forever, each time you do something, it matters less. Rather than thinking that this is the one and only time you can do something, you'd live as though each time didn't matter because you'd see it again for infinity. If you do something over and over, does it matter more because it will happen forever or matter less because it isn't unique?[6]

FRIEDRICH NIETZSCHE, PHILOSOPHER

In Friedrich Nietzsche's *The Gay Science*, he proposed a scenario in which life as we know it has already happened an infinite number of times before and will continue to happen exactly the same way an infinite number of times in the future. He used the story of a demon visiting one in one's sleep to examine how one might reconsider one's own existence—and the decisions made.

Below is the story of the demon Nietzsche used to explain this eternal recurrence, what he labeled "Eternal Return."

What, if some day or night a demon were to steal after you into your loneliest loneliness and say to you: "This life as you now live it and have lived it, you will have to live once more and innumerable times more; and there will be nothing new in it, but every pain and every joy and every thought and sigh and everything unutterably small or great in your life will have to return to you, all in the same succession and sequence—even this spider and this moonlight between the trees, and even this moment and I myself. The eternal hourglass of existence is turned upside down again and again, and you with it, speck of dust!" Would you not throw yourself down and gnash your teeth and curse the demon who spoke thus? Or have you once experienced a tremendous moment when you would have answered him: "You are a god and never have I heard anything more divine"? If this thought gained possession of you, it would change you as you are, or perhaps crush you.[7]

What if The Sun Never Went Down?

The Earth rotates on an axis (an imaginary line something turns on). You have learned that we travel around our sun. The Earth's rotation creates day and night. The day is the side of the Earth that is in sunlight. Night is the opposite side of the Earth where a shadow is created by the Earth itself.

So, "What if the sun never went down?" could also be asking, "What if the Earth stopped rotating?" (To be absolutely technical, it would

> "Then what would happen to nocturnal animals? We would have more greenhouse gasses. People will never escape sunburns."
> —Aidan, Columbia Elementary, age 10

be asking, "What if the Earth orbited the sun with the same side always facing the sun?") We'd end up being on a planet where almost half of the world would be in sunlight all the time. Almost another half would be in darkness all the time. The last little bit, the people on the border between light and dark, would live in a dim light similar to that of early morning or dusk.

> "If the sun never went down, the plants would be green, nobody would sleep, and the California drought would be horrible, and I think the world would be a horrible place."
> —Olaf, Oxford Elementary, age 9

How would society change? Think about farming. Plants need light to produce their own food. If there's no sunlight, plants couldn't grow, or we'd have to create artificial lights for the plants on the dark side of Earth. What about our sleep cycles? Your circadian rhythm is your "around day" rhythm. It's what your body goes through every day. When you get tired late at night, it's because certain hormones start to run through your body. Around 2:00 AM is your deepest sleeping time. You become alert throughout the day. Your daily rhythm changes a bit with the environment around you. You become more alert if your body knows the sun is up (and more tired when it drops and it gets dark). Think about whole societies in which the rhythm is thrown off. We'd have to set up light areas on the dark side and dark areas on the light side.

"There would be no night, and we would never see the stars or moon, and since the stars are so far away, we would never know about them, and there would not be the song 'Twinkle, Twinkle, Little Star.'"
—Francesca, Findley Elementary, age 10

How do you think we'd have to change? What else would we need to fix? What would get better if we did this?

ACTIVITY
Stay Up All Night

Ask your parents to let you stay up all night. Tell them it's OK—this book says so. Journal your experience every hour. What do you do with your time awake? How tired do you get? Do you get bored? Is it lonely when you're the only person up? Did you make it through the night?

"I would play soccer late at night."
—Edward, Columbia Elementary, age 11

"One part of the world would freeze."
—Zephyr, Columbia Elementary, age 11

"I would stay up as long as I could and play all day every day."
—Conner, Columbia Elementary, age 11

What if There Weren't Any Trees?

No trees? That's a terrifying thought! Where would birds sing? Where would squirrels play? What would kids climb? Where would you go for shade when the sun is blazing?

This scenario might not be that hard to imagine. All it takes is a quick look at pictures from one of the many deserts on earth to get an idea of what a treeless spot would look like. You could also look at photos from Mars to get an idea of what an entire planet without trees would look like. Looks kind of boring, huh?

> "Humanity would focus on algae farms in order to create an adequate oxygen supply."
> —Jonathan, Battle High School, age 17

Aside from the things we see and do with trees, did you know they serve several other functions you don't see? For example, trees make it easier for us to breathe. Not only do they breathe in carbon dioxide (what we breathe out) but they breathe out oxygen. That's right, trees use what we don't need and give us back what we need. No offense to dogs, but what if trees are humans' best friend? But that's not all—their roots, deep underground, help prevent erosion and keep ecosystems strong. Even though trees don't move a lot, they're extremely active in keeping the other living things on this planet healthy.

> "There would be no living life on Earth due to each animal and species needing air to survive."
> —Leslie, Battle High School, age 16
>
> "Then the birds would be living in caves."
> —John Ryan, Battle High School, age 15

What kinds of things could you do to make sure our planet never runs out of trees?

ACTIVITY
Plant a Tree

Here's a first step to making sure we never run out of trees: plant a tree. Depending on the time of year, you could find a seed off an existing tree. If you like oaks, look for those acorns! If you can't find any seeds, you could go to an arboretum or a plant nursery and buy one. Around Arbor Day, the last Friday in April in the United States, you can usually find some trees for free. Plant one and breathe a little easier.

JOYCE KILMER, POET

What if the pen is mightier than the sword? Or the poem is mightier than the chainsaw?

Poet Joyce Kilmer's famous poem "Trees" opens with the lines: "I think that I shall never see / A poem lovely as a tree."[8]

Three years after "Trees" was published in 1914, Kilmer enlisted to fight in the First World War. Tragically, during the battle of Ourcq, on July 30, 1918, Kilmer was cut down by a sniper's bullet.[9]

After Kilmer's death, "Trees" became even more popular among American readers. The poem and its poet became so popular that, in 1938, the US government went as far as to purchase thirty-eight hundred acres of forest in North Carolina, dedicate the land to Kilmer's

> **"Earth would look like Mars, and we would be dead."**
> —Charlie, Battle High School, age 15

memory, and stop extensive logging in the area. Today, the Joyce Kilmer Memorial Forest is one of the best examples of old-growth forests in the United States, with over one hundred different species of trees, many of which reach one hundred feet tall and twenty feet around and have been around for over four hundred years.[10]

What if People Got Energy from the Sun?

Every day, we humans have to eat. Getting food into our stomachs is a *huge* process. The sun has to shine on plants. The plants have to use a process called photosynthesis to convert sunlight into sugars they can eat. (*Photo* relates to light, and *synthesis* means "bring together to make something new.") Animals eat some of these plants. Then farmers harvest, wash, and take the plants to the store. Farmers butcher animals and take them to the store too. People buy food from the store, take it home, and then prepare it. All of this happens before we take one bite. But what if we got our energy from the sun just like plants do?

> "People wouldn't have to spend time worrying about their next meal, acquiring food, or even sitting down to eat food. Also, this function would limit where humans could live. Areas that receive less sunlight than others would be dangerous places to live."
> —Madi, Battle High School, age 15

We would just have to go outside to "eat." If you got hungry late at night, maybe you would go to the new fast food restaurant: a tanning salon. We'd probably add more windows to our buildings, so we could be full all the time.

If we only ate through photosynthesis instead of through our mouths, what else would change? Farmers would grow only decorative plants or work on biofuels (fuel made from plants). Grocery stores wouldn't exist anymore. In the transition from normal food to sunlight, we'd have so much livestock that wouldn't be eaten. What else do you think would change?

ACTIVITY
Write a News Story

Journalists are the people who write news stories. Now it's your turn to be a journalist. Write a short news story that is introducing a new species of human that can use photosynthesis. Maybe there was a government lab experiment? Maybe a group of individuals tested new drugs on themselves? Maybe someone just woke up one day and didn't have to eat if he or she sat in the sun? We don't know. But we will after you write your story.

> "We would be like plants. I would be very sad because I love food and enjoy eating."
> —Kate, Battle High School, age 15

TECHNICAL CORNER
Photosynthesis

Plants turn sunlight into energy all the time. Photosynthesis is a very complicated and involved process. We bet it's harder than the next test you'll take.

In its simplest form, photosynthesis is the process plants use to convert sunlight into usable energy. Light from the sun hits the surface of plants and gets absorbed by chlorophyll. The chlorophyll gets excited with its new energy. Through a series of chemical reactions, that energy then gets converted into sugars plants can use to grow. During the process, plants consume carbon dioxide from the air (what you breathe out) and output oxygen (what you breathe in). So, when plants are making their food, we get more stuff to breathe![11]

"World hunger would thankfully be gone; water scarcity would be even more important as it would still be required for photosynthesis."
—Jonathan, Battle High School, age 17

"I would have no energy. I do not like the sun. It would be a two-edge sword. You get large amounts of energy, and skin cancer."
—Charlie, Battle High School, age 15

What if Humans Had Elephant Noses?

If you had an elephant nose, what would you do with it: pick things up or spray water?

If you said pick things up, you might be surprised at just how many things you'd be able to grab with your trunk. Elephants can grab things as tiny as a marble and larger than a basketball.[12]

> **"I'd spray people with water more often."**
> —Charlie, Battle High School, age 15

If you said spray water from it, you're probably already imagining your brother or sister as a target. But you might also want to consider using this powerful sprayer for defense—a very dusty defense.

Did you know an elephant's nose isn't used to spray only water? Elephants use their trunks to spray dust as well. Why? Coating their bodies in layers of dust protects elephants from both the sun's rays and insect bites.[13]

> **"Slapping people would be a lot more fun."**
> —Andrew, Battle High School, age 15

Grabbing and spraying things are just the beginning of how you might use an elephant trunk if you had one for a nose. Elephants also use them to dig holes in the ground, and they show affection by caressing each other with them.

That's a whole lot of work, considering all your nose right now does is smell and collect boogers. What crazy things would you put your elephant nose up to if you had one?

ACTIVITY
Build Your New Nose

Find some cardboard and build yourself a new nose. Cardboard is an extremely versatile material. It can be cut into shapes, glued together into structures, and even be folded into a chair that can hold you up (do an image search to find some really awesome cardboard chairs). You could create a long elephant nose, a short pig nose, or a wild nose no one has seen before. Go ahead and use other materials like glue, string, and paint, if you'd like. Make sure to put a picture of yourself wearing your nose in your journal.

What if You Could See the Color of Nine?

Numbers don't have colors. Right?

Some people's brains have a condition called synesthesia. For them, senses can get crossed. Some people with synesthesia see the colors of numbers. For instance, when they see the number nine, it might always be green. Three could always be light blue. Four could always be deep yellow. Math would be pretty different if you could see how numbers relate by seeing their colors interact!

> "I would cross my sense of taste with my sense of hearing, so I could taste ice cream when someone said 'ice cream,' and I could taste screams, and if they tasted good, I would know it was happy and if it tasted bad it would be sad."
> —Schuyler, Columbia Elementary, age 11

Some people can hear colors. Orange might be a trombone playing a quick chirp. Violet might be a violin humming back and forth. Going to an art museum would be like going to a concert hall with a full orchestra!

"Yellow, with accents of mustard and sherbet orange."[14] That's the color of the hit song, "Happy," according to its artist, Pharrell Williams. Synesthesia can take over seventy different forms, such as tasting or smelling sounds, but the most common is hearing colors. Williams is part of the 4 percent of the population who have synesthesia. While synesthesia is rare among the general public, it's quite common among artists. Kanye West, Frank Ocean, and Lady Gaga are synesthetes who can hear colors, just like Vincent van Gogh, Duke Ellington, and Marilyn Monroe did before them.[15]

> "Then you could see the color of 1, 2, 3, 4, 5, 6, 7, 8, 9, 10 . . . and in math you could say 3 x 3 = yellow."
> —Vedant, Findley Elementary, age 9

If you could cross your senses, which would you cross?

ACTIVITY
Your New Senses

Seeing the color of nine or hearing red would be pretty strange for the majority of people, who have never done such a thing. For this activity, think of a few ways you could pick up a new sense. What could you do by blending sound, color, motion, taste, and touch? Write up your thoughts in your journal.

NEIL HARBISSON,
SYNESTHESIA CYBORG

Neil Harbisson was born with a syndrome called achromatopsia, meaning total color blindness. His whole world is different shades of gray. However, when he was in his early twenties, Harbisson started working with a computer scientist to change the way Harbisson perceives color. They made a third "eye" for Harbisson and attached it to his skull. The new eye sees a color, which transmits a signal to his skull, which vibrates his skull, which allows him to hear that color. Although he can't see colors

> "I would freak out."
> —Nestor, Oxford Elementary, age 9

with his eyes, Harbisson can at least hear the patterns we see with our eyes. What if you could hear what your banana's color sounded like? That's what Harbisson wondered. When he goes to the grocery store or an art gallery, Harbisson hears symphonies of sound. Both weird and awesome, right?[16]

"If I could see the color nine, than I bet it would be a tiger pattern with black and blue."
—Winnie, Oxford Elementary, age 9

"I think it would be yellow, because yellow is mellow. Nine is mellow."
—Nevaeh, Columbia Elementary, age 11

"That would be colorful! I would like that a lot. People might see different colors, or they might all see the same color."
—Calliope, Columbia Elementary, age 10

"Then I would be jealous of the people who can see the color of ten."
—Tashi, Findley Elementary, age 10

What if Humans Had See-Through Bodies?

A see-through body? Sounds pretty crazy . . . and really, really gross. Even if you had a see-through body, you wouldn't be the first animal to be transparent. Many animals in the deepest reaches of the oceans have see-through bodies. They do so because, with such little light in the depths of the ocean, being transparent makes them very difficult to see. Being see-through becomes their most effective camouflage against their predators.[17] When you consider there aren't a lot of rocks, bushes, trees, or other objects to hide behind, being able to hide in plain sight is incredibly important in the deep ocean.

> "When I ate food, would I see it digesting, or would it just disappear?"
> —Charlie, Battle High School, age 15

Not only are there already animals with see-through bodies, but scientists apparently don't believe there are enough. Some scientists are now working to create see-through mice.[18] But these aren't mad scientists. They're not making mice transparent as part of some sick and twisted experiment. Instead, they're doing it to better understand the inner workings of living things. Being able to watch bodily functions (such as digestion) as they take place could help scientists make new discoveries that might help us all live healthier lives.

If you could watch how your body reacts to and processes the different foods and drinks you put in your body, would it change what and the way you eat? If you could see how your organs performed after a good night's sleep—and after staying up late—do you think you'd change the way you sleep?

What would you do with your see-through body? Would you use it for camouflage, to gross out your friends, to learn more about your body, or something else?

ACTIVITY
Video Voice-Over

Have you ever heard a funny voice-over, or dub? That's when one video is playing, but a different audio track is playing simultaneously. Some movies use dubbed voices when the actors speak a different language than the audience speaks. Animated movies have to do this too. Those drawn or computer-generated characters aren't real people who speak, so the actors record their voices and put them over the visuals.

Find a video or record one. Then, record your voice over the visuals. You have to speak about something related to humans having see-through bodies. You could make up a conversation between two people or do a documentary-style narration. You can write out different scripts in your journal.

"Medicine would be a lot more advanced."
—Andrew, Battle High School, age 15

What if Humans Had Skin That Changed with Their Surroundings?

If you could change your skin so it matched your surroundings, you'd be invisible. Pretty cool. But what if cool powers come with heavy responsibilities? Would you use your ability to blend in with whatever was around you to protect yourself from danger? Would you use it to become a world champion hide-and-seek player? Or would you use it to spy on people when they didn't know you were there?

> "When people went hunting, they would not wear clothes. Camo would be unnecessary."
> —Charlie, Battle High School, age 15

This is an age-old question brought up by the philosopher Plato in his book *The Republic*. Plato told the story of the Ring of Gyges (a story about Gyges, who finds a ring that makes him invisible) and asked people what they would do if they had Gyges's ring. After listening to their answers, Plato could gauge how decent each person was.[19]

While Gyges's invisibility is fictional, there are real animals that can really change their skin according to their surroundings. Perhaps the most well-known is the chameleon. But did you know octopuses are expert skin-changers too? The mimic octopus, for example, doesn't

> "I'd skip class all the time."
> —John Ryan, Battle High School, age 15

change its skin color to match its surroundings—it changes its skin to look like other sea creatures'. It's been able to learn how to look like fifteen different underwater animals, such as seahorses, sea snakes, and flounders.[20]

What if You Could Give Your Pet a New Ability?

Ever wish your fish could glow in the dark or your dog could smell like roses? Which abilities would you give to which pets? Invisibility? Wings? Maybe make their own food from the sun so you don't have to feed them?

The cells in our bodies have something called DNA. DNA is made up of a sort of code, a type of chemical description for our physical features. Have curly hair? It's because your DNA tells your hair to grow in curls. If you were to change a bit of your DNA, you could change how curly your hair is, how tall you could grow, or even, to some degree, how long you could run. Your pets have DNA too. Change a bit of their descriptions, and they could have new abilities.

This is where things get really interesting. If you were able to find out how to put a piece of glowworm DNA into your fish, you could use your fish as a nightlight. If you could give your dog the right bit of fish DNA, your dog could grow gills and breathe underwater.

Researchers are exploring ways to change DNA right now! They're trying to make trees grow certain ways.[21] Imagine a seed that would grow into a bookcase! They're also modifying algae DNA so that the modified algae produce fuel for cars.[22] Rather than digging fuels out of the ground, you could just grow some at your house. Think of all the possibilities!

Would you want to change your pet? Is it right to change your pet's abilities? Is it possible to love something for what it is *and* want to change it?

ACTIVITY
Draw Your New Pet

Draw a pet with new abilities! Would you want a cat with wings? A pocket-size whale? A pink zebra? What would your new pet look like, and what would it be able to do?

TECHNICAL CORNER
Synthetic Biology

In a few short years, you'll probably be able to create your own creatures by stitching pieces of DNA together. This would work similarly to how you might create a new story by cutting and pasting pieces of other stories together. College students are already creating newish creatures in a competition called iGEM. They use, like you might one day, Bioblocks: a toolbox of genetic material. If you want your little bacterium to have a tail that spins, you just select that set of genes and have a machine stitch it together.

The field of creating new organisms and creating old organisms with new genes is called synthetic biology. It's not science fiction. It's real.[23]

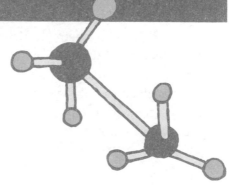

What if Ants Solved Problems Every Day?

Have you ever sat and watched ants? At first they seem to scurry around every which way. Do they know what they're doing? Look closer! Those ants are solving problems.

Ants need food like we do. When ants leave the colony, they do wander without direction. Each ant has no idea what is going on. As it turns out, most ants can't see very well, but they are expert smellers.[24] As they walk, ants lay little pheromone markers down—it's a smell trail other ants can pick up on.[25] If an ant finds food, it grabs some and walks back to the colony. Now, imagine this happening again and again. Soon there would be really strong smell trails where the ants found food and found short paths to it. There would also be weak smell trails where ants got lost or took a really long path. As the next ant leaves the colony, it wonders which way to go. Because of the smell paths, it can choose the strong one to go find food quickly. Thanks, ants! Or, *thants*![26]

But that's not all they can do. Ants build massive underground networks to live in. When trying to cross a gap, some ants build a bridge *out of other ants*. A few of them just hold on to the sides and to each other while their ant friends walk over them. There are even ants that, when dropped in water, cling together to make an ant raft. You can try to sink them, but they hold tight.[27]

Even though ants might steal food from your picnic, they do so efficiently—they are pretty good at finding the shortest path to your food! One ant can't figure out the best way. But when ants work together, they solve problems every day.

ACTIVITY
Do It the Ant Way

This one is a little messy.

First, find a few friends to play with you. Then, take paper and tear it up into tiny pieces, like breadcrumbs, and give some pieces to everyone. Next, choose somewhere in your house that will be your "anthill," your home base. (Maybe the kitchen, so you can enjoy a treat after this crazy game!) You and your friends now make trails to interesting places in your house. Each of you should start by going in a direction different from the others. As you walk, drop a trail of paper behind you. After you find somewhere interesting, walk back (following your trail) to your anthill. Now, follow one of your friend's tracks to the place that person found interesting (make sure to drop your own trail down too).

Keep doing this until you find the most interesting place. Once you find it, keep going back and forth along your chosen trail to see if your friends agree. If you all end up on the same path, you've found the most interesting place in your house. If you've been walking for a while and just can't agree, call a time out and grab a snack. There must be more than one interesting place in your house.

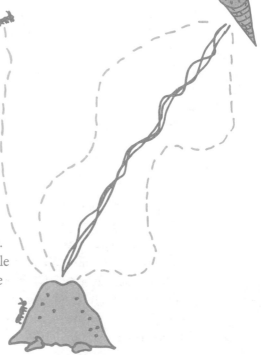

What if There Were No Luck?

Luck is tough to prove. If you could be convinced that there is absolutely no such thing as luck, what would be the first thing you'd start doing differently?

Are we too swayed by luck? If there were no luck (good or bad) and therefore no chance luck could affect anything you do, how might that change the way you live? What if how well you did on your next test, performance, or game depended on you and only you? How would this change the way—and the amount of time—you prepare for the things you do? How would this affect your future failures . . . and successes?

But what if there were a few things you could do to make you and your life at least *seem* a lot luckier? Believe it or not, people actually study luck. While their studies show luck does not exist, they have uncovered certain behaviors of people who believe they are lucky. Want to create your own luck? Follow these steps:

1. Be open to new ideas and unafraid of change.
2. Expect the unexpected. Often, what we confuse with luck is just unexpected fortune.
3. Hang out with many different people, including people from different backgrounds. Different people in our lives often deliver good news and great opportunities.
4. Break out of routines. Doing the same thing the same way keeps things the same. If you're feeling unlucky, why would you want that?

5. Be optimistic. Learn to turn negatives into positives; while it won't make you lucky, it will reduce the number of negatives in your life.
6. Expect to be lucky! What do you have to lose?

ACTIVITY
Create Your Own Superstition

Many people develop superstitions when they start believing luck is a result of routine. Create your own superstition by establishing a ritual, or routine, that you do every day. Below, make a list of the actions, words, and time of day your ritual must be done in order to bring good luck. Make it silly, fun, and useful by choosing actions that prepare you for a happy and focused day. See how many other people you can convince to take it up.

What if You Could Travel at Almost the Speed of Light?

Light travels super fast. Really super fast. If nothing is in its way, the speed of light is about 670,600,000 miles per hour! See? Really fast. The speed of light is kind of like a big universal speed limit. It's not like the speed limits on the highway, where you can still go faster. It is the fastest speed at which something can travel in the universe.

> "You would never age because you would be going so fast."
> —Mason, Columbia Elementary, age 11

When objects travel really fast, weird things happen. As you accelerate toward the speed of light, time dilates. What that means is that it kind of stretches out.

You decide to build a rocket to get you to almost the speed of light with your friend, who is the same age as you. Luckily, you get to ride the rocket while your friend has to stay on Earth. After your launch, you're zipping through space at 99 percent of the speed of light! You can't see well out of your ship because things are moving too quickly past you. After a year, you've had enough space travel and decide to head back to Earth (taking another

> "Then I would become part of the FBI or the army because it would be easy to dodge attacks/bullets, and I would be world famous."
> —Schuyler, Columbia Elementary, age 11

> "I would never be late for school."
> —Jake, Columbia Elementary, age 11

year). When you land, your friend greets you *but is fourteen years older*! Time dilated for you because you were traveling so fast. While your friend was aging normally, you were aging slowly because of how fast you were going!

TECHNICAL CORNER
Light Speed, and No Faster

Why can't we go faster than the speed of light? If you're in a car going twenty miles per hour, the driver can pretty easily speed up to sixty miles per hour. Why can't we just keep speeding up to the speed of light and beyond?

Like we learned in the question, time dilates. It expands. That means your personal clock ticks slower the faster you're moving. If you were to hit the speed of light, time would stop for you.

As you speed up, it also takes more and more energy for every additional mile per hour. To actually reach the speed of light, you would need infinite energy. Since you can't get infinite energy, you can't move at the speed of light.

Why else? The universe is having a bad day and says you can't. Not even if you say please.

ACTIVITY
Half Speed

See how long you can move your body at half speed. From walking, to lifting your arms and turning your head, move as if you're stuck in some pretty thick pancake syrup. How long can you move at this speed? Pay attention to who gets frustrated first, you or those around you.

> "There would not be any cars and planes because you could go anywhere with that type of speed."
> —Charlie, Oxford Elementary, age 9

ACTIVITY
Speedy To Dos

Take out your journal and fill out a to-do list for tomorrow if, all of a sudden, you could move at the speed of light.

"Then we could travel to Mars. Maybe even another universe. But it could do a thing or two to our skin. Plus friction can cause lots of fire."
—Aidan, Columbia Elementary, age 10

"Then I would go into space and go find 'Earth 2.0.'"
—Dillan, Columbia Elementary, age 11

"Then I would enter the running Olympics."
—Adrian, Oxford Elementary, age 8

"I would go to Europe and Antarctica and Brazil and the Spanish states."
—Olivia, Findley Elementary, age 10

"I would take vacations every day and see the moon."
—Fancesca, Findley Elementary, age 10

What if Humans Ate Insects as Our Primary Source of Food?

You think you're a picky eater now—what if the next pizza you ordered came with grasshoppers, caterpillars, and beetles for toppings? You might find it gross, but nearly a third of the planet eats insects as a part of their daily diet. The practice of eating insects is called entomophagy, and it's done by an estimated 2 billion people![28]

> "Ugh, that would be disgusting, and I don't really want to think about eating bug guts. P.S. Bug blood is green, so if I ate them, there would be green stuff all over my mouth."
> —Ceara, Findley Elementary, age 10
>
> "I tasted an ant, and it was spicy."
> —Aaron, Oxford Elementary, age 10

Not all insect eating has to be a crunchy experience. Some insects, like crickets, are ground up into flour that can then be used to bake cookies. Ready for some fresh-baked chocolate-chip cricket cookies?

Why do people eat insects? Two reasons: they're pretty healthy, and they're everywhere! Your brain may think they're gross, but your body has no problem turning insects into energy. A serving of mealworms has more protein than a serving of chicken.[29]

Another reason people are becoming interested in eating more insects is how environmentally friendly eating them can be. Compared to raising pigs, cows, chickens, and fish, insects take very little food, water, and space.[30]

"Spit them out and go get ice cream."
—Stephen, Findley Elementary, age 9

"Ew. Gross. Disgusting."
—Ervin, Findley Elementary, age 10

"Ick! Insects? Food? I don't think they really go together. But if I was forced to eat insects, and everyone else ate insects too, we would soon run out of food."
—Amy, Findley Elementary, age 9

"That would gross me out. I would never eat again. I don't care—I'd rather starve."
—Nyerie, Oxford Elementary, age 9

What if you're already eating insects? (If you love peanut butter, and you're 100 percent set against ever eating insects, no matter what reasons there might be for doing so, you shouldn't read the next sentence.) The Food and Drug Administration (FDA) allows for an average of thirty or more insect fragments per one hundred grams of peanut butter.[31]

ACTIVITY
Insect Menu

Now that you know you're already eating insects, let's get cooking! Imagine you're going to open the first insect-only restaurant in your neighborhood. Write out a menu in your journal with the soups, salads, main courses, and desserts you'll serve. In addition to giving the ingredients, be sure to name your new dishes.

"I would throw up every day and probably get stung by bugs."
—Olivia, Columbia Elementary, age 10

"Then catching bugs in a net or jar would spell the end of a bug's life and a tasty snack for you."
—Schuyler, Columbia Elementary, age 11

"We would need to eat a lot bigger portions of food because insects are not very filling."
—Cali, Columbia Elementary, age 10

"If we ate insects as our primary source of food, insects would start becoming extinct because there are billions of humans in the world. This would mean we would have to have insect farms everywhere to meet our needs."
—Hilary, Columbia Elementary, age 11

"Then it would help with bug problems."
—Adrian, Oxford Elementary, age 8

"I would like that because I get to try something new."
—Nevaeh, Columbia Elementary, age 11

"Then normal food would taste like worms."
—Carter, Columbia Elementary, age 11

"Then we would get much more protein."
—Daphne, Findley Elementary, age 10

What if You Could Taste and Smell with Your Fingers?

Why should your nose and mouth have all of the fun? You can feel with your entire body, so what if you could experience other senses, like taste and smell, with your entire body? How would your life change? Would you watch what you touched? Would you wear more gloves? Or would you be throwing away all of your forks and spoons?

If you could taste with your fingers, then you could enjoy food without having to eat it, right? What if you could just touch a piece of pizza and get pizza flavor in your mouth? Pretty cool, huh?

As crazy as this "what if" may sound, it's not all that farfetched. Not every animal smells with its nose and tastes with its tongue. For example, snakes smell with their tongues[32] and butterflies taste with their feet[33]!

"If you could smell with your fingers, people would be much more picky with what they chose to eat."
—Jaiden, Battle High School, age 16

"Handshakes and high fives, along with other hand contact would be awkward—would it be like kissing them?"
—Charlie, Battle High School, age 15

"Then when you picked your nose, it would smell really good, and you could say you were smelling your fingers."
—John Ryan, Battle High School, age 15

"People would have to be super careful wiping their butt."
—Andrew, Battle High School, age 15

"Gloves would be necessary
to go the bathroom, and cook
raw food; additionally, any job
that requires gloves, such as
working with chemicals, would
definitely need them now."
—Jonathan, Battle High School, age 17

"I would touch everything."
—Ben, Battle High School, age 17

What if Humans Only Saw in Black and White?

The world would be a pretty boring place if it were only black and white, right? Would sunsets look as stunning or mountains as majestic if they were seen only in shades of black and white? Imagine how dull a double rainbow would be without all the colors it contains.

Not only do colors convey beauty, they share information. We now use colors to signal certain feelings, warnings, and emotions. Ever wonder why stop signs are red and caution signs yellow? We've been conditioned to respond to certain colors quicker than the words written on them. Many companies and advertisers use colors to their advantage today.

Even though what colors mean today can be similar in most people's minds, the meanings colors hold haven't been the same over time. For example, if someone were to ask you what color a wedding dress is, you (and a lot of other people) would probably say white. But this hasn't always been the case. In European countries alone, the standard color of wedding dresses has been blue, pink, red, even green during different centuries throughout history.[34] If you were to start looking at the colors of wedding dresses from different cultures around the globe, you'd find even more variations. So, while colors can contain meaning, it's usually each of us who create the meaning.

ACTIVITY
Color Match

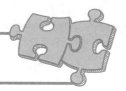

Look at the names of colors below. Get your journal out and write down the first thing that comes to your mind when you see that color. Then have a friend do the same (but don't let that person see your response!). How many things do you both associate with the same color? If you really want to test this, repeat this with as many people as you can. How often do the same colors make people think of the same things? You might be surprised at how similar your results are.

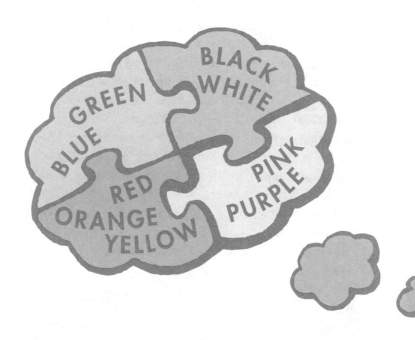

What if Everything Were an Alien Simulation?

Computers get more advanced every day. If you look at video games from 1990, they look very different from those today. We keep adding more ways to interact with games—new controllers and feedback systems. The visual quality is getting significantly better. Virtual worlds are becoming very real.

Some people think that in the future, we will be able to create a video game that is indistinguishable from the real world. We won't even need humans to play it because we could just simulate characters interacting with one another. As long as we have enough resources, we could start simulating a whole bunch of worlds. It would be hundreds and thousands and millions of virtual worlds with virtual people having virtual reactions. So much virtualness!

But what do you think these virtual worlds would *feel* like to the "people" who live there? Since the graphics are so great, and we'd be able to simulate all of our senses, it would probably *feel* real. Even though the inhabitants would be computer-based, they could still think like you and me. They might not even know they were in a simulation.

How many real worlds are there? Just one.

How many virtual worlds would there be? More than anyone can count.

Now, if you had to guess which one you were in, a real world or a virtual world, which would you guess? Chances are you're in a virtual world that feels real. You

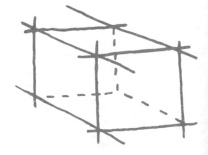

have no way of telling if you're in the year you think you are in. This simulation seems to have started just over 10 billion years ago. But there might be a civilization billions of years older than us that started the simulation.

NICK BOSTROM, PHILOSOPHER

This question is inspired by Nick Bostrom's Simulation Argument. In 2003, he published an article that shows one of three things is true.

1. Almost all civilizations die off before they reach "technological maturity." So, even though we're alive now, our civilization might end before we figure out how to use technology in an entirely responsible way.

2. Once a civilization is able to create hyperreal simulations, people lose interest in it. Even though they are able to do so, the people in the civilization don't create simulations.

3. We are probably living in a simulation.

He doesn't think we have strong evidence for which one of the possibilities is true. Maybe we're the first civilization, the people who will eventually create simulations. Or perhaps we're the first people created by the first computer simulation created by our superintelligent ancestors. Or, even more oddly, maybe we're a simulation that was started by people in a simulation themselves![35]

What if the World of the Small Seemed Very Different from the World of the Big?

Have you ever wondered what happens at the smallest level of the universe? Imagine you zoom in on your hand. Eventually you see all those cracks and ridges of your skin. You keep zooming, and you start to see your cells. Keep going, and you see the parts of your cells, then bands of molecules, then what?

Well, if you keep zooming, you see different parts of a molecule: atoms. Each atom has different amounts of electrons, protons, and neutrons (think about them as particles). Go a little farther into the protons and neutrons and you find elementary particles, things that can't be broken down any farther (though there is debate in the scientific community about this!).

At this level of the universe, things start acting really strange. Particles can tunnel through walls. If this happened at your regular size, you could push against your bedroom wall one hundred times and one of the times fall through the wall. Weird, right?

Particles can get entangled with one another. It is kind of like two particles start acting the same, and if you change one, the other changes too. If you got entangled with your friend who then moved to the other side of the world, when one of you changed direction, the other would change direction too. It'd be hard to get anywhere!

SAM DROEGE, USGS BIOLOGIST

You don't have to be as small as an elementary particle to see how the small world is different from yours. Sam Droege is a biologist for the United States Geological Survey (USGS). He also takes high-resolution images of small things, like bees. If you're wandering around outside, you will realize that most bees are too small for you to see clearly. And, even if you're an expert, it's hard to identify most bees because of their small size.[36] Tough luck if you're trying to figure out what is pollinating your plants. That's why you need Droege, because he's the guy with the high-quality bee photos.

At jumbo-size, bees show you all sorts of things: a bee's multipart eyes, their tiny hairs, and even a bunch of pollen. What else do you think we could be missing because we're too large to see it?

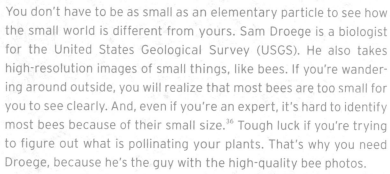

TECHNICAL CORNER
Why the Small Is Strange and the Large Is Not

Whoa. This question is really weird. How can the really small stuff in the universe be so strange when, at our size, we never see it? You've never walked through a wall or gotten entangled with a friend. If the tiny things do it, why can't we?!

There's a lot of debate in the scientific community about this. In fact, large things are understood by one kind of math, and the really, really small stuff is understood by a totally different kind of math. Physicists, those people who study physics (how things move and interact), are working to understand the universe with only one type of unified mathematics. You're right. It is weird to have two different things try to describe the same universe. The problem so far has been that, because they describe things quite differently, the two types of math don't really work together very well—yet.

One of the thoughts is that things are just calmer from far away. Think about it like an ocean. If you look at the top of an ocean really close, you see a whole bunch of tiny ripples. But, if you look at the same spot from just a little farther away, the surface seems much calmer. Then, if you look from even farther away, like from a building half a mile inland, the ocean seems even calmer. If you look at the tiniest of particles in the universe, they seem super erratic. But if you look at them from really far away, like on the moon, they seem extremely calm.

What if There Were No Mosquitos?

No mosquitos? What, no slapping your arms during the summer? No more waking up as one big itch? Fantastic!

But did you know that mosquitos are responsible for a lot more problems than red welts filled with pus? These tiny, buzzing insects are one of the world's biggest killers. Because of all that blood-sucking, they also transport deadly diseases from one person or animal to another. Every year, millions of people die from mosquito-borne illnesses.[37]

The world would be a much, much better place if we said good riddance to mosquitos, right? But what about the food chain? Isn't nature in perfect balance? Aren't mosquitos food for larger animals and pollinators for plants that we need? If all of the mosquitos were gone, it would start a spiral effect of catastrophe, right?

What if it wouldn't? Unlike other tiny nuisances (like bees) in our ecosystem, whose disappearance would spell disaster, mosquitos could disappear— many scientists don't foresee any problems with wiping out mosquitos. In fact, the only problem they can think of is, without millions of people dying from mosquitos every year, we might have too many people on the planet.[38]

> "The world would rejoice. The amount of diseases, especially in developing nations, would reduce. Also unlike other insects, mosquitoes are not integral to maintain biodiversity."
> —Jonathan, Battle High School, age 17

So, what if there were no mosquitos? Well, we'd have a new question to ponder: What if there were too many people on the planet? Which question would you rather find an answer to?

ACTIVITY
Food Web

Everything in the environment is connected. Choose a plant or animal and find out how it is connected to other plants and animals. Make a food web in your journal by drawing branches from your first choice to the new plants and animals you find. Each plant or animal is a node and each connection is a connection (pretty straightforward, right?). Keep working until you have a few loops on which, if you follow a connection away from one node, eventually you get back to your original node.

"Then fishing and hunting would
be way easier."
—John Ryan, Battle High School, age 15

"The spread of disease would
be significantly lessened, but
mosquito-eating animals
wouldn't have their food."
—Madi, Battle High School, age 15

What if All the Continents Were Joined Together?

What if there were a single "supercontinent"? What if, at one time in the Earth's history, there was? Roughly 270 million years ago, most of the Earth's landmass was huddled up together in one continent called Pangaea. Around 200 million years ago, the Earth's shifting plates started breaking this continent up, and huge masses of land started drifting across the oceans until they reached where they are now. They haven't stopped moving, either. If you've ever felt an earthquake before, it was the side effect of the Earth's shifting plates.

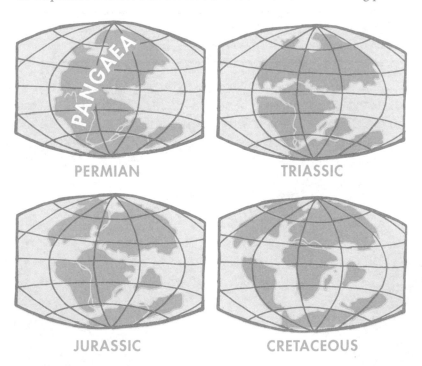

PERMIAN · TRIASSIC

JURASSIC · CRETACEOUS

Even though the location of the Earth's continents probably won't change enough in your lifetime to require you to order a World Map 2.0, the Earth is always moving. Pangaea wasn't the first or only supercontinent. In fact, scientists who study the Earth's movements believe our current continents are moving toward forming yet another supercontinent in the very distant future.[39]

Aside from the geographic changes involved with a single continent, what other changes do you think would happen if there were no oceans to separate all the humans on the planet? Would we have the diversity of cultures we have now, or would we share a single culture? Would there be more wars, or fewer? How about the history of science and learning? What if, instead of all of the smartest people studying and experimenting far away from each other, they could have worked together? What would the world look like today if it had never broken up in the past?

ACTIVITY
Earth Puzzle

What if the Earth's continents and countries were a bunch of puzzle pieces, and you got to reconstruct the Earth however you wanted? Draw a new map with new borders and locations for the Earth's countries and continents.

What if You Could Turn into an Animal?

Let's be honest, being a human being can be boring sometimes. Other animals get to climb on ceilings, soar through the air, live underwater, have claws, etc., while we humans must walk around on the ground with soft hands and very, very little fur. But we do have a supercomputer for a brain, so why not use it? Among other things, this brain allows us to wonder and ask, "What if . . . ?"

So, what if you could turn into an animal? What would be the biggest improvement you would experience while being an animal over being a human? What would be your biggest danger, threat, or disadvantage? Would there be things you could no longer do? Would there be other creatures trying to eat you? How would you survive?

Now that you're imagining yourself as an animal, what would be the first thing you do? Can you think of anything you might miss the most about not being human? Would you interact with humans? Why or why not? How? What would you tell animals about humans?

ACTIVITY
Animal You!

Draw a picture of the animal you and your new home. Where would you live? What would you eat? Who would be your friends?

What if Everything Were a Hyperlink?

Do you know where your clothes come from? What about your computers or the paper in this book?

Today, our objects get worked on from people and machines all around the world. The cotton in your shirt might have been picked in China, processed in India, woven into fabric in Vietnam, sewn together into a shirt in Brazil, packaged and sent to a warehouse in Canada, and then sent to the store you bought it from. Look at all the objects around you. They are made up of components made in different places, shipped to different places. And now, they sit quietly around you.

If everything were a hyperlink, you'd be able to investigate all the objects around you. You'd be able to learn who (or which robot) built your phone or where your food came from. If you could learn more about these, would you? Would you be interested to know the journey of all of your things?

ACTIVITY
Hyper It Up

Create a word web of ideas in your journal. Start by writing one word in the middle of a page. Then, draw five branches off it, and at the end of each branch, write a word that is related to your core word. Do that again for each of your new words. Cool. Now, do it one more time. You should have a whole bunch of words and lines connecting them. Finish your drawing by connecting any of the words that are related but don't have lines connecting them yet.

VANNEVAR BUSH, TED NELSON, AND DOUGLAS ENGELBART: THE ORIGINATORS OF HYPERMEDIA

Three guys helped start the idea of hypertext and other hypermedia: Vannevar Bush, Ted Nelson, and Douglas Engelbart. If you're at a birthday party and people ask, "What is hypermedia and who originated it?" you can inform them: "Hypermedia is a group of objects, a group of links, and a way to move between the objects through links. It's connected information that could be text, audio, video, or other things that hold information." You're surely going to be the coolest kid at the party. Well . . . you'll at least be the most informed about hypermedia.

Vannevar Bush had this idea of something called a memex. It's a device that allows you to explore your personal (mental) objects and links. Years later, Ted Nelson came around and created the actual term *hypertext*. He was thinking about how when people use *hyper-*, they are trying to extend whatever word *hyper* is connected to. So, hypertext would be text that goes beyond words on a page or screen. Around the same time, Douglas Engelbart was thinking about computers, people, and how the heck we were going to interact with each other. He realized that we both need a language, something that organizes and structures our thoughts about the world. That language, he thought, was hypertext: words and ideas connected by links. These links could be from ideas being connected or by the words themselves. Any way you look back, you'll connect to these three as the early formers of hypertext.[40]

What if You Had a Superpower?

What would your superpower (only one!) be and why? Mask or no mask? Would you have a secret identity or not? Cape or no cape? Would you rather be part machine like Iron Man or have "naturally" freaky powers like Spider-Man?

Science is constantly coming up with new ways to improve the human body. From creating new medicine to help the body function better, to designing electronic devices to put inside you, scientists are helping us become more and more "super" every day. What if there were an entire world of Hulks or Iron Men walking around?

Imagine what you could do if you were part machine? What if your legs were powered by electricity? How fast would you be able to run? What if you could pick up anything and everything?

Ever wish you had a super brain? What if you could download a book directly into your brain instead of having to read—or remember—it? What if you could be invisible? Sound crazy? Not to the scientists who are currently creating invisibility cloaks for soldiers and working on turning many other "powers" from the pages of comic books into reality. As long as we define *superpower* as an ability to do something a "normal" human body cannot do, we're all about to become a lot less "normal."

Not everybody needs to have special new parts to gain superpowers. Some are born with amazing abilities. Just look at these interesting humans born with "super" powers.

- Michel Lotito can eat anything, including an airplane!

- Ben Underwood used echolocation instead of sight.

- Tim Cridland can feel no pain.

- Mas Oyama (born Choi Yeong-Eui) was a super fighter who could kill bulls and bears with his bare hands.

"It would be something lame, like Hindsight Lad, who has the ability to tell you how something would have worked out much better if something different happened, in hindsight."
—Charlie, Battle High School, age 15

Can you find downsides to having some of these superpowers? For instance, if you can't feel pain, how will you know your stovetop is on when you accidentally put your hand on a burner?

ACTIVITY
Create the Super You

Take out your journal and draw your new super identity. What is your superpower? What is your weakness? What would your superhero costume look like? Who is your arch nemesis? What do you fight for (e.g., truth, justice, and the American way)?

What if You Could Explore Outer Space?

Space is a big place. There is a lot of room between stars and planets. There is so much room between objects in space that it can take many, many years for light to travel from one galaxy to the next. When you're outside at night, looking up at the stars, do you ever wonder what is up there?

The first question is, where do you want to go? Do you want to travel to see new stars? Look at new galaxies? Do you want to find new planets and moons? Are you looking for plants and animals too? What kinds of creatures do you think you'll find on alien planets? Do you think they'll be smarter than us? More or less advanced?

What kinds of plants would you find? Which plants grow and how they grow depends on the environment they are in. Trees that are in environments with more carbon dioxide grow larger. Some plants thrive in the sun while others can live only in shade. What new environments will you find?

The next question is, how are you going to get to your destination? You can get on a spaceship. But since the nearest galaxy is forty-two thousand light-years away,[41] it will take you forty-two thousand years—if you are traveling at the speed of light. If you're traveling for that long, you should bring more than a sleeping bag. Hopefully hibernation technology comes around, and you can sleep or be frozen the whole trip. And hopefully humanity will be here when you get back, or who will you share your discoveries with?

ACTIVITY
Sagittarius or Bust

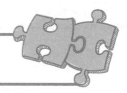

Draw where you would go and what it would look like. You could even print pictures out and paste them together to create the new landscape.

ELON MUSK, ENTREPRENEUR

NASA, essentially the United States' space exploration group, has lost a percentage of its funding, making it harder to explore space. After selling PayPal, Elon Musk started a company called SpaceX. According to its mission, "SpaceX designs, manufactures and launches advanced rockets and spacecraft. The company was founded in 2002 to revolutionize space technology, with the ultimate goal of enabling people to live on other planets."[42] Why should we go to other planets? Musk thinks that there are a few things that fit on an evolutionary scale: single-cell organisms, differentiation of plants and animals, life moving from oceans to land, mammals, consciousness, and finally life becoming multiplanetary. That's the first part. The second part is that if something is important enough to be put in the history of evolution, maybe we should put some of our resources toward achieving it.[43]

What if You Could Engineer at Planetary Proportions?

You might have heard of engineers. They are the people who build highly technical structures like medical devices, bridges, skyscrapers, robots, spaceships, submarines, traffic systems, and nuclear power plants. They solve problems and build things precisely.

The Burj Khalifa, the tallest building in the world at 2,716.5 feet,[44] is still miniscule in comparison to the size of the Earth. Really, anything engineers build is pretty small. But there are now a few engineers who are trying to engineer our whole planet.

Realizing we might have to take drastic measures to stop climate change, some engineers have been thinking about clouds. If part of the problem with the climate is that too much heat is getting trapped in the Earth's atmosphere, what could we do to reduce the amount of heat coming in? Light from the sun comes in through our atmosphere and warms what it hits. But since only some of the sun's light makes it through the clouds and the rest bounces back into space, the Earth heats up less than it would without clouds. These cloud engineers are finding ways of creating both more clouds and more reflective clouds.[45]

Other engineers are working on plans to help the algae in the oceans grow, thereby reducing the amount of carbon in the atmosphere and reducing the planet's ability to hold extra heat.[46] Even though plans are being made and experiments are being performed, nothing major has been implemented. Since geoengineering affects all of us, scientists take lots of precautions.

ACTIVITY
What Would You Build That Was the Size of a Planet?

Planets are pretty big. If you could build something that big, what would you build? Or if you could change Earth, how would you change it? Draw pictures and write in your journal.

WANGARI MAATHAI, DRIVEN ENVIRONMENTALIST

You don't have to be a geoengineer to change the world's climate. With a PhD in veterinary anatomy and a background in biology, Wangari Maathai started an organization called the Green Belt Movement.[47] She saw that other women in Kenya were losing their food supply and water resources, and had to walk farther and farther to get firewood. Maathai started the Green Belt Movement with a simple, yet powerful idea: trees help keep the "soil [together], store rainwater, and provide food and firewood," so let's plant some trees.[48]

In the years since its foundation in 1977, Maathai's organization has helped rural Kenyan women plant trees to better their own communities. And, in 2004, she received a Nobel Peace Prize for her work.[49] Maathai wanted to make the world a better place. She found a simple idea that resonated with others, and then she helped that idea spread in order to change her community.

What if You Experienced the Unknown?

You have five senses. You can see, smell, hear, taste, and touch. Everywhere you go, you bring these senses with you, to experience the world. But what if there is more than what you can experience?

Take sight. We see reds, blues, greens, purples, and all sorts of colors—what physicists call visible light. What we see is part of a larger spectrum of electromagnetism. X-rays, microwaves, ultraviolet light, radio waves, and infrared light are also on the spectrum, but we just can't see them! Some bugs see ultraviolet light, and to them, flowers are very different colors than they are to us.

Hearing is similar. We can hear up to a certain high pitch and down to a certain low pitch. If you have a dog, you might have noticed it can hear more than you can.

It's hard to imagine what other colors of light would look like or what sounds are beyond what we can hear. What if we were to change our senses even more?

Think about your eyes. They have been looking forward out of the front of your head for your entire life. They help you walk around and guide your hands. Your brain is used to them. What if you could move your eyes outside of your body? Weird! You might be able to hold one eye in each of your hands and move it around independently. You could look around corners just by rolling your eyes around the corner.

You could also put your eyes really close to the ground to feel like one of your pets. Or you could put your eyes really high in the sky to be like a bird. You could put your eyes a few feet above your head and behind you such that it would be like you're playing a third-person video game when you walk around. You could put your eyes in the back of your head so you could see behind you. You could flip your eyes upside down to flip the world upside down (but remember, you'd still be standing upright). You could put your eyes into special lenses that would allow you to see all around you at the same time. You could put your eyes on a wall and walk around a room as though you were seeing out of a fly's eyes!

It doesn't even have to be sight that you're extending. What if you could feel via touch if you were going to get sick? Or what if your big toe vibrated when someone was calling you?

ACTIVITY
Real Surrealism

What would you do if you could remove your eyes from your head? Where would you put them? What would you want to experience if you could experience more?

Conclusion

Thank you! You've hung out with us through a book full of questions, activities, and interviews. You're officially a curious person. Boom! The book is running out of pages, but that doesn't mean the curiosity has to be over.

Now it's on you to go out into your world and ask deep questions —or silly ones! No matter how the question starts, finding an answer can take you to different edges of your mind and the world.

A question is a powerful thing!

Empires have been built on questions, and they've fallen with questions. It's OK to not know the answer sometimes. We don't always know. Even the experts had to start somewhere. Don't be nervous—be proud that you're courageous enough to question everything!

The questions in this book shouldn't just spur deeper thinking —they should spur conversations. Conversations can change the world—especially when those conversations turn into actions. That's where the power of this book lies: in its ability to spur and further conversations about difficult and new subjects so that we may cocreate a better future.

If you'd like to get connected with a global community of What Iffers who are already working together to turn big ideas into even bigger actions, go to whatif360.com to learn more. You'll also be able to explore the questions people have asked in the past, find an event near you, or even sign up to speak at a What If . . . ? 360 Experience.

We're looking forward to hearing your world-shaking question!

We'd also love to bring a What If . . . ? 360 Experience to your school, so you can join the other schools around the world turning ideas into actions by asking, "What if . . . ?"

If you use social media, you can find us on Facebook, Twitter, YouTube, and Google+.

#WhatIf360

Facebook: facebook.com/TheWhatIfConference

Twitter: @WhatIf_360

Google+: What If . . . ? 360

YouTube: youtube.com/TheWhatIfConference

We'd Like to Say Thanks

What if there are far too many people to thank than could possibly fit in the pages of this book? For a start, though, I'd like to thank my agent, Jessica Regel, who has been helping me make my dream of becoming a writer come true over and over again. I'd also like to thank our editors, Lindsay Easterbrooks-Brown, Emmalisa Sparrow, and Kristin Thiel at Beyond Words, for believing enough in the power of asking, "What if . . . ?" to help us put it on some pages between a couple covers so we could share it with the world. I'd also like to thank the ever-growing global community of What Iffers who refuse to accept the way things are and continue to commit their thoughts and actions to cocreating a better world, not just for tomorrow but for today. Thank you! Lastly, I'd like to thank my wife, Seung Ah Lee, for putting up with all my craziness. That is all.

—Matt

Thanks to everyone who stuck with us on both the What If . . . ? journey and our personal ones. Thanks to our editors, Lindsay Easterbrooks-Brown, Emmalisa Sparrow, and Kristin Thiel, for helping us craft and realize our vision. Thanks to our agent, Jess Regel, for advising us along the way. Thanks to my mother, Stephanie McHugh, for helping me through tough times. Thanks to my various clients and employers for such a flexible schedule while I was writing. Thanks to my friends who have provided feedback and shot me resources, especially to Caroline Slavin for her Ada Byron spotlight suggestion. Thanks to Ben Cairns for helping edit early drafts of the book. Thanks to Dr. Selcen Phelps, a dear friend and always-mentor. Thanks to each of my teachers; you were the reasons I was able to write well about so many things. And a special thanks to my partner Abby Stokes for her continued encouragement, support, edits of drafts, feedback, interview transcriptions, resource locating, and citation formatting. Finally, thanks to all of you for picking up a copy of this book and helping active curiosity thrive.

—Andrew

Notes

Special note: All kid answers were collected in the months of September 2014, January 2015, and April 2015. These students came from a variety of places, from Columbia Elementary in Bellingham, Washington, and Oxford Elementary School in Berkeley, California, to Findley Elementary School in Beaverton, Oregon, and Battle High School in Columbia, Missouri. All of these kids rock!

Special note #2: Though none of our material was taken directly from *What If . . . ?: Collected Thought Experiments in Philosophy* by Peg Tittle, we referenced this book to remind ourselves of many of the questions that ended up in our own book. *What If . . . ?* directed us to some of the sources cited, saving us a good chunk of time.

History

1. "Top 10 Misconceptions about Dinosaurs," Smithsonian National Museum of Natural History, accessed September 1, 2014, http://paleobiology.si.edu /dinosaurs/info/misconceptions/mis_4.html.

2. "Dinosaur FAQ," Smithsonian National Museum of Natural History, accessed September 1, 2014, http://paleobiology.si.edu/dinosaurs/info/faq /faq_2.html.

3. Ibid.

4. DinoBuzz: Current Topics Concerning Dinosaurs, "Are Birds Really Dinosaurs?," University of California Museum of Paleontology, last modified January 22, 1998, http://www.ucmp.berkeley.edu/diapsids/avians.html.

5. Ben Waggoner, "Mary Anning (1799-1847)," University of California Museum of Paleontology, accessed August 10, 2015, http://www.ucmp .berkeley.edu/history/anning.html.

6. Invictus, "The Mongol Empire," All Empires Online History Community, last modified February 2007, http://www.allempires.com/article/?q=The_Mongol_Empire.

7. Abby Rogers, "The 10 Greatest Empires in the History of the World," *Business Insider*, November 9, 2011, http://www.businessinsider.com/the-10-greatest-empires-in-history-2011-9#2-the-mongol-empire-was-the-largest-contiguous-empire-the-world-has-ever-seen-9.

8. Crash Course World History, "Wait for It . . . The Mongols!," YouTube video, 11:32, posted by CrashCourse, May 17, 2012, https://www.youtube.com/watch?v=szxPar0BcMo.

9. Rebecca Brayton, "The History of the Mongol Empire," WatchMojo.com video, 2:50, May 23, 2010, http://www.watchmojo.com/video/id/8258.

10. Evan Andrews, "10 Things You May Not Know about Genghis Khan," History.com, April 29, 2014, http://www.history.com/news/history-lists/10-things-you-may-not-know-about-genghis-khan.

11. Hillary Mayell, "Genghis Khan a Prolific Lover, DNA Data Implies," *National Geographic News*, February 14, 2003, http://news.nationalgeographic.com/news/2003/02/0214_030214_genghis.html.

12. "How Did America Get Its Name?," Library of Congress, August 2003, http://www.loc.gov/wiseguide/aug03/america.html.

13. Ibid.

14. Mat Barkhausen, "Native Americans Influenced American Political Thought," PowWows.com, September 29, 2011, http://www.powwows.com/2011/09/29/native-americans-influenced-american-political-thought.

15. David Yarrow, "The Great Law of Peace: New World Roots of American Democracy," Kahonwes.com, September 1987, http://www.kahonwes.com/iroquois/document1.html.

16. Cristen Conger, "10 NASA Inventions You Might Use Every Day," Long Beach Unified School District, accessed September 1, 2014, http://www.lbschools.net/Main_Offices/Curriculum/Areas/English_Language_Arts/docs/Common_Core/14-15/NASA%20inventions.pdf.

17. Claire Suddath, "A Brief History of: Velcro," *Time*, June 15, 2010, http://content.time.com/time/nation/article/0,8599,1996883,00.html.

18. Conger, "10 NASA Inventions."

19. Ibid.

20. "Neil deGrasse Tyson—We Stopped Dreaming (Episode 1)," YouTube video, 5:19, posted by "Evan Schurr," March 9, 2012, http://youtu.be /CbIZU8cQWXc.

21. "Neil deGrasse Tyson: On the First Moon Landing," YouTube video, 7:24, posted by "Alfonso J. Ramos," July 28, 2012, https://www.youtube.com/watch ?v=Q6ClA5f5uu0.

22. "Neil deGrasse Tyson," Hayden Planetarium, accessed November 1, 2014, http://www.haydenplanetarium.org/tyson/profile/about-neil-degrasse-tyson.

23. Tom Benson, "Brief History of Rockets," NASA, last modified June 12, 2014, http://www.grc.nasa.gov/WWW/k-12/TRC/Rockets/history_of _rockets.html.

24. Michio Kaku, *Physics of the Impossible: A Scientific Exploration into the World of Phasers, Force Fields, Teleportation, and Time Travel* (New York: Doubleday, 2008).

25. Michio Kaku, *Hyperspace: A Scientific Odyssey through Parallel Universes, Time Warps, and the 10th Dimension* (New York: Doubleday, 1994).

26. Ibid.

27. David Toomey, *The New Time Travelers: A Journey to the Frontiers of Physics* (New York: W. W. Norton & Company, 2007).

28. James Gleick, *The Information* (New York: Pantheon Books, 2011), 38–39.

29. Rachel Grate, "Science Has Great News for People Who Read Actual Books," Arts.Mic, September 22, 2014, http://mic.com/articles/99408 /science-has-great-news-for-people-who-read-actual-books.

30. Alison Flood, "Readers Absorb Less on Kindles than on Paper, Study Finds," *The Guardian*, August 19, 2014, http://www.theguardian.com /books/2014/aug/19/readers-absorb-less-kindles-paper-study-plot -ereader-digitisation.

31. Grate, "Science Has Great News."

32. "Vision / Strategy," Seasteading Institute, accessed October 27, 2015, http://www.seasteading.org/about/vision-strategy/.

33. "Floating City Project," Seasteading Institute, accessed January 10, 2015, http://www.seasteading.org/floating-city-project.

34. Jonathan Miles, "The Billionaire King of Techtopia," *Details*, September 1, 2011, http://www.details.com/culture-trends/critical-eye/201109/peter-thiel -billionaire-paypal-facebook-internet-success.

35. "FAQ," Seasteading Institute, accessed January 12, 2015, http://www
.seasteading.org/about/faq.

36. "About," Seasteading Institute, accessed January 12, 2015, http://www
.seasteading.org/about.

37. "About the Fellowship," Thiel Fellowship, accessed January 10, 2015, http://
www.thielfellowship.org/about/about-the-fellowship.

38. "The Six States," Six Californias, accessed January 12, 2015, http://www
.sixcalifornias.com/the_six_states.

39. Joel Stein, "Billionaire Tim Draper's Mad Plan to Blow Up California,"
Bloomberg Businessweek, July 31, 2014, http://www.businessweek.com
/articles/2014-07-31/six-californias-a-tim-draper-idea-just-as-madcap-as
-the-others.

40. Ibid.

41. "About," Six Californias, accessed January 12, 2015, http://www
.sixcalifornias.com/about.

42. "About Draper University," Draper University, accessed January 12, 2015,
http://draperuniversity.com/about.

43. "America's 10 Deadliest Wars," MarketWatch, May 25, 2014, http://www
.marketwatch.com/story/americas-10-deadliest-wars-2014-05-23.

44. Mark Juddery, "What If? 19 Alternate Histories Imagining a Very
Different World," *Mental Floss*, January 9, 2014, http://mentalfloss.com
/article/54464/what-if-19-alternate-histories-imagining-very-different-world.

45. Ernest B. Furgurson, "Churchill Imagines How the South Won the Civil
War," *HistoryNet.com*, August 3, 2011, http://www.historynet.com/churchill
-imagines-how-the-south-won-the-civil-war.htm.

46. Gary Gene Fuenfhausen, "Missouri's Little Dixie," LittleDixie.net, January
2009, http://littledixie.net.

47. "Once You Know . . . Fulton, Missouri: History," City of Fulton, accessed
January 9, 2015, http://fultonmo.org/once-you-know/history.

48. "Milestones: 1776–1783: French Alliance, French Assistance, and
European Diplomacy during the American Revolution, 1778–1782," US
Department of State, Office of the Historian, accessed January 8, 2015, https://
history.state.gov/milestones/1776-1783/french-alliance.

49. "Milestones: 1776–1783: Benjamin Franklin: First American Diplomat,
1776–1785," US Department of State, Office of the Historian, accessed
January 8, 2015, https://history.state.gov/milestones/1776-1783/b-franklin.

50. "World War II History," History.com, accessed January 10, 2015, http://www.history.com/topics/world-war-ii/world-war-ii-history.

51. "An Interview with General Otto Ernst Remer," by Stephanie Shoeman, trans. Mark Weber, *Journal of Historical Review* 10, no. 1 (Spring 1990): 108–117, http://www.ihr.org/jhr/v10/v10p108_Schoeman.html.

52. Timothy Snyder, "How Hitler Could Have Won," *New York Times Sunday Book Review*, June 17, 2011, http://www.nytimes.com/2011/06/19/books/review/book-review-the-storm-of-war-a-new-history-of-the-second-world-war-by-andrew-roberts.html?_r=0.

53. "Joseph Stalin," National Cold War Exhibition, accessed January 10, 2015, http://www.nationalcoldwarexhibition.org/the-cold-war/biographies/joseph-stalin/ (page discontinued).

54. Palash Ghosh, "How Many People Did Joseph Stalin Kill?," *International Business Times*, March 5, 2013, http://www.ibtimes.com/how-many-people-did-joseph-stalin-kill-1111789.

55. Nigel Jones, "From Stalin to Hitler, the Most Murderous Regimes in the World," *Mail Online*, October 7, 2014, http://www.dailymail.co.uk/home/moslive/article-2091670/Hitler-Stalin-The-murderous-regimes-world.html.

56. "Joseph Stalin," National Cold War Exhibition.

57. Daniel R. Headrick, *When Information Came of Age: Technologies of Knowledge in the Age of Reason and Revolution, 1700–1850* (New York: Oxford University Press, 2000), 217.

58. Gerard J. Holzmann and Björn Pehrson, *The Early History of Data Networks* (Los Alamitos, CA: IEEE Computer Society Press, 1995), 51.

59. Headrick, *When Information Came of Age*, 156–157.

60. Rus Shuler, "How Does the Internet Work?," last modified 2002, http://web.stanford.edu/class/msande91si/www-spr04/readings/week1/InternetWhitepaper.htm.

61. "George Lucas on Mentors and Faith," *Moyers & Company*, August 9, 2012, http://billmoyers.com/2012/08/09/moyers-moment-1999-george-lucas-on-mentors-and-faith.

62. Steve Persall, "Move Over, Odysseus, Here Comes Luke Skywalker," *St. Petersburg Times*, 1999, http://www.folkstory.com/articles/petersburg.html.

63. Joseph Campbell, *A Joseph Campbell Companion: Reflections on the Art of Living*, (San Anselmo, CA: Joseph Campbell Foundation, 2011), Kindle eBook, "In the Field."

64. Joseph Campbell and Bill D. Moyers, *The Power of Myth* (New York: Doubleday, 1988).

65. Kevin Kelly, *What Technology Wants* (New York: Penguin Group, 2010), 11.

66. Ibid, 272.

67. Steven Johnson, *Where Good Ideas Come From: The Natural History of Innovation* (New York: Riverhead, 2010).

68. Ray Kurzweil, *The Age of Spiritual Machines: When Computers Exceed Human Intelligence* (New York: Penguin Group, 2000).

69. "Nikola Tesla's Idea of Wireless Transmission of Electrical Energy Is a Solution for World Energy Crisis," Tesla Memorial Society of New York, accessed September 1, 2014, http://www.teslasociety.com/tesla_tower.htm.

70. "Tesla: Life and Legacy—Tower of Dreams," PBS, accessed June 25, 2015, http://www.pbs.org/tesla/ll/ll_todre.html.

71. Ljubo Vujovic, "Tesla Biography: Nikola Tesla, the Genius Who Lit the World," Tesla Memorial Society of New York, July 10, 1998, http://www.teslasociety.com/biography.htm.

72. Ibid.

73. Ibid.

People

1. Arghavan Salles, "Ephemeroptera: Mayflies," University of California Museum of Paleontology, August 4, 2000, http://www.ucmp.berkeley.edu/arthropoda/uniramia/ephemeroptera.html.

2. "Births and Natality," Centers for Disease Control and Prevention, last modified May 14, 2015, http://www.cdc.gov/nchs/fastats/births.htm.

3. Aubrey de Grey, interview by Andrew R McHugh, September 13, 2014.

4. Aubrey D. N. J. de Grey, "Ending Aging," YouTube video, 1:05:13, from Talks at Google on April 7, 2014, posted by Talks at Google, April 11, 2014, https://www.youtube.com/watch?v=tXJzvo0Jekc.

5. Stephen W. Stathis, "Federal Holidays: Evolution and Application," CRS Report for Congress, last modified February 8, 1999, http://www.senate.gov/reference/resources/pdf/Federal_Holidays.pdf.

6. Ibid.

7. Peter Tyson, "Bear Essentials of Hibernation," *NOVA*, December 18, 2000, http://www.pbs.org/wgbh/nova/nature/bear-essentials-of-hibernation.html.

8. Ibid.

9. "Fun Hibernation Facts," Scholastic, accessed September 1, 2014, http://www.scholastic.com/teachers/article/fun-hibernation-facts.

10. Nola Taylor Redd, "How Long Does It Take to Get to Mars?," Space.com, February 13, 2014, http://www.space.com/24701-how-long-does-it-take-to-get-to-mars.html.

11. "World's Largest Digging Machine Is Huge," *Geekologie*, August 19, 2008, http://www.geekologie.com/2008/08/worlds-largest-digging-machine.php.

12. Ariel Schwartz, "10 Jobs That You Could Have in 2030," *Co.Exist*, June 2, 2014, http://www.fastcoexist.com/3031225/futurist-forum/10-jobs-that-you-could-have-in-2030.

13. Sugata Mitra, "The Child-Driven Education," TEDGlobal 2010, 17:13, filmed July 2010, https://www.ted.com/talks/sugata_mitra_the_child_driven_education.

14. Vinod Khosla, "Technology Will Replace 80% of What Doctors Do," *Fortune*, December 4, 2012, http://fortune.com/2012/12/04/technology-will-replace-80-of-what-doctors-do.

15. "A Futurist on Why Lawyers Will Start Becoming Obsolete This Year," *Wired*, March 28, 2014, http://www.wired.com/2014/03/geeks-guide-karl-schroeder.

16. Paul Ingrassia, "Look, No Hands! Test Driving a Google Car," *Reuters*, August 17, 2014, http://www.reuters.com/article/2014/08/17/us-google-driverless-idUSKBN0GH02P20140817.

17. M. Paul Lewis, Gary F. Simons, and Charles D. Fennig, eds., *Ethnologue: Languages of the World*, 17th ed. (Dallas: SIL International, 2014).

18. Ibid.

19. Ibid.

20. Suzanne Kemmer, "Major Periods of Borrowing," Rice University, accessed September 1, 2014, http://www.ruf.rice.edu/~kemmer/Words04/structure/borrowed.html.

21. Mark Rice-Oxley, "The Germans Have a Word for It—And It's a Very Long One," *The Guardian*, September 21, 2012, http://www.theguardian.com/world/2012/sep/21/germans-word-long-language.

22. Ker Than, "L. L. Zamenhof: Who He Was, Why He's on Google," *National Geographic News*, December 15, 2009, http://news.nationalgeographic.com/news/2009/12/091215-ll-zamenhof-google-doodle-esperanto-150th-birthday.html.

23. "Five Fun Facts about Esperanto," *Bloomsbury Linguistics* (blog), Bloomsbury Academic, May 22, 2014, http://bloomsburylinguistics.typepad .com/continuum-linguistics/2014/05/five-fun-facts-about-esperanto.html.

24. Jonathan Jenkins Ichikawa and Matthias Steup, "The Analysis of Knowledge," *The Stanford Encyclopedia of Philosophy*, Spring 2014 ed., last modified November 15, 2012, http://plato.stanford.edu/archives/spr2014 /entries/knowledge-analysis.

25. Jane Jacobs, *The Death and Life of Great American Cities* (New York: Modern Library, 2011), 440–484.

26. "Jane Jacobs," Project for Public Spaces, accessed January 10, 2014, http:// www.pps.org/reference/jjacobs-2.

27. Adi Robertson, "Scientists Turn Dreams into Eerie Short Films with an MRI Scan," *Verge*, April 4, 2013, http://www.theverge.com/2013/4/4/4184728 /scientists-decode-dreams-with-mri-scan.

28. "Profile: Malala Yousafzai," *BBC News*, December 10, 2014, http://www .bbc.com/news/world-asia-23241937.

29. "Malala and Kailash Satyarthi Win Nobel Peace Prize," *BBC News*, October 10, 2014, http://www.bbc.com/news/world-europe-29564935.

30. Kathryn Schulz, "On Being Wrong," TED2011, 17:51, filmed March 2011, http://www.ted.com/talks/kathryn_schulz_on_being_wrong.

31. James Gleick, *The Information: A History, a Theory, a Flood* (New York: Pantheon Books, 2011), 106.

32. Ibid., 111.

33. Ibid., 104–105.

34. Ibid., 116.

35. Thomas Hobbes, "Of Identity and Difference," *The English Works of Thomas Hobbes of Malmesbury*, vol. 1 (London: John Bohn, 1839), Part II, 136–138, http://books.google.com/books?id=Gr8LAAAAIAAJ.

36. David Eagleman, interview by Andrew R McHugh, October 21, 2014.

37. "The Woman Who Designed The Swoosh," Women You Should Know, June 12, 2012, http://www.womenyoushouldknow.net/the-woman-who -designed-the-swoosh/.

38. Kaku, *Physics of the Impossible*, 62.

39. Alexander Osterwalder, "Why I Want My Kids to Fail," *Business Innovation Factory* video, 17:06, 2010, http://www.businessinnovationfactory.com

/summit/video/alexander-osterwalder-why-i-want-my-kids-fail
#.VI4yhGTF-m0.

40. Alexander Osterwalder and Yves Pigneur, *Business Model Generation: A Handbook for Visionaries, Game Changers, and Challengers* (Hoboken, NJ: John Wiley & Sons, 2010).

41. Osterwalder, "Why I Want My Kids to Fail."

42. Alexis Ohanian, *Without Their Permission: How the 21st Century Will Be Made, Not Managed* (New York: Hachette Book Group, 2013).

Stuff

1. "Nanorobotics," *ScienceDaily*, accessed January 8, 2015, http://www.sciencedaily.com/articles/n/nanorobotics.htm.

2. "Particle Sizes," Engineering ToolBox, accessed January 8, 2015, http://www.engineeringtoolbox.com/particle-sizes-d_934.html.

3. "Size and Scale," UW MRSEC Education Group, last modified May 20, 2015, http://education.mrsec.wisc.edu/36.htm.

4. Ibid.

5. Jason Dorrier, "Can DNA Nanobots Successfully Treat Cancer Patients? First Human Trial Soon," Singularity HUB, January 8, 2015, http://singularityhub.com/2015/01/08/can-dna-nanobots-successfully-treat-cancer-patient-first-human-trial-soon/#.VK8coaCxTvY.facebook.

6. "Cellular Surgeons: The New Era of Nanomedicine," YouTube video, 1:27:59, posted by Word Science Festival, August 1, 2014, https://youtu.be/FzFY5ms3AUc.

7. Alex Madinger, interview by Andrew R McHugh, September 11, 2014.

8. Amber Case, interview by Andrew R McHugh, September 19, 2014.

9. GPS.gov, "How GPS Works," accessed November 1, 2014, http://www.gps.gov/multimedia/poster/poster-web.pdf.

10. Sherry Turkle, *Alone Together: Why We Expect More from Technology and Less from Each Other* (New York: Basic Books, 2011).

11. Ibid.

12. Dr. K. Gudmundsson, "The Many Uses of Nanobots," Enlil Science DBD Research Institute, accessed January 8, 2015, http://dbdresearchinstitute.com/the-many-uses-of-nanobots (page discontinued).

13. Ibid.

14. Lawrence Osborne, "The Gray-Goo Problem," *New York Times*, December 14, 2003, http://www.nytimes.com/2003/12/14/magazine/14GRAY.html.

15. CMStewart, "Our Grey Goo Future: Possibility and Probability," *Singularity* (blog), January 6, 2012, https://www.singularityweblog.com/our-grey-goo -future-possibility-and-probability.

16. Patrick Farrell and Kassie Bracken, "A Tiny Fruit That Tricks the Tongue," *New York Times*, May 28, 2008, http://www.nytimes.com/2008/05/28 /dining/28flavor.html.

17. "How Does Our Sense of Taste Work?," PubMed Health, last modified January 6, 2012, http://www.ncbi.nlm.nih.gov/pubmedhealth/PMH0033701.

18. Stephen P. Thornton, "Solipsism and the Problem of Other Minds," *Internet Encyclopedia of Philosophy*, accessed November 1, 2014, http://www.iep.utm .edu/solipsis.

19. Online Etymology Dictionary, s.v. "awesome," accessed April 12, 2015, http://www.etymonline.com/index.php?search=Awesome.

20. Ibid.

21. "The Official Harvey Milk Biography," Milk Foundation, accessed August 10, 2015, http://milkfoundation.org/about/harvey-milk-biography/.

22. Ibid.

23. Ibid.

24. Robert Nozick, *Anarchy, State, and Utopia* (New York: Basic Books, 1974), 42–43.

25. Peter Rubin, "The Inside Story of Oculus Rift and How Virtual Reality Became Reality," *Wired*, May 20, 2014, http://www.wired.com/2014/05 /oculus-rift-4/.

26. Adi Robertson and Michael Zelenko, "Voices from a Virtual Past: An Oral History of a Technology Whose Time Has Come Again," *Verge*, August 25, 2014, http://www.theverge.com/a/virtual-reality/oral_history.

27. Jemima Kiss, "Oculus: Facebook Buys Virtual Reality Gaming Firm for $2bn," *The Guardian*, March 25, 2014, http://www.theguardian.com /technology/2014/mar/25/facebook-buys-virtual-reality-gaming-firm-oculus.

28. Bertrand Russell, *The Analysis of Mind* (London: George Allen & Unwin, 1968), 159.

29. "The Next Black: A Film about the Future of Clothing," YouTube video, 46:55, posted by AEG, May 21, 2014, http://youtu.be/XCsGLWrfE4Y.

30. Blaine Brownwell, *Transmaterials: A Catalog of Materials That Redefine Our Physical Environment* (New York: Architectural Press, 2008), 167.

31. Ibid., 166.

32. John Haugeland, "Semantic Engines: An Introduction to Mind Design," in *Mind and Cognition: An Anthology*, 3rd ed., eds. William G. Lycan and Jesse J. Prinz (Malden, MA: Wiley-Blackwell Publishing, 2008), 195–212.

33. Brian P. McLaughlin, "Computationalism, Connectionism, and the Philosophy of Mind," in *The Blackwell Guide to the Philosophy of Computing and Information*, ed. Luciano Floridi (Malden, MA: Wiley-Blackwell Publishing, 2004), 135–151.

34. David Cole, "The Chinese Room Argument," *The Stanford Encyclopedia of Philosophy*, Spring 2014 ed., last modified April 9, 2014, http://plato.stanford .edu/archives/sum2014/entries/chinese-room.

35. Tejvan Pettinger, "Billie Holiday Biography," Biography Online, May 28, 2010, http://www.biographyonline.net/music/billie-holiday.html.

Nature

1. Scott A. Stockwell, "Scorpion Facts," Walter Reed Biosystematics Unit, accessed September 1, 2014, http://www.wrbu.org/scorpions/sc_sting.html.

2. Michele Berger, "The Most Painful Insect Stings," The Weather Channel, July 10, 2014, http://www.weather.com/news/science/most-painful-insect -stings-20130717?pageno=11.

3. "Box Jellyfish," *National Geographic*, accessed September 1, 2014, http:// animals.nationalgeographic.com/animals/invertebrates/box-jellyfish.

4. Berger, "The Most Painful Insect Stings."

5. Erica Roth, "Wasp Sting," *Healthline.com*, August 22, 2012, http://www .healthline.com/health/wasp-sting#Overview1.

6. Kathleen O'Dwyer, "The Challenge of Eternal Recurrence," *Philosophy Now*, November 1, 2014, https://philosophynow.org/issues/93/The _Challenge_of_Eternal_Recurrence.

7. Friedrich Nietzsche, *The Gay Science*, trans. Walter Kaufmann (New York: Random House, 1974), Section 341, 273.

8. Joyce Kilmer, "Trees," Poetry Foundation, accessed April 12, 2015, http:// www.poetryfoundation.org/poetrymagazine/poem/1947.

9. "Joyce Kilmer," Poetry Foundation, accessed April 12, 2015, http://www .poetryfoundation.org/bio/joyce-kilmer.

10. "Joyce Kilmer Memorial Forest," United States Department of Agriculture, Forest Service, accessed April 12, 2015, http://www.fs.usda.gov/recarea/nfsnc /null/recarea/?recid=48920&actid=70.

11. Crash Course Biology #8, "Photosynthesis," YouTube video, 13:14, posted by CrashCourse, March 19, 2012, https://www.youtube.com/watch?v=sQK3Y r4 Sc_k.

12. "The Elephants of Africa: Tale of the Trunk," *Nature*, November 16, 1997, http://www.pbs.org/wnet/nature/elephants/trunk.html.

13. Ibid.

14. Holly Williams, "How Synaesthesia Inspires Artists," *BBC.com*, October 21, 2014, http://www.bbc.com/culture/story/20140904-i-see-songs-in-colour.

15. Ibid.

16. Neil Harbisson, "I Listen to Color," TEDGlobal 2012 video, 9:35, filmed June 2012, http://www.ted.com/talks/neil_harbisson_i_listen_to_color.

17. "Marine Life You Can See Through," *New York Times*, accessed September 1, 2014, http://www.nytimes.com/slideshow/2014/08/19/science/seethrough-fish .html.

18. Ruth Williams, "Next Generation: See-Through Mice," *The Scientist*, July 31, 2014, http://www.the-scientist.com/?articles.view/articleNo/40636 /title/Next-Generation--See-through-Mice.

19. Jon Dorbolo, "Plato: Ethics—The Ring of Gyges," Oregon State, 2002, http://oregonstate.edu/instruct/phl201/modules/Philosophers/Plato/plato _dialogue_the_ring_of_gyges.html.

20. Fox Meyer, "How Octopuses and Squids Change Color," Ocean Portal, accessed September 1, 2014, http://ocean.si.edu/ocean-news/how-octopuses -and-squids-change-color.

21. Mitchell Joachim, "Don't Build Your Home, Grow It!," TED2010 video, 2:56, filmed February 2010, http://www.ted.com/talks/mitchell_joachim _don_t_build_your_home_grow_it.

22. Tuan C. Nguyen, "Scientists Turn Algae into Crude Oil in Less than an Hour," Smithsonian.com, December 31, 2013, http://www.smithsonianmag .com/innovation/scientists-turn-algae-into-crude-oil-in-less-than-an-hour -180948282.

23. Marcus Wohlsen, *Biopunk: DIY Scientists Hack the Software of Life* (New York: Penguin Group, 2011).

24. David Salisbury, "Ants Have an Exceptionally High-Def Sense of Smell," *Research News at Vanderbilt*, September 10, 2012, http://news.vanderbilt.edu /2012/09/ants-have-an-exceptionally-high-def-sense-of-smell.

25. "Planet Ant—Life Inside the Colony," BBC video, published on March 13, 2013, https://www.youtube.com/watch?v=8n0SkIGARuo.

26. Joke taken from "Water," *Look Around You*, directed by Tim Kirkby (London: BBC, 2010), DVD.

27. Emily Singer, "The Remarkable Self-Organization of Ants," *Quanta Magazine*, April 9, 2014, http://www.simonsfoundation.org/quanta/20140409 -the-remarkable-self-organization-of-ants.

28. Khalil A. Cassimally, "Why Should We Eat Insects? It's the Future of Food," *Labcoat Life* (blog), June 6, 2013, http://www.nature.com/scitable /blog/labcoat-life/why_should_we_eat_insects.

29. Daniella Martin, "Your Post-Workout Protein Shake Should Be Loaded with Insects," *Slate*, April 28, 2014, http://www.slate.com/articles/health _and_science/science/2014/04/the_benefits_of_eating_bugs_they_re_a _sustainable_efficient_and_tasty_source.html.

30. "Grub's Up," *Economist.com*, May 14, 2013, http://www.economist.com /blogs/graphicdetail/2013/05/daily-chart-11.

31. "Defect Levels Handbook," US Food and Drug Administration, accessed September 1, 2014, http://www.fda.gov/food/guidanceregulation/guidance documentsregulatoryinformation/sanitationtransportation/ucm056174.htm.

32. "Do Snakes Really Smell with Their Tongues?," AnimalSmart.org, accessed September 1, 2014, http://animalsmart.org/kids-zone/jr-animal -scientist-e-news/do-snakes-really-smell-with-their-tongues-.

33. "Arthropods: Butterfly," San Diego Zoo Animals, accessed September 1, 2014, http://animals.sandiegozoo.org/animals/butterfly.

34. "Wedding," Historical-costumes.eu, accessed September 1, 2014, http:// www.historical-costumes.eu/en/10_wedding_dresses.html.

35. "Nick Bostrom: The Simulation Argument," YouTube video, 23:27, Future of Humanity Institute, February 21, 2013, posted by Adam Ford, https:// youtu.be/nnl6nY8YKHs.

36. Jane J. Lee, "Intimate Portraits of Bees," *National Geographic*, accessed April 10, 2015, http://www.nationalgeographic.com/features/140114-bee -native-macro-photography-insects-science.

37. "Mosquito," *National Geographic*, accessed September 1, 2014, http://animals.nationalgeographic.com/animals/bugs/mosquito.

38. Janet Fang, "Ecology: A World without Mosquitoes," *Nature*, July 21, 2010, http://www.nature.com/news/2010/100721/full/466432a.html.

39. Charles Q. Choi, "How Earth's Next Supercontinent Will Form," *LiveScience*, February 9, 2015, http://www.livescience.com/18387-future-earth-supercontinent-amasia.html.

40. Thierry Bardini, "Hypertext," in *The Blackwell Guide to the Philosophy of Computing and Information*, ed. Luciano Floridi (Malden, MA: Wiley-Blackwell Publishing, 2004), 248–260.

41. Robert Nemiroff and Jerry Bonnell, "Astronomy Picture of the Day," NASA, November 4, 2007, http://apod.nasa.gov/apod/ap071104.html.

42. "About," SpaceX, accessed April 19, 2015, http://www.spacex.com/about.

43. "Elon Musk: The Case for Mars," YouTube video, 1:02, posted by SpaceX, July 9, 2013, https://youtu.be/Ndpxuf-uJHE.

44. "The Tower: Facts and Figures," Burj Khalifa, accessed January 10, 2014, http://www.burjkhalifa.ae/en/the-tower/factsfigures.aspx.

45. "Geoengineering to Combat Global Warming," United Nations Environment Programme, May 2011, http://na.unep.net/geas/getuneppage witharticleidscript.php?article_id=52.

46. Ibid.

47. "Wangari Maathai," The Green Belt Movement, accessed August 10, 2015, http://www.greenbeltmovement.org/wangari-maathai/biography.

48. "Who We Are," The Green Belt Movement, accessed August 10, 2015, http://www.greenbeltmovement.org/who-we-are.

49. "Wangari Maathai," http://www.greenbeltmovement.org/wangari-maathai/biography.

Curious Resources

Now that you know curiosity can take you anywhere, you might need some places to go. We've compiled resources for you to check out. Some of these resources are for adults, others for kids. Some of these resources are videos, some are articles, some are just interesting places on the internet. We put them all in because with a healthy dose of curiosity, you can learn anything. Remember, if you ever need to look something up, Wikipedia is an excellent place to start your knowledge quest. Speaking of which . . .

Your Curiosity

We're listing many resources here, but the most important—*beyond anything else*—is your own curiosity. Even though you live with yourself all day long, there are still new things to find and learn. Maybe a food you didn't like before now tastes great. Maybe you never realized you could achieve something your heroes do. The best way to explore yourself is to continue to try new things, learn from mistakes, and always ask questions. Your curiosity will lead you to places you've never imagined. Curiosity will disobey rules other people set up for you. It will unlock your world.

Your Local Library

Libraries not only have great books, but they also have magazines, newspapers, videos, and some even have makerspaces (community workshops with tools anyone can use). Also, they have librarians who are expert information detectives.

Books and Movies

If you ask scientists who or what inspired them, many of them will talk about science-fiction books and movies. Read new books and watch new movies. You might just be inspired to become something you never expected. Some of our favorite books are *Einstein's Dreams, Incognito: The Secret Lives of the Brain, Mrs. Frisby and the Rats of NIHM, Every Minute on Earth* (Matt's first book), and *The Boxes.* Our favorite curiosity-charging movies are *Star Wars, 2001: A Space Odyssey, Interstellar,* and *Raiders of the Lost Ark.* And, of course, the other books we mention in this section!

You can use bookshelves too. Bookshelves, really? Yep. Here's how: a bookshelf holds together many different, though usually related, ideas. Have you ever been in a library and, after finding the book you were looking for, found another really cool book in the same area? That's one way bookshelves keep your curiosity up. One of the things we find useful is that whenever we're working on a project, we can look at our bookshelves and be reminded of ideas we might have forgotten. It even helped us write this book.

Illustrated Dictionary of Cyborg Anthropology

If you appreciated the technology questions, you might want to check out Amber Case's *An Illustrated Dictionary of Cyborg Anthropology.* It inspired some of these entries. You can read more about anomie, extended nervous systems, identity production, junk sleep, persistent architecture, and more.

Physics of the Impossible

Some of our scientific entries were inspired by *Physics of the Impossible: A Scientific Exploration into the World of Phasers, Force Fields, Teleportation, and Time Travel.* The author, Michio Kaku, explains how things we've seen in science fiction might one day become reality. Or how something might never come to fruition.

What If . . . Collected Thought Experiments in Philosophy

If you liked the philosophical thought experiments and wanted to read about more, *What If . . . Collected Thought Experiments in Philosophy* by Peg Tittle is a great book to check out. Every two pages there's a new thought experiment and something new to consider.

CitizenFour

citizenfourfilm.com

You might think our section "What if Your Phone Always Knew Where You Were?" an interesting question and want to know more about what is possible with this technology. In 2014, Laura Poitras produced a documentary called *CitizenFour* that outlines a whistleblower's experience releasing private information. (Whistleblowers are people who release information to the public, in the interest of the public good, that a company, organization, or government doesn't want released.) As explained in this recounting of a true story, Edward Snowden released information that showed that the United States government has been secretly spying on American citizens and people from all over the world. This documentary is a great insight into not only what is possible but what is (or was) happening.

Cosmos

channel.nationalgeographic.com/cosmos-a-spacetime-odyssey

In 1980, Carl Sagan, a leading astronomer, had a television show that explored the quirkiness and amazingness of the universe. It was called *Cosmos*. More recently, in 2014, Neil deGrasse Tyson released an updated version of the series with him as the guide. If you want to learn more about our universe's history, human evolution, how the world works, and other oddities of our lives, *Cosmos* is the place to start.

Podcasts

Podcasts are like radio shows on the internet. Just about every subject has a podcast. If you have some free time, podcasts are great ways to keep up to date on the things you care about. Some podcasts you might enjoy are: *99% Invisible, This American Life, Song Exploder*, and *Planet Money*. Each one sheds light on things we don't always think about and does it in a way that is enjoyable and understandable.

Wikipedia.org

Encyclopedias used to be a huge collection of books with short descriptions on everything. Both of us remember when we had to look up information in a paper encyclopedia. Since 2001, the people of the internet have been contributing to a collectively built encyclopedia: Wikipedia. It has information on just about everything and is an excellent place to get started learning about something.

Like any body of work, it can sometimes have errors or biases (your teachers might remind you of this). But, when errors or biases come up, users are able to mark them so other users are aware, working together to create an always current and accurate resource. Wikipedia is where many people start a quest to learn more about something. Be sure to follow citations and never rely on only one source when you're learning about something.

DIY.org

If you liked our activities, check out DIY.org. These grouped activities can help you continue to learn about new things while also getting your hands dirty.

Business Model Generation

businessmodelgeneration.com

Have an idea for a business or nonprofit, product or service? Business Model Generation has a tool called the Business Model Canvas. It's helped both of us craft and refine our ideas. It'll probably help you too.

Crash Course, Khan Academy, Coursera

youtube.com/user/crashcourse
khanacademy.org
coursera.org

Crash Course is an online web series that gives really brief, really entertaining lessons in subjects ranging from chemistry to history to biology to psychology to literature. If you need a short video introduction to a subject, this is a great place to start.

Khan Academy and Coursera are two more places to investigate if you want to learn about something. Khan Academy is a little more math focused, and Coursera is for late high school and college students (but that doesn't mean you can't give it a shot!).

Cellular Surgeons: The New Era of Nanomedicine
youtu.be/FzFY5ms3AUc
If you're curious about nanotechnology in general or learning more about nanomedicine, you should watch this talk. Three researchers chat back and forth with a moderator about what nanotechnology is, how it works, and where their research is going.

littleBits
littlebits.cc
If you liked any of the questions that had to do with electronics, littleBits is a great way to start learning about circuits and prototyping. Each "bit" easily snaps to other bits, allowing you to build contraptions that actually do something.

Kerbal Space Program
kerbalspaceprogram.com
This video game helps keep up your adventuring spirit. We had a few questions on space, rockets, planets, the sun, more space stuff, and adventure. Here, you'll build rockets and send them into space. The destination and goal are yours to choose. Do you want to explore all the planets? Do you want to set up colonies on new planets? Do you want to create a space station? Do you want to drive rovers across alien landscapes?

Story of Stuff
storyofstuff.org/movies/story-of-stuff
Ever wonder where all this stuff around you came from? Who made it? How did it get to you? What's going to happen to it when you're done with it? This short video explains the lifecycle of the products around us with links to find out more.